Bengali Girls Don't

Based on a True Story

L.A. Sherman

Blue Sari Press

Cover photo by Z.M.S.

Cover design by Sherry O'Donnell

http://twitter.com/lukysherman

ISBN: 0615520774

ISBN-13: 978-0615520773 (Blue Sari Press)

DEDICATION

To my hubby: thank-you for sticking by me all these years
and for helping me to slosh through my memories.

CONTENTS

ACKNOWLEDGMENTS

I'd like to thank my family for being so supportive and God for giving me a life worth writing about.

AUTHOR'S NOTE

In the summer of 1947, exactly 24 years before my story begins, the British left India, giving rise to two new nations: India and Pakistan. But back then, Pakistan didn't merely comprise the western zone of India as it does today, but the eastern zone as well, under the name of East Bengal, then later as East Pakistan, before becoming a free nation in and of itself during my birth year, in 1971, under the name of Bangladesh.

Now, before that fantastic moment of liberation, when Bangladesh was still called East Pakistan, West Pakistan, which had less of the population but all the political power, treated East Pakistan and its people as the unwanted step-siblings, as the impure Muslim cousins from the east, as the speakers of an impure tongue (we spoke Bangla and they spoke Urdu), as the people who constantly needed help due to cyclones and floods.

In other words, they couldn't stand us.

To make matters worse, on March 25, 1971, the day before my country, East Pakistan, declared independence, the government of West Pakistan sent in their soldiers to rape and slaughter their way through Dhaka, our capital city, to instill fear in the hearts of the people, leaving the Bengalis no choice but fight back and defend themselves. It was five months after this that I came into the world on a mud floor in a remote village, and four months more until Bangladesh won liberation.

At a February conference in 1971, shortly before the war broke out, General Yahya Khan, then president of Pakistan, when referring to the Bengalis to a reporter named Robert Payne, said, "Kill three million of them and the rest will eat out of our hands [like dogs]." (The dogs part is my own personal addition, but I always pictured him saying it whenever I heard this quote). Just like other maniacal dictators had done throughout history, he used genocide as a means to control his population. Anyway, this was the world I was born into and the place where my story begins.

P.S. Certain names in the book have been changed at my discretion, and faces in the photo section blurred, to protect identities, and I promise (truly, I promise) that I have tried to write everything exactly as how it all happened, based on my own memories and feelings of the events, as well as the memories and feelings of certain family members whose brains I picked with a fine surgeon's scalpel. However, and to be quite honest, it's possible I may have gotten a few minor details mixed up or mistaken (though not *too* mistaken), such as exact dates or times, but for the most part, I believe that everything I have written in these pages happened in the exact way that I've described.

Part I. Birth. East Pakistan. 1971. Summer.

1

They race through the doorway, two boys and their parents. They scamper over a pathway to check in on a neighbor, thirteen other Bengali families in tow, their eyes never leaving Rahman's solid frame. The neighbor isn't there. Thank God, Rahman says to them. Must have already left.

Backtracking, Rahman motions for them to follow, but they barely have an opportunity to round the corner when they see a group of soldiers flanking a motored vehicle and approaching fast, though still 150 to 200 meters off. Rahman knows they came from the market. Knows what they did there. What they did to his sister. *What they tried to do to him.*

Instinctively, they rush toward the tree line, leaving Rahman's home in the rear-view. They know the Pakis won't follow after. When they reach the forest, they stash themselves amid the thick brush where the undergrowth is as dark as it is dense. The women restrain their children by cupping their hands over their mouths and the men, vigilant, edgy, remain helpless. *But how to run farther.* Yet they cannot run farther. Why? Look to the tree tops. Hear those black things cawing? If more movements below, then more alarms in the air. And if that happens, the soldiers will have no choice but to turn their guns toward the forest, open fire, and revel in the clinking sound of shell casings hitting each other at their feet. So, for the time being, they are content to stay low, stay quiet, and wait.

All except Rahman.

Sunia, his wife, notices he is not among them. The others do too. "Where is he?" they keep asking. "Where…?"

"There," someone whispers. "Up against the tin."

The people look.

"Rahman…Rahman," they call. Though not too loudly, so as not to alert the soldiers, who are still heading in their direction.

No answer. Nothing. Rahman remains stolid, his back resting against the outer wall of his home, his mind lost in some thought or paralyzed by some unknown fear, but not bothered by any worries. In a moment, he'll look to his left, toward the jungle, where he'll see his family and other Bengali families motioning for him to come to safety. He'll then look to his right, toward the soldiers, where he'll see nothing but foreign pigs encroaching onto their land, their homes, and into their lives. He'll hate them at that moment. Hate them for the rest of his life.

"Rahman…Rahman," they call to him again, but just like the last time, they receive the same answer.

Rahman looks straight ahead now and stares into the lush expanse he calls home, wonders if he'll ever be back. His eyes become watery, and they close. He wipes them, but his vision remains cloudy so he blinks. When it clears, he sees he's no longer squatting at the edge of civilization, about to flee for his life and his family's lives, but he's at the market buying naan, cilantro, jackfruit and mangoes, and two other items no Bengali household can do without: betel nut and paan, all of it to take to his sister.

He routinely goes to the market after morning prayers to buy things for his sister. She's married, but lately her husband's been ill. Been in bed resting for the past couple of weeks. Rahman helps out whenever he can, considers her husband a brother. He bargains for some jalebis, his sister's favorite sweet, and hears some commotion down by the water. Walking closer, he sees people screaming and running and knocking things over. He hears gunshots. He runs, though not for safety, but for his sister, her husband. He knows his own family will be safe, at least for a little while longer, as they're situated farther away from the main hub of the village.

Rahman runs.

He reaches the home of his sister and quickly looks around. Nothing's afoot. He removes his sandals. Opens the door.

And the image he sees is one that will haunt him for the rest of his life. A woman. Her hands bound. Her lower half completely bare. The rusty blade of a machete buried deeply into her most private of parts.

Rahman steps toward the body.

The ground upon which she lies is soggy, squishy even, under Rahman's barefeet. He wonders who this woman is in his sister's home.

Surely, it can't be my...

He raises his right leg, pulls his foot up over atop his left knee and scans the bottom of his sole. Wipes it with his hand. Blood. All blood.

He notices a man in the corner, his sister's husband, lying face down in a pile of vomit. His hands bound behind his back. A single bullet hole through the back of his skull.

Oh no, they couldn't have. Not to him, not to her, not to my...

Rahman bends down, slowly pulls back the woman's sari, for it had been covering her head, and looks into his sister's lifeless eyes.

Sons of bitches! Goddamned bastards!

He drops to his knees, gasps for air, and is about to cry out to Allah for justice when he hears voices outside. Men's voices. Saying something about going back in for another ride.

He rises to his feet.

And tears mingled with rage stir rebellion.

He reaches for the machete.

The bootsteps grow louder.

He slips to the shadows.

The soldiers enter with smiles.

He holds the blade ready.

The soldiers step forward.

He leaps from the shadows with a grin.

"Rahman! RAHMAN!"

For a moment, he can't remember where he is or what he is doing squatting alongside his home. His head feels muddled, but when he glances toward the tree line and sees his wife and others motioning, waving for him to come over from behind a patch of closely knit bushes and shouting his name no less, he remembers. Only then does it all come flooding back.

He takes one more look at the soldiers—more of them coming now. He counts two more vehicles, two more trucks. More foot soldiers. Carrying rifles with bayonets. Rahman doesn't waste any more time. He scurries off into the forest and then, as everyone else had been doing, crouches down low and waits, and is thankful it is no longer raining.

The vehicles drone by and then stop. Soldiers disembark and begin shouting. They order everyone in the trucks to get out and everyone complies.

Sunia watches a small contingent of soldiers enter nearby homes. A few even enter her husband's home, but soon reappear as there wasn't much left to see. Looking at the trucks now, she counts twenty-one men, all Bengalis, making their way from the rear of the farthest truck to the clearing adjacent her husband's home. They walk quietly, eyeing only their barefeet, seemingly resigned to their unaccustomed fate. Some will welcome what is about to come. Some of their losses probably too great to bear.

In the clearing, they are ordered to stop. Thick black bands are wrapped around their heads to cover their eyes, and they are made to stand in single file, one behind the other, so tightly that not even an inch of space can pass between them. Yet why so close? Sunia wonders.

A solider with a rifle walks to the front of the line and shouts at the men to open up their gobs.

Defeated, they obey.

The soldier cocks his rifle and buries the tip of it into the first man's mouth.

Sunia whispers something to her children, Abir and Saqir: Close your eyes. Then covers their ears and prays that no one in her company makes a sound, as even the faintest little din could put *all* their lives in jeopardy.

The soldier yells, "Allahu Akbar." God is great.

The air about them turns grim.

"Allahu Akbar," the soldier repeats the mantra.

"Allahu Akbar." Sunia closes her eyes.

The soldier pulls the trigger.

A single shot leaves the barrel and enters the first man's mouth and exits through the back of his head, doing so, more or less, to each and every one of the prisoners, knocking them over, killing some, injuring others.

When Sunia opens her eyes, a ghastly scene awaits her vision: 21 bodies being doused with some sort of fluid and a single soldier lighting a match. Horrified, she watches the match.

Minutes later, the pile of human flesh is afire, the byproduct thereof a dark-gray smoke plume, a testament to its vulgarity. But the soldiers, in their vehicles now, never look back, never feel guilty concerning their fellow Muslim brothers whom they charred; and in the bushes only silence and blinks.

2

Hours pass. Night falls.

The children are beyond restless and cranky, and all they beg for is sustenance. But there is no sustenance. Even Abir loses his cool and screams out in pain because he is hungry. Saqir does too, but his screaming is more from him not getting his way than from hunger. Though soon dreamland overtakes them and all is quiet.

Sunia remains restless. She wonders after her baby's discontent, its uneasiness as it roils about its temporary home. She feels its tiny appendages protrude her tummy; she places a palm over the spot where it touches and wonders whether a hand or a foot is the culprit behind the jutting. The thought makes her glad, and for the first time all day she smiles, but only briefly, as a piercing gun blast in the distance boils her with worry. When she was little, she could always count on her mother to sing her a lovely ghazal each time she was scared or worried, but now…

Another kick. She knows the baby would enjoy the soothing effects of a song, but how could she possibly sing one? Not now. Too dangerous. Because of *them*. And so, for tonight, her baby's only tune will come from the empty part of her belly.

A troubling sign. Sunia notices that many of the others have departed. *But why?*

A rustling in the shadows. Sunia watches a woman round up her children and shuffle them away to the darkness to where her husband, who is standing with scant belongings in hand, is waiting. The woman's husband scoops up one of the children, a little girl, and softly plants a row of kisses on her cheek.

"Allah hafiz," Rahman calls out to the man, his final parting words. May God be with you.

"Allah hafiz," the man replies back.

Sunia watches them walk away and disappear to the blackness. She never sees them again.

Rahman walks to where Sunia is sitting and tells her that no one else will be leaving. "I promise," he says to her. "They have nowhere else to go."

Sunia presses her palms to her face and offers a heartfelt prayer to Allah. She is grateful they will not be alone on this journey, and this makes her feel a little more secure.

A low growl. Sunia's stomach rumbles and she thinks of her children. If only I had something to give them, she pines. But she doesn't have anything, and her only solace is their snores.

A little while later, it is Sunia who closes her eyes. It had simply been a long and tiring day.

At some point, Abir awakens and sees his father speaking to a band of three or four men, and though he can't quite tell, it seems as though they are shaking their heads.

His father turns away from the men.

"How are you doing?" Rahman asks him as he kneels down after walking over and places a hand on his shoulder, a partial smile on his lips.

"Thik acche, Abba," Abir replies, looking down. I'm okay, father.

"Bhalo, good. Now I need to ask you a question."

Abir looks up and sees Abba's uplifted brows, his head tilted questioningly to one side.

"Now listen, because it's important," Abba says sternly. "Have you seen your Uncle Polash?"

"No," he says in Bengali. Na.

Abba sighs and runs his fingers through his curls. "Accha," he says. All right. For a while, he stares at his son's face and wishes that things were different.

"You can lie down now if you want to, but be ready. We may have to move fast."

Abir nods in understanding.

"Bhalo. That settles it then." Abba pats Abir's shoulder reassuringly. "Now get some rest."

"Accha, Abba."

"Allah hafiz," Abba says.

"Allah hafiz, Abba."

Abba stands and goes to turn around.

"Abba—"

"Yes?" he whispers.

"I thought they were Muslims."

"Kita?" What?

"I thought they were Muslims."

Abba brushes a few stray locks from his eyes. "Who?"

"Those men. I thought they were Muslims."

Abba nods; he understands. He comes back to Abir's side and wraps both arms around his body and pulls him close and whispers something in his ear. "I did too, my son. I did too."

Minutes later, Abir hears Abba say asalaam alaykum to the men, peace be unto you, and the men's reply, wa alaykum asalaam, and unto you be peace. He watches them shake hands and embrace. Then Abba creep off into the darkness, into the lurid Bengali night, and disappear like a shadow among shadows.

Lying down again, Abir looks once more to the black forest but sees nothing. He wonders where Abba has gone to and yawns. He struggles with his eyelids. It rains.

3

A pang deep inside Sunia's womb tears her from her slumber and she cries out in agony. She glances around but cannot remember where she is or how she came to be in this place, but when another pang, even more severe, belts her tummy from within, she remembers, only then does it all come surging back: the soldiers, the running, *the pain*. Soon it becomes unbearable, and she senses that something isn't right with the baby. This can't be happening, she thinks. Not yet. I haven't been pregnant long enough to...

Awake.

Abir's eyes open and he chases the remaining drowse with his fingers.

A scream.

He sees his mother kneeling on the forest floor, gagging, her left arm wrapped around her tummy, her right hand planted firmly on the ground; the hand is the only thing keeping her from tumbling.

"Amma!" he screams, forgetting where they are. "Are you all right?" And when she raises her head and removes her hand from her belly and places it atop of his shoulder, that's when he notices her eyes; and from that moment on, even as an old man, Abir would always wonder how her tears were so clearly visible, even in the night's rain.

Two women scurry over, one to Sunia's side. "Kita hoisay?" one of the women asks. What's the matter? "Are you okay?" The other woman goes to Abir and Saqir to shoo them away. "Give your Amma some room," she growls. But Saqir starts crying and has to be dragged away by the arm, while Abir goes willingly, head bowed, but dying to take a look-see.

A few quick breaths by Sunia and she winces.

"Calm down, calm down," the woman says. "You need some rest. Too much running not good for the baby."

The baby, the baby. Her mind races from one thought to another.

Relief. The pain passes. *But when will it return?* She thinks about every bad thing that could happen when she hears a voice. A woman's voice. Saying something about her husband looking for a man. Immediately, her eyes widen. There isn't any need to even ask. But before she can ponder any further, a commotion beyond the tree line startles their quiet and they all turn to see Rahman running like the whirlwind, the moonlight shining on his tired face. Making his way past the clearing where the charred bodies still lie. Shouting something about his brother being a razakar, a traitorous Bengali, and that it's time to move out. He heads straight for Sunia and drags her body to its feet.

Gunshots. Instinctively, they all freeze — except for Rahman.

"Is anyone listening to me?" he bellows without worry. "We gotta make our escape. They're coming. *He* betrayed us. Are you ready? We gotta get to Shonapur. We gotta go."

An explosion.

"Hurry," Rahman says to them. "Move!"

They run through the forest.

More gunshots.

"Don't stop," he says. "Keep going."

But Sunia is having trouble keeping up. With each stride, her tummy bounces one way and then another, forcing her to stop and wrap her arms around it like a melon and rest. But no matter what, she cannot seem to stop it from shaking, which cannot be a good thing for the baby, and she cannot stop running altogether because of their pressing need to hurry. If only she could fall asleep and come to on the day prior, before this whole ordeal came to fruition, before *they* came, then she and her family could...

Her husband is calling to her now, begging her to keep moving, that it's not much farther. Only her legs are aching and she doesn't think she can make it, doesn't think she can make it, and there's barely any light except for the moon rays, so how can she see where she is going?—and the darkness is blanketing her to the bone. She wishes she were home instead of fleeing for her life, from her government. Where are the others? she wonders. She doesn't see them anymore, doesn't even sense their presence. They must have gone on ahead, she thinks. Deep down, she wishes she were like them, able to keep apace, not pregnant. She fears being left out here, surrounded by the darkness, forgotten, of being captured by those beasts.

"Come on," Rahman calls to his wife again, this time a little louder and a bit more forceful. "We're almost there. It's not much farther."

Under her breath, she curses the soldiers and their guns. Wonders why they had to alter *their* lives, why now, why ever...

Again, Rahman calls to her: "You gotta keep moving," he says. "Come on. It's just up ahead."

"I can't," Sunia tells him, "go any farther. My breath, my breath..." She pauses, inhales deeply, then continues. "I have terrible shooting pains coming from my belly, and my feet are muddy and sore, and I cannot, for the life of me, chance to take another pace." To make matters worse, everything is soggy, wet. Even the rock upon which she now sits is damp, cold even. It sends shivers raging through her body, and if a white flag were placed in her hand at the moment, she would parade it across the sky in surrender. In a single day, she has lost control over her own body, her entire life; and after wetting herself she cries more tears.

She watches her husband remove his shirt from his torso; his bare chest, wet from the rain and partly from a little sweat, glistens in the moonlight. The sight of it causes Sunia to hide a portion of her face, particularly her mouth and nose area, with a piece of her sari in shyness, and this despite the fact she'd been running all night and in pain.

She remembers the first encounter she had had with her husband, the first time her eyes had taken account of his whole being. It was during her wedding (at the tender age of fifteen) when her Amma had placed a mirror in her hand and slowly removed the veil from her face. Oh, the shock of it all, she remembers, the increase in her heart rate, the nervousness in her stomach as she saw not only her own reflection but that of another's: her husband's, Rahman's. He was her raj kumar. Her prince. And she his sootoh raj kumari. His little princess. *There was also the blushing.* For his dark eyes, smooth complexion, and curly black locks had simply been too much for her vision to bear.

While still looking in the mirror, she had heard the voice of her sister-in-law ask him, "Tell us, brother. What do you see?"

Sunia had watched his lips as he spoke.

"I see the new moon. A brightness more stunning than ten thousand fiery suns. A sight more stunning, more splendid even, than one million shiny shaplas," or water lilies, "falling from the sky like rain."

She had almost cried, had fallen in love with him immediately.

Now here she is, staring at the man she calls husband, still happy to be his bride.

He takes his shirt and tears it and wraps it around her body like a waist-belt, to keep her tummy from moving.

"Now come on," he says after tying it tightly, maybe even a little too tightly. "Keep moving. Only a little ways to go."

Sunia nods. "Okay." And follows after.

It is no longer raining.

4

Sometime later, Rahman asks Sunia, "Are you all right?" And when she says, "Yeah, I'm fine," he asks the boys the same thing.

Minutes later, Sunia loses balance and falls to the ground. Rahman's feet stop running and his body reverses trajectory and darts in the direction of his wife who has fallen.

"Give me your hand," he shouts.

"I can't," she whimpers.

"Come on. It's not too far."

"It…" Her voice trails away.

"What? What is it?" he asks her. "What's the matter? Please tell me."

She reaches for her belly. "I think I'm gonna have the baby."

Rahman reaches for his wife and grabs her by the arm and shouts at the boys to keep moving. He drags her to her feet; she screams. He places her left arm over his shoulder and tells her to hang on; she holds onto her breath. He lifts her onto his back so that she is face down across his shoulders, her tummy squished and in turmoil. Again, she screams. Wonders if anything inside her body will burst.

Rahman tells her they are close to the river now, and that the others are just up ahead. *Finally, there is something to be happy about.* She silently praises Allah.

Alhamdulillah. Praise God.

Alhamdulillah. Praise God.

She knows they'll be in a boat soon.

Able to rest.

Far away from them.

We're almost there.

Rahman reaches the others and orders two of the men in the group to go on ahead and secure a paddle boat, to get it ready. "But be careful," he says, "and don't let anyone see you." After that, Sunia says, "I need to get down. I feel sick." But when he removes her from his shoulders and sets her on the ground, she reaches for her mouth and vomits. *The baby, the baby.* She cannot remember when the baby stopped moving. Only knows it was before Rahman lifted her and began running, and that was maybe an hour ago, or maybe two. She can't remember. *Oh little one, where have you gone?* She loses all faith, and even Rahman is moved by her tears.

The two men return from the river and tell Rahman the boat is ready, that everyone is ready. Rahman nods. Says, "Thik acche," okay. "Guide them to the water." He looks at Sunia, knows the night hasn't been too kind to her. But what else can he do? They have to go and they have to go now, to the boat.

When he tells this to her, she doesn't even acknowledge his presence, doesn't even look in his direction. Her body is simply too weak, her strength nearly lost.

"Don't worry," he says to her. "I'll carry you in my arms."

Which he does.

For after bending over and hoisting her to his bosom, he makes his way through the remainder of the forest—

Through the yet darkened night.

Toward the boat.

To the river.

Where the others are waiting.

"Alhamdulillah," Rahman says to Sunia. "You'll be resting soon. Just hold on a little longer. We're almost there."

At the shoreline, three men and Rahman steady the boat in the water while the children and the women board first. Their mood is somber.

Rahman tells them Shonapur isn't too far away, and that the soldiers shouldn't be there. "Much too far for them to follow," he says, and when the men begin paddling, no one in the boat says a word.

Much later, they reach the outskirts of a village: Shonapur. All is quiet. Rahman tells them to hide in some bushes while he and another man scout the perimeter, just to be on the safe side.

They return sometime later, only to find Sunia on all fours, vomiting all over the ground, all over her hands, crying moaning and snot bubbles popping from her nostrils. She lurches and then collapses, rolls onto her side and then screams, "It's coming, the baby!"

The women try and calm her, but it doesn't help.

Oh little one, please don't leave me. Not now. Your Amma's sorry about all the running. I know it was too much for you, but what else could I have done?

A pain frolics across her lower back and sidles to her fragile womb, toward her baby's home.

Oh, Allah, please release me from this agony.

Rahman pulls her from the dirt and carries her to one of the nearest homes, one that he knows well but hasn't been to in some time. He pounds on the door. It opens and an elderly lady ushers them inside, telling them to hurry in out of the rain, for it had started up again. Rahman nods and steps through the doorway, Sunia hanging on to his neck. He gives his salaam to the lady and goes to explain the situation, but the lady waves him off and tells him that she understands.

Rahman looks relieved.

The lady retrieves a mat from somewhere and lays it on the earthen floor and shouts at a woman to grab some water and cloth. But Rahman doesn't hear her when she tells him to set Sunia down because he is thinking about the soldiers.

"Rahman!" the lady screams. "RAHMAN," she yells again, louder. "You can set her down now, thik acche. We'll take it from here."

"Accha," he says, all right, and lays her on the mat.

A scream.

All eyes on Sunia. They rush to her side and ask her how she is feeling, but never receive an answer, though they think they hear a gurgle or a cough.

5

Awake.

"I know her name," Sunia screams, opening her eyes. "It's Lucky. It's what she tried to tell me earlier, only I didn't understand. But now I know. It's Lucky, it's Lucky, it's..." Her voice runs out of sound.

Two woman scurry over. One carries a dampened cloth, the other a pitcher of water. The lady with the cloth begins dabbing Sunia's forehead and cheeks.

"Shhh, it's all right," she says. "Don't worry. Everything's gonna be just fine. We thought we lost you for a moment there."

"But..." Sunia can't stop thinking about the little girl and how she was just lying there, trembling, her childish frame being pressed to the ground, her legs like a wishbone, the soldiers thrusting...

"I'm just gonna raise your head up a bit so you can take a sip of water."

Sunia waits for the water.

"There," the woman says. "Not too much now." The woman lowers her head again. "You're almost there."

"But the girl?"

The woman scrunches her brows and scratches her nose. "What girl?" she asks, puzzled.

"The Lucky little girl," Sunia answers back, wildly. "Haven't you seen her?"

"I don't know what you're talking about," the woman replies. "Just calm down, relax. Keep pushing. You're delirious. It's been a long night and you're tired and about to have a baby."

"No, listen to me," Sunia counters. "The soldiers had her and wouldn't let her go."

"Slow down, slow down. You need to hold it together a little while longer and keep pushing." The woman looks away. "I need another cloth," she says.

"Here, use this." The elderly lady places a rag in her hand.

"Dhonyobad," the woman says. Thank you. Then dries Sunia's eyes.

"Some more water?"

"No, I think I'm gonna…" She reaches for her mouth and presses her hands there, but her efforts are in vain as some watery substance, yellowish in color, forces its way through and drapes itself across her cheeks, her chin, and in between each of her fingers. The others can only look on as the woman with the cloth wipes away the emittance.

"Not to worry. We'll clean it."

The elderly lady tells the men to wait outside, that only the women can remain, and when she points to the door, the men start to leave.

Rahman asks one of the guys to watch over his boys and the guy that he asks leads them to the door. The others file out as well, one by one, leaving Rahman as the only guy left. Oh, how he wishes to stay inside, to make sure all goes well with his wife and, Allah willing, his baby, but he knows he cannot, for his two boys, who are both tired and hungry and scared, need him, need him more. So, with heart-heavy reluctance, he pulls the door open and steps outside to where it is raining.

Sunia had watched her husband walk across the room, had even watched him pause, albeit briefly, to take a final glimpse back at her before opening the door and skirting to the beyond. She had wanted to ask him why he was leaving when a pang jolted her abdomen from within, causing her breath to falter. It had been excruciating, so much so that she'd nearly lost consciousness, resulting in her inability to voice questions. But now that the pain's a bit more tolerable, she calls out to her husband, even doing so by yelling his first name, Rahman, which is something she has not ever done before, nor is it something she would ever do again.

"Don't scream," the other women tell her. "It's not good for a woman to raise her voice and surely never wise for a woman to speak the name of her husband."

Sunia doesn't listen. "Rahman!" she calls out again, a little louder this time, more forceful even, the sound reeling him through the doorway.

"Kita hoisay?" he asks. "What's wrong? What's wrong?"

Sunia motions for him to come closer. He leans in.

"Maf Korben," she whispers to him. Please forgive me. "If I've ever done anything wrong, maf korben."

"Accha," Rahman says while nodding. "I forgive you."

Sunia adds, "I know the little girl's name. It's Lucky."

"What?" Rahman asks her, not understanding. "What are you talking about?"

"The little girl," Sunia begins. "Her name is Lucky."

Rahman looks to the other women, questioning them with his eyes, one by one, searching for answers, but the only answers they have are shoulder shrugs and head shakes.

Now Sunia, who'd been watching this entire fiasco, turns her gaze away from her husband and instead eyes the women. "I told you earlier," she says to them before looking again to her husband. "I told you all earlier that her name was Lucky." She turns back to the women. "I told you, you, and you," she says while pointing at each one of them in turn, then back to her husband, her finger like an arrow, "and you."

Rahman wishes to console her, but isn't sure what to do. He looks to the women. "You mean to tell me no one knows what she is talking about? None of you do?"

The woman holding the cloth shakes her head. "We're clueless." The others ape her bewilderment.

"Well, who is this girl, then, that's so lucky? Does anybody know her?"

The elderly lady chimes in. "Perhaps she is talking about the baby. After all, it's possible she dreamt about it. Remember when she passed out earlier? I bet she saw the baby in her sleep and the baby told her its name was Lucky, because it was born during the Shangram." The fight for freedom. The lady pauses for a second. "It's possible, isn't it?"

Rahman doesn't answer, only stares at the lady's eyes. The lady lowers her gaze and inches her feet backwards a few paces, just in case he...

Rahman sighs.

He hears the lady's words over and over again in his mind. *It's possible, isn't it?* And he knows of a certainty that it is. He remembers the words of his own Amma shortly before she passed away; it was the day he had told her he wanted to live abroad as an adult, to live the good life, the posh life. She had told him that if he studied hard, worked hard, and that if he read all of his surahs and did all of his daily namaz prayers, that *anything would be possible for him,* and in the end it was. His Amma's words came true, each and every last. He even got permission from the British consulate a few months back to move to England, to begin a new life, to start a new job, and all he did was simply walk in and ask for a voucher, and that was it. He was awarded one on the spot, that very same day.

"Thik acche," Rahman says to everyone within hearing, again thinking of the voucher and how happy it made him feel just a few short months ago. "It's settled, then. If it's a girl, her name will be Lucky. It's a bhalo nam." A good name.

"So be it," the elderly lady agrees. "Now please go and wait with the others. I'll call you with any news."

6

"What's taking so long?" Rahman wonders from outside the doorway. "What the hell is going on?"

Inside the home is commotion.

"Calm down, calm down," the women tell Sunia. "Everything will be all right. Everything always happens according to Allah's will. You're doing well," they say. "Just keep pushing, and keep reciting your ayats," your verses, "and insha'Allah," god willing, "everything will be fine."

Sunia pushes. Her insides are in agony and her stomach feels as if it is about ready to explode. She takes quick breaths. She pushes.

"Allah's with you, my dear," the elderly lady says to her. "Just keep pushing down. It's almost…"

A scream.

Though not from Sunia, but the baby. *The lucky baby.*

"Kita Kuboor?" Rahman bellows from the door-side. What's the news? He pounds on it with all his might. "Kita Kuboor? Kita Kuboor?" No answer.

The others tell him to calm down, that these things take time.

The door opens.

"Everything's okay, brother," a woman tells him. "But your wife needs to rest. Lost lots of blood." She pauses and lowers her gaze to the ground. "And—" she swallows— "fourie hosai." You had a girl.

Rahman steps back.

The door closes.

He feels a hand on his shoulder.

"Rahman—"

His head turns. "What is it?" he asks. "Kita?"

"They're coming…"

Rahman frowns.

"…coming this way…"

His teeth clench. His jowls tighten.

"…be here in less than half an hour."

His eyes narrow.

"…have to move."

His hands form themselves into fists.

"…we've no time to…"

Rahman is no longer listening to the man. He is already inside the home, shouting that they are coming, that the bastards are coming. He tells the women to hurry, to swaddle the baby and carry it to the boat. He bends down and pulls Sunia by the hand, but she doesn't move, doesn't even wake. He picks up a jug of water and dumps it on her face. Still no movement. He slaps both cheeks. "Come on!" he says to her. "We gotta go. They're coming."

"Brother," one of the women says, "I don't think we should move her."

"I don't care what you think! What choice do we have?"

The woman doesn't answer.

"Now I can't promise we'll make it." He looks away for a moment, to the door. "But if we stay here, we'll die. Each and every one of us." He looks again to the woman. "A miserable and wretched death." He picks up Sunia. "But I know a safe place…"

On the boat, someone tells Rahman that he's bleeding.

"Don't worry," Rahman says to the man. "Probably just a flesh wound." Though deep down he knows otherwise. Knows the wound isn't even his, but Sunia's. Yet what else can he do, except pray they get to Rangarchur (where Sunia's family is at) before she…

Abir and Saqir's grandmother, their Nanu, had nearly passed out when she first heard the sordid news, that the soldiers had entered Rajanpur, her son-in-law's village, and terrorized it. Even her two sons, Leelu Miah and Abdul Noor, couldn't console her shuddering frame; she was simply too sorrowful, too mournful concerning the probable loss of her daughter and her daughter's family.

Oh, Allah, I pray they haven't yet perished. And please don't let the soldiers get them, those wicked kafirs. Confound their evil ways, and guide my family to safety. Oh, Allah, please guide them to my home.

A voice.

Nanu sees a man holding a little girl, a woman standing beside him. In the woman's arms is a small boy, two more behind her, each trying to capture quick peeks of their surroundings.

The man says he's from Rajanpur, and that he knows her son-in-law. Says they spoke to each other only yesterday. "We were hiding in the jungle," he says. "Many of us were, just outside Rajanpur with our families, and Rahman was there, along with his wife and sons, and they were holding up all right, all of us were, and Rahman—well, he and a few others actually—had been planning on going to Shonapur to hide out…guess he knew someone there. Only I…" The man looks away for a moment, into the youthful eyes of his daughter, and smiles. "I came here to look for my brother, but—" he breaks off again and glances toward the clouds— "he apparently came looking for me. I found out he was captured and marred beyond recognition, gutted by his own damn blade."

Nanu approaches the man and tells him how extremely sorry she is about his brother, and that Allah will one day exact revenge on those responsible.

The man smiles. "Your words bring me much comfort, and I appreciate your loving kindness and your heartfelt sympathy, so now I will say to you what your son-in-law last said to me: Allah hafiz." The man turns and walks away to the forest, his family like a tail. Nanu watches them go with sadness.

The next day, Nanu stands at the river's edge, the wind at her face. She stares at the water in hopes of catching sight of her two boys, who, at any moment, should be returning home with her daughter and her daughter's family. "Where are they?" she pines. "Where?" She doesn't see them. Knows their trip shouldn't have taken this long.

Oh, Allah, I pray they are okay. I pray they are all right.

She thinks about her grandchildren and wishes she could go out and look for them. Wonders how many more days and nights she'll have to endure before they...

Suddenly, she sees a boat paddling in her direction and her hearts skips a beat. She begins trotting along the river's bank, slowly at first, before gradually picking up speed. *Is that them?* she wonders. *Maybe, but I can't tell because of the sunrays. So what should I do?* In a defiant counter measure, she tears off her hijab and raises it like a visor to block out the brightness, and when her eyes, unhindered, hover about the bow again, she notices someone waving.

"They're home," she cries. "My boys! They're finally home."

The boat comes to a halt near the side of the bank, and from a commanding position near the boat's bow, Rahman leaps into the rushing waters, another man by his side. Together, they grab the craft and draw it closer to the shore.

When Abir and Saqir step off the boat, the first thing they hear is Nanu crying out their names and pleading with them to come hither, and when Nanu holds them close, they hold her even closer.

"Don't worry about those two," Rahman shouts from the boat-side. "I need you to take care of the baby."

The baby? Nanu just stands there, mouth agape, watching some lady hand to Rahman a small bundle, which he promptly carries over.

"Ittah ki?" she asks. *What's this?*

"Your grandchild."

"Already? But how? Did she have it on the boat?"

"No, in Shonapur. The running caused it." He steps forward with the baby and places it in Nanu's arms.

"Masha'Allah. Masha'Allah," Nanu says, smiling. "God has willed it. God has willed it!" She kisses the baby on the forehead and also on the cheek. "You're a lucky little baby," she coos. "Bless Allah who has kept all the hairs on your head safe." She looks to Rahman and the others. "What's her name?"

"We'll get to that later," Rahman says. "Right now, we've got to get them inside." He motions to Sunia and the baby.

"Is she—?" Nanu asks, trembling.

"Oy," yes. "She just needs some rest, that's all."

At home, Nanu says, "Are you listening to me?"

"Maf korben, I—"

"Maf nai!" No forgiveness. "I just want to know if you saw my boys."

Rahman shakes his head. "We never crossed paths. But if you want me to, I can go and look for them."

"No, no. You're not going anywhere. Sit down. I'm not about to lose another member of this family. Insha'Allah," god willing, "they'll be back soon."

7

Abir and Saqir's two uncles return home deflated. Even the normally confident Leelu Miah seems to be at a loss. The entire boat ride home had been spent in grim silence, and even after reaching Rangarchur and securing the boat to the shore and walking through the village toward home, the brothers remained aloof from one another, neither knowing what to do or say.

They reach the door. All is quiet. All is dim. Leelu Miah goes to push it open, but his brother grabs him by the arm.

"What are we gonna say?" Abdul Noor asks, nervously.

"The truth."

"Which is?"

"That we couldn't find her and she's gone."

"Just like that?"

Leelu Miah nods. "Now remove your hand, brother, or I'll remove it for you."

Abdul Noor lets go.

They enter.

A scream.

Someone curses.

"Let go of me!"

"Who's there?"

"Get off!"

"It's me."

"Who?"

"Abdul Noor."

"Bhaiya, brother? Is that you?"

"Yes, it's me. Sunia? Is that you? You're alive? And Rahman too? And the children? Oh alhamdulillah. Alhamdulillah! Why, only a moment ago, we thought we lost you forever."

"Get a light!"

"Well, you didn't lose us. We're alive."

"Quickly, goddammit!"

"Thank god."

Someone fetches a lamp.

Nanu grabs both boys and cries on their collarbones. "Promise me you'll never leave me again."

"We promise," they say.

"Are you hungry?" Nanu asks them.

"Starving."

A few weeks later, Abdul Noor comes crashing through the door in a complete state of panic, breathing heavy and gasping for air and sweating profusely and smelling afoul of all things even remotely pleasant and babbling on about something or someone at some new location and telling everybody how they're planning and scheming and getting ready to...

"Slow down," Rahman tells him. "Your garbling is beyond all comprehension. Take it easy. Relax. We can't understand a single word you are saying."

Abdul Noor takes a seat and Sunia hands him a cup of water and he drinks it.

"Now tell us what's wrong?" Rahman implores him. "What did you see?"

"I saw *them*," he begins, "about three and a half kilometers away, I saw them. They were bringing in weapons and supplies and stockpiling them in a clearing. I saw them unloading their trucks and covering them with camouflage colored canopies and hewn branches of trees, and they were doing the same with the crates." He goes to take another sip of water but realizes he has already drunk it; instead, he buries his face in his palms. "I think they were getting ready to attack, which means..."

"Which means *we*," Rahman rises to his feet, "should be leaving."

After nightfall, Sunia picks up the baby and kisses it on the forehead and sets out for Gurushpur with her family. For them, this is the last stop, the place where all running will conclude.

8

"Can you hear it?" a woman asks Sunia a few months later, out of breath on this dry and sunny afternoon.

"Kita? Hear what?" Sunia replies, looking over everything as though her head were on a swivel.

"The noise."

"…"

She grabs Sunia by the hand and leads her away from the place they are standing, farther away from the center of the village and closer to the sound. "How about now?" she asks her. "Can you hear it now?"

"Uh-uh. I don't…"

"Come on. It's getting closer."

"What is? Ami bujhte na." I don't understand.

The woman runs, pulling Sunia behind her. "We're almost there. Hurry."

"To what?"

"You'll see."

The woman stops altogether and Sunia stumbles and falls.

"Here, give me your hand."

"Shhh! I think I hear something."

"Of course you hear something."

"Quiet. What's wrong with you? They'll hear us." She turns to leave. "We have to go back and warn the others."

"No, we don't," the woman says. "You don't understand. It's not them. I swear. I'm telling you the truth."

"But…"

A noise.

Sunia hears it again and wonders… The woman, reading her thoughts, smiles. "Come on. I'll show you." She leads her a little farther out, and when Sunia hears people shouting some type of phrase or slogan, one that her husband oft repeated on more than one occasion, she understands. Joy Bangla, Joy Bangla, Joy Bangla. Victory for Bangladesh, Victory for Bangladesh, Victory for Bangladesh. And when she turns and sees others repeating it, others like her Amma and bhaiyas, she knows that Bangladesh, that is, East Pakistan, has finally won its freedom.

The procession of people coming forward is headed by a man named Iskunder, one of the Bangladeshi captains, a brave man, a kind man, and a dear friend of Abdul Noor's. When Rahman sees the captain, he runs to his side, the baby still in his arms. And when the captain sees Rahman, he smiles and wipes the day's sweat from his brow.

"I caught him you know," the captain says as he approaches.

Rahman looks to the baby, "I know…" Then back to the captain. "But you will spare him? For at the end of the day, he is still my brother."

The captain places a compassionate hand atop Rahman's shoulder. "I will see what I can do."

Rahman smiles and gives the captain his salaam. Then steps out of the way so as to let him and his troop pass. The celebratory shouts continue: Joy Bangla, Joy Bangla, Joy Bangla.

For today is a happy day.

A day of much celebration.

Rahman raises the baby high above his head. He tells her again and again how she helped bring about liberation and freedom and independence, and that, because of her, all Bangladeshis will be free to live their lives and pursue their futures. He lowers her to eye level. "You did it, amar sootoh Amma," he whispers. My little mama. "You did it." He kisses her on the forehead. "You brought about liberation. You brought about freedom." He gives her another kiss. "Yes, yes, my little Amma, you did it, you brought about freedom and liberation to us all."

And as the sun dips behind some lonely hill, the glorious birthday of their independence comes to a close and Rahman, sitting in a broken hovel all alone, his palm under his chin, momentarily ponders the day's earlier events; and after reminiscing through the ups and the downs, he realizes that life, starting on the morrow, will be quite different from how it was yesterday.

Joy Bangla, Joy Bangla, Joy Bangla.

Part II. Life. Growing up Muslim in England. Visiting my Grandmother in Bangladesh. Falling in Love with a Pakistani. 1979-1986.

1

Summer.

They are living at eighty-eight Little Horton Lane, all nine of them, in between a Pakistani couple and some English folks. The English folks are all renters and mostly keep to themselves, unless, of course, they feel the need to say something mean to their neighbors. The Pakistani folks are, well, Pakistani and, as such, not very friendly to the Bengalis, which is not surprising when you factor in that the Pakistanis fought against the Bengalis during the war. Outside the house is a girl on roller skates. She is eight years old. The roller skates are blue with yellow wheels and have those stripes on them. Inside the house is an angry mother.

"Get in here!" Amma screams, opening the door, her eyes all crazy like a mad woman. "How come you were outside the gate?"

"I was trying out my—"

"No, no, no," Amma points to the wheeled monstrosities in her daughter's arms. "Girls don't wear those things. I already told you."

"They *do* though," she cries. "All the girls—"

"Only white girls do," Amma says. "Bengali girls don't. And besides, what'll happen if you break your legs, huh? What then? You'll be finished. Because no one wants a handicapped girl for a wife. Now get in here—" Amma points to the front entry hall— "before you hurt yourself. And remember, your Abba will be coming back from zuhoor namaz soon," from noon prayers, "and we still need to set the table for his and your brother's lunch."

Luky steps through the doorway and presses her skates to her heart even tighter and wishes that things were somehow…

"Are you coming?" Amma asks from the long narrow passage, leading to the kitchen.

"Oy," Luky replies, her body still closer to the door than to Amma. "Be right there." Only she doesn't want to go inside or help with the cooking. Instead, she wishes she were racing up and down the street on her skates, feeling the wind's gentle caresses on her body and listening to its murmurs. She longs to purchase ice cream and candy and crisps from the corner store with her friends and peek in the windows of the…

"What's wrong with you?" Amma shouts. "How come you're not moving?"

"I am," Luky frowns.

"Well, hurry up. You need to slice the onions." Amma disappears to the kitchen.

"Fine," Luky says. *Walk, walk, walk* but stops when Saqir, the younger of her two brothers, pops out of the dining room, blocking her path.

"Give 'em back," she yells.

"Why should I?"

"They're not yours."

"So what? I don't give a shit."

"You *better* give 'em back to me!"

"Or what?" he asks, sarcastically. "Is the stupid cow gonna tell?"

Just then, the main door opens and Abba enters with guests from the masjid, or mosque. He ushers them into the front room after they've taken off their shoes and closes the door. Saqir, knowing his judgment is nigh, shoves the skates into Luky's chest and hightails his feet to another location, while Luky hits the wall, boom.

After hearing a disturbance, Abba exits the front room and goes down the passage. He walks past the living room and the dining room, almost all the way down to the kitchen, on the opposite side of which sits the door to the basement. He squats down next to his daughter. Asks her, "What's the matter?" Kita hoisay? No response. He leans in closer. Places a reassuring hand on her shoulder and says, "What's wrong, sootoh Amma? Maybe you'd like a packet of crisps?"

Luky sniffles and wipes something from her nostrils. She opens the packet of crisps and starts eating.

Abba watches with amusement. "Feeling better?" he asks.

Luky nods.

"Bhalo, good." He clears his throat. "So tell me, how come I saw you on the ground and Pilton," which is Saqir's nickname, "going into the basement? Did he hit you?"

"Mm-hmm," she nods. "Then he took my skates and pushed me."

Abba rises and goes to the basement.

Moments later, one of the guests in the front room asks one of the other guests in the front room, "Did you hear that?"

"Yeah."

"What was it?"

"Dunno."

"Do you think—?"

"Maybe."

"Yeah, it sounded like a—"

"Yeah, yeah, like a—"

"—scream."

One week later, Luky calls Salena from the bottom of the stairs. "Whaat?" she answers from the second floor, a bit bothered.

"Come on. Mum said we could play outside in the back garden."

"Okay, boro affa." Big sister. "Be there in a minute."

"Hold on, Salena! Wait! Don't come down yet."

"Why?" she asks, still upstairs.

"Cuz you need to make sure you get *all* the dolls this time."

"Okay, boro affa. I will."

Salena flies down the stairs with the dolls and hands them to Luky who takes them and enters the dining room through the door adjacent the stairs. She walks past the sofa, the table and the shoddy black and white picture tube. The stone hearth, which is inset into the wall on the house's north side, and into the kitchen past Amma's washer and dryer. She then exits through the rear exit door and scampers across the garden to a miserly stone shed, which is just to the left of the back gate, beyond which lies an alleyway.

Salena follows.

Inside the shed, they scan the walls for bugs and other creepy crawlies whose ickiness turns their stomachs oofhtah, upside down. After deeming it safe enough to continue, they drag out four plastic folding chairs and a raggedy white sheet. Salena comments that the sheet is more yellow and brown now than white and stinking of old moth balls. "I don't care," Luky says. "It'll do." After, they haul everything to the house and set up shop by the steps and place the chairs in a square and cover them over with the sheet, and presto! They have a doll's house. Luky enters and begins to separate the dolls by putting the mommy next to the daddy, the two boys next to the mommy, and the girls she puts in a group of their own.

Luky grabs one of the dolls and so does Salena.

"I'll be this one, boro affa. She's seven, like me."

"What's its name?"

"Shazia. Mum says it means fragrant."

"You can't name her that, Salena. Our dolls are shada, remember? And white girls don't have Bengali names. They have cool names like Alice or Susan or—"

"Annie?"

"Yeah, like Annie."

"All right then. I think I'll name her Elizabeth, after the queen."

"That's fine."

"What's yours, boro affa?"

"Mine? Mine's Karen. And Karen's gonna be a nurse when she grows up and marry a cute doctor, one that can speak perfect English and take her out to fancy restaurants—" she shuts her eyes and smacks her lips together— "and kiss."

"Eeewww, boro affa, that's gross. Girls aren't supposed to do stuff like that, remember? You know what Abba would say…"

"Yeah, he'd call her a whoonga bastor," a damn bastard, "and a trashy low-lifer from the rubbish class."

Both girls laugh.

"But Karen's different though," Luky continues. "And so is her Abba. She'll get to wear short skirts like the nurses do and go on dates and marry a fit guy like—"

"Mr. Andrews?"

"How—?"

"Cuz I heard you say he was cute to Suja after her mum left the other day."

"Yeah, well…"

"Don't worry, boro affa. I won't tell. I promise."

Luky smiles and grabs another doll. "Salena, I think we're missing one. Didn't I tell you to bring all of them?"

"I did, boro affa. I swear. Maybe you dropped one."

Luky sighs. "All right. I'll go and check in the shed. You stay put." She exits under the sheet. *Walk, walk, walk* but stops when something beyond the gate, on the other side of the cobblestone alley, catches her eyesight.

"Luky!" Amma calls from the doorway, Salena standing next to her, the dolls piled in her arms. "Hurry!"

"Why?" she screams, snapping out of her spell. "What for?"

"There's rubbish people out there! Unclean, filthy humans!"

"What dirty people? Where?"

"Forget it," Amma says, not wanting to draw any further attention to the shada people's indiscretions. "It's nothing. Just come in and get ready for your namaz." Amma walks to the kitchen and Salena follows, leaving the door ajar. Luky walks across the yard to the steps and up the steps to the kitchen, but not before another glance back to the alley, where a boy and a girl have their hands all over each other's bodies, their lips all over each other's lips, their bodies like two wrestlers grappling, but not taking each other down.

2

They turn the telly on today. Luky makes Salena hold the antenna. But none of the channels—BBC1, BBC2, or ITV, come in, but remain fuzzy, with zigzags across the screen. So Luky pounds the side of the set with her palm and the picture begins to clear. On it, she sees people. White guys and white girls. Dancing. Wearing tight dresses and tops. All glittery, showy. The men in flared trousers.

"Salena!"

"What, boro affa?"

"Stand still!"

"I am. It's the telly."

"Well, it went out again."

"But—"

"Stop moving!"

"I—"

"Salena!"

"What?"

"Turn the dial."

"But—"

"It's clearing."

"What is?"

"The show."

"What show?"

"*The* show."

Salena looks to the screen. "Boro affa, we shouldn't be watching that. If dad comes home he'll—"

"What?" Abba enters the room, fresh from namaz. "Abba kita korbo?" I'll what?

Salena drops the antenna.

Luky switches the knob to off.

They both stay silent.

"So—" Abba looks from Luky to Salena— "what will Abba do?" He looks to the telly. "*Nothing?* Okay, I guess I'll just sit here at the table and eat these crisps by myself." He opens a bag of Skip's Prawn Cocktail crisps and pops a couple in his mouth. He does the same thing to a bag of Walker's Cheese and Onion, Salena's favorite.

The girls run. Salena reaches for the Cheese and Onion and Luky the Prawn Cocktail. Like vacuums, they inhale.

Abba laughs. "You're welcome," he says to them after they hug him. "Would you two like to hear a story?"

The girls smile.

Abba lights a cigarette, takes a couple of puffs, a couple of drags. Then tells them about a man, a brave man, and a tiger, and how the man, while traveling to his wedding, had been attacked by the implacable beast shortly after sundown.

"It was raining," Abba begins, "and the man decided to stop for a while to rest." Abba brings the butt of his cigarette to his lips and breathes in before removing it again and blowing out a hazy cloud of gray to the ceiling; then, in a voice barely above a whisper, says, "But the tiger sprang at the weary traveler without warning and tore into his fleshy ribs, his arm, his shoulder, with teeth and claws like iron, ending his breather."

The girls inch closer, their eyes like the moon.

"Incredibly," Abba continues, "the man broke free and the tiger retreated; still, it continued to circle." Abba flicks the tip of his cigarette over an ashtray and takes another drag. "The man tried to stand but was unable to. Yet after crying out to Allah for power—" Abba reaches for a crisp and the girls wait patiently for him to swallow— "he willed himself to the soles of his sandaled feet, held onto his breath, and formed his hands into fists." Abba pauses for effect. "And when the tiger charged, the man bull rushed it. And when the tiger growled, the man bellowed out a war cry: 'Allahu Akbar. Allahu Akbar. Allahu Akbar.' And when the tiger leapt, it opened up its jaws and bared its razor sharp teeth, all of which were coated with the man's blood." Abba turns away and stares at nothing in particular, as if lost in some thought he'd rather not dispense.

"Abba, Abba," the girls tug on his sleeve. "Ere foray kita hoibo?" Then what happened?

"Well," Abba says, clearing his throat, "the man leapt at the tiger."

"*And then?*"

"The two met as one, like this—" he bangs both fists together as though two trains were colliding— "in the rainy air before falling in a frantic fit of violence to the earth."

Abba takes a measured breath and scratches the bottom of his chin. "In the early morning hours, they found him. A half dying man. Laying atop the unmoving carcass of a tiger, the man's fingers, his hands, still gripping its discomfited jaws."

Luky closes her eyes. She replays the story again and again, but each time she gets to the part where the man kills the tiger, she pictures it's her Abba tearing apart its jaws.

"Do you lot know why he was able to kill the tiger?" Abba asks.

Luky opens her eyes.

"It's because he had big muscles like your Abba." Abba flexes. "Go ahead," he says to them. *"Feel* them."

The girls giggle and reach for their daddy's muscles. The moment recalls a time some years ago when they were playing in the living room and Abba came in and said *look at daddy's muscles, feel them* and Luky thought *wow, my Abba's so big and strong, he can beat anybody.*

Abba lights another cigarette and puffs it; he exhales the foggy vapor through his lips. "You know," he says to his girls, "in life there are many tigers, and sometimes the only thing at your disposal is your own body. But don't worry. If you work hard, study hard, and do all of your namaz prayers, you can do anything, be anything. You can grow up to be doctors."

Abba turns away and ponders some distant memory, sighs and then casts his eyes to the floor. "Your Abba never got to go to school, you know." He takes another puff and looks at his girls and tells them to go upstairs and do wudu, their ritual ablution, because it's time to do asr or late afternoon prayers.

"Okay, Abba," Salena says, and removes herself from his lap and rushes upstairs to the bathroom. But when Luky goes to follow, Abba says, "Come 'ere." And when she goes there, he places a hand on her shoulder and tells her to study hard and become a doctor, "Because daddy never had an education, never had the opportunity to do something like that, but if you get an education, you can be a doctor or a lawyer or an engineer and you won't have to work in a factory all night long like your Abba and you get no sleep." He brushes the hair from her eyes. "It was my dream, you know, to be a doctor." He pauses before continuing. "If you're a doctor and I get sick, you can heal me and give me your medicine, and if you're a *good* doctor, you can cure everyone back in Bangladesh and make them all better because they get really sick over there," he says, "and they'd be happy to have a bideshi doctor," a foreign doctor, "somebody from London, to help them."

Luky smiles and Abba pats her on the head. She hugs him around the ribcage and exits the room. But Abba remains in the same chair, rubbing the right side of his body, his eyes shuttered, his mind lost in some distant memory or nightmare, his cigarette still burning, the ashes waiting to fall.

3

A dream.

Luky looks down and sees her barefeet in the sand. She looks up and sees a tower in the distance. Blackpool Tower. And it stretches forever into the English sky. She wonders what it would be like to stand at the top of it and look out on the people, the cars and the houses, but Amma calls to her from where the water meets the shore, and when Luky looks to the place, Amma waves. Her sisters do too, and then continue on with their sand castles, while her two brothers, Abir and Saqir, are nowhere to be found.

A voice.

Someone yells "Luky," but when she turns to see who it is that is calling, all she sees is a giant beach ball flying in her direction, the sun right behind it. She watches it bounce a few times and dribble to a halt at her feet, and when she looks up, Abba waves.

"Throw it back," he says, clapping his hands together twice real fast, so she does.

Luky wishes that things could always be this way, that they could always go to the beach and play games like the shada families.

"Abba," she asks him, "can we do this again next weekend?"

"Sorry, sootoh Amma," he replies, "but you know how difficult it is, taking the bus and all. Maybe next summer, when you're off, then we could come back." He catches the ball and throws it. "How's that sound?"

Luky smiles. She already cannot wait for next year's trip.

Awake.

Luky looks to the clock and hears Abba singing, which is all part of his nightly bathroom routine before he sets off for work. She sees him in her mind's eye, standing bare-chested in front of the mirror, his silver razor covered with cream, the sink water running. She feels the melody of his music on her body, feels it rushing over it like the evening tide the shore.

Abba sings.

About a raja, a king, whose beautiful wife and son were lost under the waves of the Kushiara River when their boat suddenly capsized and sank to the bottom one day in December. Oh, the tragedy of it all. How, upon hearing the distressing news, the man became full of distraught and despair, but rather than face his pain and be comforted by the community, he fled from the eyes of the living and made his permanent home in the hills.

Abba sings.

About the day the raja found something in his garden, a
mirror, buried beneath the soil. It was attached to a small
handle of gold and fitted with a circular piece of obsidian,
polished down and burnished smooth like glass. When the
raja held it to his face, he saw for the first time in many,
many years his own reflection, but instead of seeing a man
full of vigor and youth and piercing eyes of dusky-brown, he
saw an elderly old beggar, all gray-faced, with eyes akin to
fog. *Where have my chiseled features gone to?* he wondered.
Because the image that stared back at him was not the same
one he remembered. Then, suddenly, it all came back: his
wife, his son, the accident, the anger. And in a knee jerk
reaction, spawned mostly from regret and heartache, he
smashed the mirror and threw it to where he had found it
and covered it over with dust, so as to hide it forever, and
stood up all tired like and walked to a small cut-out in a hill,
his home for the last thirty years, and curled up on his side in
the fetal position like an unborn baby and cried.

Abba buttons the last of his shirt buttons and exits the
bathroom, and Luky dreams another dream.

Saturday.

Two days later. A knock.

"Time to do namaz," Abba says. "Time to get up."

Luky opens her eyes. She hears Abba's footsteps in the
hallway, knows he'll have a cup of tea in the dining room at
the table before making his way to the masjid for fajr or
morning prayers.

The clock reads 4:47 in the morning and Luky goes to the
bathroom. She washes her face and rinses out her nostrils.
She wets the grooves and lobes of each ear. She washes her

forearms, from her wrists to her elbows, and passes the backs of her hands over her nape. She scrubs the bottoms and tops of her barefeet, from her ankles to her toes, then dries off the wetness. Then it's back to her bedroom again, where she grabs her jai namaz or prayer carpet from the top drawer of her dresser and does fajr; after, she jumps into bed at 5:22am and goes to sleep. Only to be woken up again three hours later by another knock.

"Luky na, Luky na!" Amma screams, grabbing her daughter by the shoulder and pushing the front door shut and locking it. "What are you doing?" she asks. "Are you crazy? They're out there."

"Who is?" Luky asks, puzzled. Ke bai ray? No answer. Because the wrought iron knocker pounds the door like thunder and Amma goes all cold. "Shhh," she says out of nowhere, her finger pressed to her lips. *"It's them."*

Again, the wrought iron knocker hits the door and Amma jumps. But this time, she takes Luky by the hand and drags her to the front room, all the while cringing as someone opens the letter box and asks whether Rahman's home.

"It's the Jam-e-khans," Amma whispers. The Jamaicans.

"Kita?" Luky asks, not sure what the heck Amma is talking about.

"Jam-e-khans ai-say!" Amma yells back. The Jamaicans are here! "...have to hide!" She creeps her way to the window and motions for Luky to follow. They peek through the curtains and see four men near the door.

"Why aren't they leaving?" Amma asks. "Why, why, why? And where is your Abba? Oh, Allah."

She tears Luky away from the window. "Run!" she says, dragging her to the hallway.

"But—"

"Shhh," Amma counters. "Move!" They run past the living room and the dining room. Past the kitchen—for their lives. All the way to the storage closet at the end of the hall, which is on the same side of the wall as the door to the cellar, where they end their fearful flight and hunker.

A scream.

Something is touching Luky's shoulder.

"Boro affa, it's me," Salena says. "Don't worry."

"And me," says Mumtaz, the third sister.

"And me," says Taz, the fourth.

"And me," says Gully, the youngest and the fifth.

"All of you be quiet!" Amma shouts. "They'll hear us."

"But Amma—" Luky begins.

"Sooboh!" Amma tells her. Shut up! "Jam-e-kahns bai ray roi say." They're still out there. "And if you're not quiet—"

"But Amma—"

"Shhh! Don't talk."

Minutes pass.

Amma opens the door and peers down the passage, but does so in reservation. She calls for Salena using her nickname, "Lahbi, Lahbi," or Lovely, Lovely, and tells her to "Come here."

Salena steps forward.

"Go to the front room," she tells her, "and see if they're still out there. And Lahbi," she adds, "be careful."

Luky watches Salena disappear into the front room. She wonders what she is thinking as she stares through the window.

"Lahbi, na!" Amma hollers from in between the closet doorposts, her face turning pale from what she is seeing. "Come back, Lahbi. What are you doing? Nooooooo!"

The girls cower and hide. All except Luky. Their hearts beating.

Another knock.

Luky skirts past Amma. "No!" she warns her sister. "Don't do it!"

Amma reaches for Luky's shoulder. "No! We gotta hide. Don't go. They'll—"

"Salena!" Luky calls. "Don't open it!" *Stumble, trip, stumble.* "Salena!" she yells, but it's too late, and all she can do is watch from the floor as two shadowy figures enter and grab her sister; that and listen to Amma in the background, her frantic body still halfway in the closet, the only sound from her mouth a scream.

4

Asalaam alaykum uncle, Salena says to King George as he and Abba step through the doorway. Wa alaykum asalaam, King George says to Salena, kicking off his shoes. He lifts her to the top of his shoulders and walks to the front room.

Luky's sisters follow.

In the front room, they see two bags of hard candy and three two-liter bottles of soda lying on the coffee table. They race to the candy, grabbing handfuls, and then to their dad's best buddy, a man they consider an uncle.

"How are you doing?" he asks them.

"Good," they say.

He asks them about school, their prayers, about their likes and dislikes, and they in turn ask him about their aunty and his daughters.

Amma comes in with tea. She, like her husband, sees King George as a brother. Also sees the candy and the soda on the table. "Why do you have to always bring that stuff for? We have things for the girls."

"Aah, these are my kids too, you know," he says. "Why shouldn't I?"

He sets Salena down and makes his way to the sofa and falls backwards into its cozy embrace. Gully jumps into his lap and giggles. He positions her onto his right leg and holds her steady by holding onto her hands. She smiles and he smiles back and begins to sing her one of his favorite nursery songs while bouncing her up and down on his knee:

See saw mother-in-law.
This is the way to London town.
This way up.
And this way down.
This is the way to London town.

As soon as he finishes, Taz, Mumtaz and Salena beg for him to sing *Baa Baa Black Sheep* or *Diddle Diddle Dumpling, My Son John* or another of the nursery rhymes with catchy little tunes. They plead for him to swing them around and around or carry them on his shoulders or toss them to the couch-cushions like ragdolls. Though after some time, King George says, "I should be leaving."

Luky would always remember King George and his songs. His kindly demeanor, his gentle heart. But what she'd remember most would be that wintry night in February when he said he'd be back in the morning to take them to a hill. "To go sledding," he had said. And that was it. Morning never came for King George, and the next time anyone ever saw him was when some burley beat cop found him two days later in the dumpster behind St. Luke's Hospital, his body still clothed in its parka, his hands still fitted in their gloves.

They tried to piece together the events of the night prior and finally came to the conclusion that he was hit over the head with a beer bottle, mugged, beaten, and then left to die. Leaving a wife without a husband, three small children without a father, and five little girls without their songs.

"Please stay, please stay," the girls beg Abba's best buddy not to leave. "Okay, okay," the best buddy says. "I'll stay."

Though when he does leave, the girls rush to their rooms and Amma goes to the kitchen and Abba says, "I'm going to the masjid for asr."

Upstairs, Salena unfolds her jai namaz and watches Luky turn on the radio.

"Luky!" Amma screams. "Get down here. I need you."

Luky sighs and makes her way to the kitchen and sees Amma working with the onions and slicing them and tossing the pieces in a pan.

"Over there are the potatoes and a knife," Amma says to her. "And here's the cilantro. I need you to chop it up and sprinkle the bits in the curry. After that, I need you to wipe down the counters and help me set the table and clean the stove and sweep the floor."

Luky rolls her eyes. "Aw, why do I have to do it for? How come you never ask—?"

"Because it's your duty, that's why. You're the oldest daughter, and once you learn, you can teach your sisters."

"But—"

"What?"

"I don't have time for this."

"No?" Amma asks, bewildered. "Then what are you gonna do when you get married and go to your mother-in-law's place? Or when she shouts at you because you're a good-for-nothing?" Amma shakes her finger. "Well, I'll tell you. You'll think back to this day and wish you'd taken the time to learn." Amma shakes her head. "Someday, you know, your in-laws are gonna say we never taught you anything, and it's gonna be a disgrace." Amma pauses. "Now just do what I told you."

"Fine," Luky says.

"Bhalo. Now hurry, because your Abba will be back soon with guests."

Luky slices the potatoes, chops the cilantro, and mixes the pieces in the curry. She wipes down the counters and helps set the table, but wonders why Amma always has to wear that same purple sari, though quickly forgets about it when a hand snatches three beef kabobs from the table.

"Put those back bi-shab, brother. They're Abba's."

"Who cares? You're not getting any. The meat's for the guys."

Luky looks away, disgusted, says nothing and instead reaches for a piece of chicken.

"What do you think you're doing?" Saqir asks her. He smacks the back of her hand. "I said the meat's for the guys." He steps closer, jabs her in the shoulder and grabs two more kabobs. "Now get me a drink, beybootah," you dummy, "or I'll kick your head in."

"Get it yourself," she says, crossing her arms.

"Why are you answering your brother back for?" Amma asks, annoyed. "What's wrong with you? Get him something to drink. And you," she points to Saqir, "sit down and eat your food like a human. Quit acting like a dog."

Saqir sits.

"And don't finish all those kabobs either," she adds. "Your Abba's coming home and he still needs to eat."

"Idiot."

"Whud she say to me?"

Saqir reaches for his sister.

"Nothing."

Amma plays referee.

"She was just getting you your drink."

In the kitchen, Luky opens the refrigerator and pulls out a two-liter bottle of soda and carries it to the counter. She twists off the top and hears the fizz fizzing and then grabs a medium size glass from the cupboard and fills it to the brim. She turns just in time to see Saqir walk in from the dining room.

"What's taking so long?" he asks.

"Nothing's taking so long," she quips. "Here...take your stupid drink," but accidentally spills it on him. *The ire in his eyes like lava.*

"Jah, jah!" Amma says to Saqir, averting the next world war. "Go upstairs and change. And you," she points to Luky, "clean this mess and call your sisters down to eat."

"Saleeeena! Mumtaz! Taz! Gully! Mum wants you down here. It's time to eat."

The girls come running.

They sit on a white sheet that is laid out on the floor in the dining room, in between the table and the fireplace; Luky finds a spot next to Salena. The girls wait like little birds as Amma mixes the curry into the rice using her fingers; they wait like little birds for her to stuff little bits of it into their mouths.

"Refill!" Saqir yells from the table. "I'm thirsty."

Luky gives him the look of death.

"Jah!" Amma cries, her eyebrows like N's. *Go!* "Don't make faces at your brother."

Luky rises. *I'm sick of it* she mumbles. *Why's he so laz—?*

"Whud you say?" Saqir asks, pushing away from the table.

"None of your—"

"What?" He steps closer.

"Nothing."

"I didn't think so."

Luky walks to the kitchen, Amma right behind her. "It's your duty, you know, to do these types of things. The men come first. *Always.* Remember that. Especially when you're married."

"I'm never getting married."

Amma laughs. "Just remember what I told you."

After eating, the girls wash plates and Amma sits on her ottoman, a bowl of leftovers in her hand, and eats.

Sometime later, they hear Abba.

"Boro affa, dad's home!"

"Where is he? In the front room?"

"Mm-hmm," Salena nods. "He just walked in."

"With guests?"

"Yep."

"I'm going upstairs."

"Me too."

"No, you have to stay put and help mum."

"But—"

"You have to make the tea!"

"Ami goro ai see," Abba's voice bellows through the hallway. *I'm home.*

"Asalaam alaykum, Abba," they say as he enters the dining room.

"Kita koro shaub?" What are you all doing?

"Kitchu na." Nothing.

Abba looks to Amma.

The girls watch her rise from the ottoman and set her half-eaten bowl of leftovers on the table and give Abba her salaam.

"Amar shahtay dui-jon mammon ai-say," Abba begins. I've two guests here with me. "Bhalo kori-cha ar-nastha bah-now." So make us some good tea and some snack.

Amma nods. "Thik acche." Then walks to the kitchen.

"Ar-ami dosh minute foray aye-moo," Abba adds, letting her know that he'll be back in ten minutes.

"Accha," Amma says, looking over her shoulder. "I'll have everything ready for you on a tray."

Luky switches the telly to on and plops on the couch next to Salena. Abba exits the room but comes back ten minutes later for the tray.

"Make sure you turn the telly off before maghrib," or sunset prayers, he says to them. "And do your namaz on time. Don't get carried away and forget."

"Thik acche, Abba."

Abba leaves.

Salena scoots off the couch and tells boro affa that she's going upstairs to do wudu, then namaz. Tells her, also, that she should come up too.

"All right," Luky replies. "Be there in a minute."

Nineteen minutes later. A commercial airs onscreen. A girl takes a bite out of a candy bar and a guy reaches for...

"Turn that thing off!" Amma shouts. "What are you still doing watching it? How come you're not doing namaz? You know the good angels won't come in here if the telly's on during maghrib."

Slowly, Luky trembles past Amma's glistening glare and switches off the telly. She covers her nose as she breathes in the purple sari, hopes her shada friends never have to smell it. Upstairs, in the bathroom, she does wudu; in her bedroom, namaz. After, she goes back down to the dining room and switches on the telly.

Abba, who had earlier gone with his guests to the masjid to pray maghrib, comes home and removes his sandals and climbs the stairs to his room.

Amma warms his food on the stove and tells the girls to re-set the dining room table. "Okay," they say, following orders.

Abba comes downstairs and enters the dining room, says asalaam alaykum to the girls and takes his favorite place at the table, his white genji or wife-beater on his body, his black kufi on his head, and his light-blue lungi, woven in a pattern of checks and squares, wrapped around his waist like a kilt.

Wa alaykum asalaam, the girls reply and then disappear like mice to their rooms.

"Just where do you think *you two* are going?" Amma asks Luky and Salena, her two oldest daughters, her hands resting on her hips. "These need to be folded."

Luky looks to Salena. "I can't do it. I have homework."

Salena looks to Amma. "Me too."

"Liar."

"Am not."

"Are too."

"Sooboh!" Amma loses her temper. "What are you two arguing about? I said 'fold the clothes,' so fold them."

Luky looks away. Whispers "Stupid cow, I hate you" to Salena after Amma leaves, and Salena whispers back "I hate you too."

They stare at the basket for some time.

Luky speaks first. Says, "I'll fold the big stuff."

"Okay," Salena agrees.

So Luky folds the pillowcases, the sheets and the towels, and Salena the knickers, the socks, the saris, the hijabs, the...

"I'm done!" Luky cheers.

"But I can't find the matches to these socks, boro affa. Can you help me?"

"No way. Get lost."

"But, boro affa, I—"

In her room, Luky thinks about Abba and how he came home the other day from the masjid, shortly after maghrib, and took his usual place at the table, and after only one or two bites of his dinner, began saying *the food's horrible today, what happened? didn't you take your time?* and Amma apologizing profusely for not paying enough atten...

"Luky!"

"Whaaat?" she answers from her doorway, pissed that she had to get up from her bed and break her concentration.

"I need you to sweep the hall and tidy the living room."

"Why?"

"Because I said so."

"Ask Salena."

"She's folding."

"I have a test to study for."

"You want me to tell your Abba?"

"Fine." *It's not my fault she takes so freakin long folding the clothes.* "Saleeeena!"

Amma goes to the kitchen.

"What, boro affa?" Salena enters the hallway.

"Mum wants you to sweep the living room and tidy," Luky says, coming downstairs.

"No, she doesn't," Salena says.

"Yeah, she does," Luky counters, "and if you don't do it, I'll beat your head in." She pounds her palm with her first.

It's not fair Salena thinks, reaching for the broom. *Why do I always get stuck?*

Upstairs, Luky prays to Allah. "Please keep Nanu safe, and don't let Pilton hit me in the arm when he's angry, and tell Luton," which is Abir's nickname, "to change his mind about going to uni next September, or else I'll be the saddest little girl on the planet. Besides, Manchester's too far away, anyway."

She turns on the radio, but not too loudly, as she knows Salena will be up any moment to do isha, her nightly namaz, as soon as she enters the room.

She looks to the schoolwork on her dresser and ignores it. Yawns and looks to the clock and sees that it's just after nine, which means Abba is still at the masjid.

Salena enters the room and grabs the jai namaz and prays. Downstairs, Amma finishes eating and wipes the counters and checks the doors to make sure they are locked and turns out the lights. Upstairs, she asks the girls if they've done their namaz. "Shaub namaz for so-ni?"

"Oy," they say.

"Then turn out the light. You're wasting electricity."

All quiet. Salena asks, "Boro affa, are you awake?"

"No. Go to sleep."

"But, boro affa…"

"What?"

"Why does John have only one shoe?"

"Whaat?"

"Why does John have only one shoe?"

"Who the heck is John?"

"From the nursery rhyme, the one King George sings us."

"I don't know, Salena. It's just a song."

"You think he lost it?"

"For God's sake, Salena, shut your face."

Luky scooches to the edge of her bed and pushes the covers off her body. She sits on the bed's brink and touches her barefeet to the floor and paces forward in the dimly lit darkness after standing and pulls open the bedroom door and walks down the hall to the bathroom. She enters and searches with her fingers for the light switch. Bingo. She raises the toilet seat cover and sits on the seat part to pee. She reaches for the medium sized pitcher that sits on the floor next to the toilet and fills it with warm water and pours it over her privates, her fingers playing the role of toilet paper as the water rushes over. She repeats the process two or three more times, each time rubbing her privates. Then she sets down the pitcher and rises and pulls up her knickers, her pajama bottoms up over her knickers, and flushes the toilet and turns out the light.

In bed, she thinks about tomorrow and Suja's brother and Mr. Andrews and falls asleep.

5

Winter.

The girls love it. Everything about it. Especially Luky, who admires the tinsels. But what she loves more than anything is when Abba takes them to the city centre each year to see Father Christmas, his red suit like a bullseye, the girls' eyes like darts when they spot it, his shiny black wellies like nighttime compared to the snow. Too bad they never get to sit on his lap, though. Against their religion or something. Anyhow, there's always the snowpeople to mess with. With their orange carrot noses and sticks and stones for eyes and arms. You know the girls love making those things. Not to mention ice balls for snow fights, though hate it when their sootoh bi-shab, Saqir, joins in their innocuous games, turning them into ordeals of survival and of terror and of dread.

Winter is also when they receive their free tickets to the Alhambra Theatre, which is on Morley Street at the bottom of Great Horton Road. Abba's employer gives them to his employees each year for Christmas, along with boxes of chocolate-covered biscuits. Last year's biscuits, according to Luky, had been marvelous, almost as good as the actual trip to the theatre had been. She remembers the ride there, the snow along the roadway, all of them, even Abba, in their winter gear: their gloves, their boots, their hats; the bus pulling to the curbside, the people filing out to the street: some to the theatre, some to another venue; the dome, the columns, the free concessions...

Hey, boro affa, look at this. Hey, boro affa, look at that. Oh, Taz, watch what you're doing because you're spilling all of your pop!

At the front of the theatre, the girls had talked excitedly for what seemed like ages, glancing around at the others in attendance and up at the ceiling and drinking and eating and kicking the seats in front of them with their boots and bothering the people behind them with their antics, until, suddenly, the light began to fade and grow thicker and more substantial with each passing tick of the clock, and when all the sound and the murmurs in the place had officially ceased their racket, there arose a spot of light in the center of the stage and a man smack dab in the middle of it, a black suit on his body, a matching hat on his head, and in his hand was a...

The girls had sat transfixed, mesmerized. On the brink of their seat-cushions. Bright-eyed. Utterly captivated by the performance and the performers. Oh, how they loved the array of multi-colored lights! The orchestra. The female stage dancers, who kicked their legs up to the ceiling. The thunderous cheers. The smoke and the large stage-curtain. But what stood out the most that night wasn't the hula-hoop dancers or even the part about the rabbit. No, it was when a male performer grabbed a female performer and bent her over his knee-tops and spanked her. By far, it was Luky's favorite. But how come Abba didn't tell them to shut their eyes as he normally did when anything even remotely objectionable came into view? Who knows? Only one thing was certain: that night at the Alhambra Theatre marked a turning point in Luky's young life. It was then that she realized it was okay for boys and girls to...

"Boro affa, didn't she look beautiful, the one with the red costume? And what about the one dressed like Cinderella, wasn't her dress really nice?"

"Yeah, boro affa, wasn't she so pretty?"

At home, the girls had discarded their gear by the shoe pile and dissipated to their rooms, where they acted out many of the night's earlier scenes. Yet it was only after everyone fell asleep that Luky realized Amma never got to go to the shows. Of course she wondered why but fell asleep before she could pursue the reason. Though that was last year. This year, no one would be going to the Alhambra Theatre but to a faraway land with a green flag, a red circle in the middle of it, forever.

Indeed. Abba had been sending money back to Bangladesh for years, the plan being to build a high-end home in Hasan Nagore, in Sunamganj, where his children could readily adapt to foreign life, and also to where he could ride out the rest of his days near the village of his birth, his youth, and live the good life, the posh life, like a raja. It had long been his dream to return home after such a considerable journey away. (He left shortly after the war, in the year 1971, at the end of December. His wife and two sons and baby daughter left three years later). His wish was to settle them (his family) there first, in Sunamganj, and then return to England to labor for a year or two, or maybe even more, before returning to his homeland for good.

"Asalaam alaykum," Abba says to Akrum Khalu, his brother-in-law, at the airport in Sylhet, and wa alaykum asalaam is the reply he receives back.

"How was your trip?"

"Long, tiring, but it's good to be home."

"Well, it's good to have you home."

They load a baby taxi with the luggage and Heron, the only son of Abdul Noor, Amma's late younger brother, sits on the seat next to it, keeping a watchful eye, while everybody else fills the seats of three others.

One of the drivers says, "Probably in about two hours, insha'Allah," God willing, "give or take, we'll arrive in Sunamganj."

"Thik acche," Abba replies. "Two hours."

They reach Akrum Khalu's home three hours later and the first thing they see is Rabiya Khala, Akrum Khalu's wife, standing beneath the lintel of the door, in between the two doorposts, smiling, eagerly awaiting their arrival.

"Sunia!" she cries.

"Rabiya!"

The two sisters run to each other and meet in a teary embrace. "Oh, Sunia, look at you. You've changed so much. Did you miss us? We've read every one of your letters and never want you to leave." Rabiya takes her by the arm. "Come now, come inside. I've made fresh fish from the Surma River and you must come now and sit." She looks to the others. "Please, all of you must have something to eat." She leads them to the house.

They follow.

Evening passes in increments relative to an inchworm, as do the people claiming to be their relatives from before their eyes, but when Akrum Khalu summons the ricksha-wallahs the next day and tells them to take Abba and his family to Hasan Nagore, where Abba's new home is at, they breathe a sigh of relief, especially Luky, who knows they will pass by the former home of the famous poet and raja.

"Bhaiya, brother," she asks Abir when they pass it, "what ever happened to him?"

"He never came back from the hills."

Just then, Abba's ricksha narrowly misses another ricksha racing by from the opposite direction. Luky watches the driver of the approaching ricksha careen around the curve, his face so certain, his brow so sweaty, his oversized calves like iron blocks.

"Amra ai see," one of the drivers says to no one in particular. We're here.

Luky looks to the two-story, solid-brick structure and hears Amma say, "We're home."

Abba grabs the luggage, or most of it anyway, and enters the home through a set of double doors, his family reminiscent of a brake van; and for the first time in days, they're alone.

The next day, they set out for Rangarchur, Amma's birthplace, by heading to the river and boarding the launch, a large boat propelled by a rickety engine. Their plan is simple: to stay in Rangarchur for a couple of days and then to return home with Nanu.

When they arrive, which is four hours later, they grab their things and step onto a makeshift dock and praise Allah for getting them there safely. Then they walk along dirt roads and paddy fields, all the way to Nanu's door.

"There she is!" someone yells. "There's Nanu!" A plain white sari on her body, a wellspring of tears in her eyes.

That night, Luky fights with her eyelids because earlier in the day Pilton had told her she wasn't allowed to sleep next to Nanu: "Girls don't have priority," he had said. "Only boys do." But Nanu had secretly told her not to worry: "As soon as he falls asleep, I'll pull you over next to me."

In the morning, Amma tells her, "Your bhaiyas have gone hunting with their uncles, your Abba to the bazaar, and your sisters are playing outside like fahgol nees"—like crazy girls—"in the mud."

Luky runs.

Sometime later, Nanu asks Luky and Salena, "Would you two like to help Nanu pick fruits from the forest and gather little sprigs for the fire, so we can cook lunch and dinner?"

After asr, the boys ask Nanu if they can go to the market to buy mishtis, or sweets.

"Ooh, ooh, can I go?" Luky begs.

"No, no," they say, "girls aren't allowed."

"Are too."

"Ah, let her go," Nanu goads them. "What's the harm?" She turns to Luky. "Here—" she puts in her hand ek taka, one Bangladeshi dollar— "bring me back something delicious, maybe an am," a mango, "or some other kind of fruit."

"Okay, Nanu." She pauses. "What about Amma?"

"What about her?"

"Won't she be mad?"

"About what? You going to the market?" Nanu chuckles. "She shouldn't be. After all, I'm your Amma's Amma and I say you can go."

Coming back, Luky runs into trouble.

"Where were you?!" Amma screams. "You know better than to tag along with your bhaiyas. What if someone saw you, a girl, wandering around the market? What would people say?"

"Oh, it's all right," Nanu cuts in. "I asked her to go to the market and bring me back something. Now quit running your mouth, and I'll go boil water for their ghusls," their baths.

Luky smiles, but does so from behind the safety net of her palm, for the big one had spoken, and she loved it.

After isha, Luky asks Nanu, "Why do you always sleep on the floor?"

"Because our bodies are part of the earth, my dear, and one day, after we're buried, we'll become one with it."

"But how?"

"Remember earlier when Nanu was using her broom to sweep away the dust?"

Luky nods.

"Well, the earth uses its own type of broom, one that's invisible, to sweep away our flesh from its bones, and over time our bodies and the soil merge with one another, and if you've lived a good life, a worthy life, pretty flowers of all colors will sprout from it and bloom."

Luky climbs onto Nanu's lap and smiles. "Would you like to hear a kitcha?" Nanu asks. A story.

"Oy, oy, oy!" Mumtaz and Taz and Salena say out of nowhere, interrupting. "We do. We do. We do!"

Enter Saqir, whose presence gives Luky the cringes.

"Let go of me!" she barks. "What are you doing?!"

"What's it look like I'm doing?" he asks.

"Get away." She pushes at his hand. "Jealous."

"Me, jealous?"

She sticks her tongue out and says something about Nanu liking her more.

"You little…" He drags her to the floor and kicks her in the thighbone. Reaches for her hair and pulls it.

Luky's eyes fill with water.

"Stop it, you two!" Abir yells, grabbing Saqir by the shirt collar and pulling him backwards. "What's wrong with you?"

"She was—"

"Who cares?"

"But—"

"Jah!" Nanu rises, pointing to Saqir. "Your sister's crying and she's hurt." She takes Luky by the hand and tries to calm her. "Shhh," she whispers in her ear. "It's okay. Don't worry. When he falls asleep, remember, you'll be next to me." She looks to the others. "Now who wants to hear a kitcha?"

Me, me, me they all cry, except for Saqir, who exits the room.

"Well, a long time ago," Nanu begins, "there lived in a certain city a divorced woman who worked as a prostitute, and every time the people saw her they would spit in her face and slap her. But one day, this woman did something compassionate before the eyes of our prophet."

"*What was it?*" they ask.

"It was…"

"*What, what?*" they cry.

"…something…"

"*What, what?*" they demand.

"…that no one else would have done."

"*What, what?*" They cannot take it any longer.

"She gave water to a thirash kutah." A thirsty dog.

6

They leave Rangarchur for Hasan Nagore, and after a two week hiatus, the kids start school. Amma helps ready them in their uniforms. She sits with them while they wait for the Jee, their paid escort, a service only Londoni families can afford.

A knock.

Salena goes to answer it.

"Asalaam alaykum. How are you?" asks the Jee, stepping through the doorway. "Are you lot ready to go to school today?"

The Jee wears a plain white sari with a black border, though sometimes she wears one that is white with red.

"Oy," they say.

"Good."

The Jee leads them to the rickshas, which are waiting outside, and when they get in, the ricksha-wallahs drive away. First stop: the boys' school, and when the ricksha-wallahs arrive, the girls see the boys playing leap frog and tag and some others hanging-out by the swings.

"Ow," Luky screams, reaching for her shoulder blade. "I hate you!"

"So what," Pilton chides, showing no sympathy. "I hate you too."

"Pilton!"

"Whaaat?"

"What's wrong with you?"

"Nothing."

"Then stop it!" Abir orders. "Want me to knock your block off?"

Saqir mumbles something beneath his breath and walks away.

"Are you all right?" Abir asks.

"I'm fine," Luky says.

"Good." He looks to his sisters. "Well, have a good first day at school." He looks back to Luky. "All of you."

Next, they go to the girls' school, and when they arrive, the Jee steps down and helps them deboard.

Breathe, breathe Luky tells herself. But how, when all she can think about is her old school back in Bradford and her friends?

"Luky," calls the Jee. "Are you coming?"

Luky nods but wavers when she sees a young woman with a kolshi—a water pitcher, the water from it slipping down the sides. Instantly, her mind trails away to an earlier scene, one that she saw along the way; but long gone are the details of it, and it's all because of that driver, who kept running over craters like they were 1-Ups in a video game, blurring her vision and jolting her neck bones and back, and all she could think about the entire time was holding on to the sides for dear life.

"Are you okay?" asks the Jee. "You've been acting sort of strange."

"I'm fine," Luky says. "Just thinking…"

"Look!" says Salena, pointing to an open area next to the school. "They're about to call the roll."

The girls line up on the grass according to the level of their grade and a women dressed in a white sari calls out their names. After, she makes them perform a series of physical exercises such as jumping jacks, then tells them to line up again in single file and make their way into the building. Inside the building, she tells them, "Get to your classes," and they go.

Luky enters the room.

The instructor begins by teaching them Bengali language skills, followed by math, science and writing. Then it's on to folk songs. When the bell sounds, the children run outside for recess to play skipping ropes or hopscotch or tag, and they love it.

The rest of the day flies by, and when the final bell rings, the Jee is back to pick them up. She helps Luky and her sisters into their seats and asks them how their day was. She leads them in song on the way to pick up the boys.

Kabadi, the boys love it, especially its roughness. The girls see Abir audibly repeating the words ha du du du while attempting to tackle one of the opposing players, without so much as taking a single breath. They see him bring down the player, scoring a point for his team.

The girls cheer.

Abir looks up and sees his sisters on the ricksha, along with the Jee, waiting for him and his brother, so he yells to Saqir to *come on.*

The ride home seems faster—doesn't it always?—though in reality it takes roughly the same amount of time. But time's a fickle sort of thing, innit?—and as the ensuing days and weeks transpire, everything starts to feel like a giant blur: the school, the boys, the Jee. Why, even trying to pinpoint the exact date Abba went back to England leaves Luky's head reeling, and all she can do, even though she doesn't want to, is think about the bags and the tears. Gosh, she misses her real home back in Bradford and her friends and the park with the fountain and Abba and the feeling she had on the steps that day when her little hand was in his.

"Luky," Nanu calls.

Luky turns her head and sees Nanu approaching from the rear. "Hey, Nanu. Why are you so sweaty?"

"Your Nanu's so fat she needs to be up in the batash," the air. She laughs and points to the ceiling. "Where it's cooler and where I won't always be in such heat." Nanu smiles and fans herself with one hand and tugs a portion of her sari away from her sticky flesh with the other. "Your Nanu's just always so hot." Another laugh and they walk hand in hand to the stairs and up the stairs to the roof.

On their backs, they stare at the stars, counting them and singing songs about their splendor. It is then Nanu learns the words to *Twinkle Twinkle.* Though after some time, only the cicadas and a few other night creatures care to sing.

"Nanu, could you tell me a story?"

"What would you like to hear?"

"Something about a king and a queen," she says. "Or maybe something about a prince and a princess."

"Okay," Nanu nods. "Are you ready?"

"I'm ready."

"Well," she begins, "years ago there was a lonely servant girl who fell in love with a handsome prince, and one day, while she was retrieving water from the tube well, the prince appeared along the path after traveling a great many miles and asked her for a drink of water. When the servant girl saw who it was, she nearly fainted from the shock of it, and when the prince saw the servant girl, he was struck by her exquisite fairness, by the alluring hue of her pleasant eyes, and by the kindly look of her smiling lips. To him, she was the beauteous vision of the absolute and his heart was like a prisoner in an unbreakable cage. Undoubtedly, they belonged to one another, and in due time," Nanu says, "they were married with much pomp and festivity, and eventually the prince became the king and the servant girl the queen."

"Then what happened?"

"They made babies, and eventually their babies grew up and had even more babies."

"Then what?"

"The queen, when she was old and gray, spent the remainder of her days telling stories to her grandkids on the roof of her son-in-law's home."

Luky smiles and Nanu places a hand on the side of her head. "You're gonna marry a prince someday," she says.

"I'm never getting married."

"Never?"

Luky shakes her head. "Uh-uh."

"But if you get married, your husband can look after me."

"Why's he gonna look after you for?"

"Because your Nanu's gonna get really old and she'll need someone to care for her. I'll be a bura beti," an old lady, "and—"

"Oh, all right. I guess he can look after you too," Luky concedes, nestling into her grandmother's side.

Nanu laughs. "And when you're ready to get married, you can come here and Nanu will pick out a guy for you, a prince, and we'll have a huge celebration."

"Okay, okay," Luky nudges her with her arm, "but I'm still not sure I wanna get married."

"Well," Nanu leans in closer and smiles, "maybe one day something or someone will change your mind."

7

More guests arrive today, and all Luky can do is wonder when it'll end: the countless visits from strangers, the constant inquiries concerning England.

She brings one man his tea and overhears him say that he wants to build a new home for his family. The next day, it's someone who wants to replace the thatch on their roof. Then it's someone with a sick so and so, who's been unable to the see the doctor for lack of sufficient funds. "Well, I just need a couple hundred takas," they begin, "that's all. And if you could ask your husband," or, "if you could ask Londoni bi-shab to help me out." And Amma's reply? "Well, Luky's daddy has gone back to England, and I don't have the money to give you, but when I talk to him again," that is, when I speak to your Londoni bi-shab again, "I'll let him know about your situation."

In the meantime, Amma never lets anyone leave the house without first filling up their bellies, which is why she and the girls are always in the kitchen, and even with the help of Nanu and the housemaids, they can barely keep up.

A knock.

Some guy at the door.

"Hello. How is everybody? How's the kids?" the man asks after Amma opens it.

Everybody runs from the kitchen.

"I need some money to open up a little grocery shop in the market," he says to her.

"Get lost," Amma tells him.

"Not until I get my money."

The neighbors rush over to intercede.

"Amma, who was that man?" Luky asks with an air of confusion.

"The goonda."

"The who?"

The villain. "Your Abba's brother, Polash."

At night, she overhears Amma say something to Nanu about Rajanpur, Abba's birthplace. She hears the two of them talk about war and foreign soldiers with heavy boots. About things normally left unspoken. Then she hears them say something about *him*, how he had deserted them in their most pressing hour of need, though then they go quiet and nothing further is mentioned.

Atop the concrete flooring of the tabular roof, underneath the glistening stars, Nanu massages oil into Luky's hair. They sit on morahs, two round woven seats made from cane and bamboo, and converse about a woman's beauty.

"Nanu, I don't like the coconut smell of the oil."

"You don't?"

"It stinks."

"It's good for you, though. It'll make your hair grow."

"And stink."

"Besides, your husband will like it when you're married."

"I'm never getting married."

"One day," Nanu says, "you will. Maybe to a doctor. Yes, a doctor. You'll become a doctor and marry a doctor."

"But I wanna be a nurse."

Nanu laughs. "But if you're a doctor and Nanu gets sick, you can give me your bideshi medicine from England and make me feel better. I'll even get to brag about the pretty doctor who healed me."

"Nanu, will you stop."

"Oh, all right," Nanu says, getting ready to change the subject. "Is England a nice country?"

"Mm-hmm," Luky nods. "I miss it too."

"But isn't it always dark there and cold and raining all the time?"

"Not all the time," Luky says. "But I bet it's cold there right now. I bet they even have snow."

"Then how do they keep from turning into ice blocks?"

"Huh?"

"The people, aren't they always nude?"

"No," Luky says. "They wear clothes."

"We hear they're always bare."

Luky laughs. "That's only when they're at the beach or when it's really hot outside, like in summer."

"Oh," Nanu replies, wondering what the beach is. "Do they ever talk to you a lot?"

"Yeah, sometimes, but only in English."

"Not in Bengali?"

"No."

"Not at all?"

"Not unless they're Bengali."

Nanu points to a tree, asks her if they have the same kind in England.

"Uh-uh."

"Really?"

Luky shakes her head. "Ours lose their leaves before winter."

"They do?" Nanu closes her eyes and tries to picture the falling scene. "I bet it's so nice," she says, then asks about the food.

"Mostly the same," Luky says. "But the chickens we get aren't live like the ones you lot get here. Ours are already cut."

"Already cut?" Nanu asks, shocked. "How?"

"The butcher."

"Not the women?"

"Nope." Luky shakes her head.

"Wow, everything is such a luxury." Nanu tries to comprehend it. "What about the people, how are they?"

"Bhat thear motton shada," Luky says, matter-of-factly. White like the rice.

"Really? Are they really white like that? I hear they're the most beautiful people in the world, and that some of them even have hair like the bura manoush." Like the old people.

"You mean blonde, and it's not just old people that have it, young people have it too. Even some kids are born with it."

"Really? They even have shada suil hair when they're born?"

"It's not called white hair though," Luky says. "It's called blonde. Picture sonali, Nanu." Gold.

"Ooh, it's gotta be so nice then if it's golden. Does it look like my bangles, like this color gold?" Nanu asks, all excited.

"No. It's not as shiny as that."

Nanu looks disheartened. "Well, I hear those people are taller than anything."

"Some are," Luky says, "but the Jam-e-khans are even taller."

"The Jam-e-khans?" Nanu asks. "Who are they?"

"Some folks from Africa."

"Are they nice looking?"

"They look like khallah bandors."

"Like black monkeys?"

"Mm-hmm," Luky says. "With big lips, wide noses, and curly hair."

"Uggghhh." Nanu makes a face. "Do they ever talk to you?"

"To Abba."

"He knows them?"

"A few."

"And their language?"

"Not really. He makes a lot of hand gestures."

"Oh."

Nanu ties a red ribbon to a braid. "Is it true that back home you lot bathe in hot water that comes from an indoor tube well?"

"It's comes from a faucet."

"Who heats it?"

"No one."

"No one?"

"You turn a handle."

"Is that where you wash your clothes?"

"No. We do that in the washing machine."

"The washing machine?"

"Yeah."

"It cleans them?"

"All by itself."

"Who taught it?"

"No one."

"No one?"

"You press a button. It's the same with the dryer."

"The dryer?"

"Yeah. It dries things."

Nanu looks puzzled. "But where does the gorom batash," the hot air, "come from? How is it drying—?"

"It just does, Nanu."

"But—"

"*It knows.*"

Nanu steers the conversation toward food.

"Fish and chips," Luky replies. "They have these little shops you can buy it from too, but Abba hates it. He gets fishes from the store and puts them in the fridge."

"The freege?" Nanu asks.

"Yeah. It keeps everything cold."

"But how? Is there snow inside of it?"

"Just ice," Luky says.

"Well, why doesn't Amma cook the fishes on the same day that Abba brings them?"

"She does, but he normally brings too many."

"So they never spoil in there?"

"No. That's what the snow…er, I mean ice is for."

"But won't that make them hard?"

"It's what keeps them fresh."

Nanu pictures the stiffened fish and cringes. "But they're dead in there, right?"

"Of course."

"So you lot eat dead fish then?"

"Doesn't everybody?"

Nanu takes another ribbon and ties it to another braid. "I wish we had a machine like your freege here to keep things cool because your uncle, you know, he catches so many, and with a freege like your Abba's, Nanu wouldn't have to cook so many all at once."

Luky smiles and Nanu pulls her into her arms. "Are you gonna take me to England someday?" she asks.

"Yeah, we're gonna take you someday."

"To London?"

"Yeah. Even to London."

8

July. 1980.

Luky gathers her sisters and escorts them from the yard to the house and into the house through the door. She leads them into the kitchen, where they sample what is left of the mishtis, where they wish a final Eid Mubarak to the stragglers, who are getting ready to depart for the masjid or to home. She smiles when a woman says *I love your dress. Where did you get it from?* But after doing wudu and changing into another outfit, a hand embroidered salwar, maroon in color, with a matching kameez, and doing her namaz, she suddenly laments the encroaching onset of darkness, which means an end to her favorite day. She also wonders "Is Abba going to call?" Even now, she sits by the phone, hoping to hear its ring.

But she never does.

Because he never calls.

She thinks if only she had held him in her arms that day he waved goodbye and stepped onto the airplane...

Under the covers, she thinks about the story behind the night of power, which was three days ago on the twenty-seventh day of Ramadan, and how the prophet Mohammad went to Jerusalem on a night journey on a flying horse named Buraq to meet with the prophets of oldtime prior to his ascension; and the day after that, which was two days ago on the twenty-eighth day of Ramadan, she remembers when the ferry-wallah came with his suitcases full of new saris and how she and her sisters had been allowed to choose from an array of motley colors and fabrics; and the day after that, which was one day ago on the twenty-ninth day of Ramadan, she remembers, clearly, how Nanu had bargained for some bangles and trinkets from some women who carry baskets full of jewelry atop of their heads. She also remembers the startled faces of the two housemaids, not to mention the Jee, when they got their new clothes shortly after asr, and the smiling faces of the neighbor boys and girls as they played in the yard with no cares or worries on the west side of Abba's home. But the incident that came after that, which happened shortly before maghrib, when she asked of another girl *how come you're not wearing a new dress for Eid?* and the girl replied *because our daddy's not a Londoni daddy like your daddy is* made her feel less than well.

On her side now, she hugs her pillow to her body and wonders if Abba got new clothes. *It's over,* she thinks. *Eid. It's really, really over.* Although she wishes it were Eid every day.

Three weeks later.

"Oh, Allah, please don't let my daughter die," Amma begs. "Please don't take her away. I'll do whatever you want me to. I'll read the Quran. I'll give up every part of my body. If only you let her recover. If only you allow her to live." Amma collapses and she sobs and she sobs. While Nanu pulls her granddaughter closer to the edge of the bedside, so that her head is hanging off of it. She then places a large empty bowl on the floor while reciting verses from the Quran. "Please," Nanu prays, wrapping a blanket around Luky's body and grabbing a pitcher of water to pour over her head, "heal my Luky. For what is an old grandmother's life worth anyway, without the beautiful face of her grand-daughter?" She turns to Amma. "The medicine in this country is crap," she says, "and you know it. She needs Londoni medicine. Otherwise…" Nanu uses her hand as a tissue. "My grandchildren don't belong here. They deserve to be in luxury."

Apparently, Amma agrees. Even now, she's dialing Abba's number.

"Hello?" Abba answers the phone.

"Asalaam alaykum, ami." It's me. Amma's voice cracks.

"What's wrong?" Abba asks. "Why do you sound like that?"

Amma sniffles, begins to cry. "It's Luky. She—"

"Wha—what's wrong with her? What's happened?"

"…been sick for days." Amma makes a throat noise. "And the doctors—" she shakes her head— "don't know what they are doing." She swallows. "They're at a loss."

"How come you didn't call me earlier?"

"I thought she was going to get better." Amma's voice fluctuates. "I didn't want to be a bother."

"Is she stable?"

"...has diarrhea. High temperature. Don't know how much longer—"

"Okay, okay," Abba says. "I'll get a plane ticket immediately and call you when I arrive."

"Accha," Amma whispers. "But hurry. Your daughter needs to go home."

—*How is she?*

—*Ill, very ill.*

—*How long do you think?*

—*Not long, especially if she stays here.*

—*What should we do then?*

—*Take her to England, where she belongs.*

—*But this is where she belongs.*

—*Sorry, dahman* (son-in-law), Nanu says to Rahman, *she is dying, and if you don't take her back as soon as possible, she won't make it. Why can't you understand that? This place is foreign to her and she deserves better. None of my grandchildren are adjusting, not to the food, the weather, the endless queue of relatives, arriving, departing, without any kind of regard for their privacy, their time; coming and going, in and out, in and out, carrying all sorts of disease and begging. I tell you, dahman, there is no end in sight to this madness. You'll be working your ass off forever to support these people. You might as well open your own hotel here, for that's what this place, this house, is beginning to become. And my daughter, all she does all day long is slave away in that kitchen, trying to feed those bottomless baskets. They're like hungry wolves, and who can fill them? And where is all your hard work and earnings going to? It's going down the shitpit so long as these animals keep chawing away at your trough. There's no point in staying. Your best bet is to return to England where my grandchildren can live in peace. Besides, the girls miss you, especially Luky, and I know that you miss them too.*

—Well, my first concern is my daughter, and if she isn't doing well, then I probably need to take her back. I probably need to take them all back. After all, I don't want anything to happen to my children.

Abba picks up his little girl and carries her to the living room. He tells everyone to pack, to take only what they need.

At the airport, Leelu Miah (Amma's older brother) stands a short distance away from Nanu's right flank. Heron is there too, as is Jooshna (Leelu Miah's eldest daughter), and they are all crying, except for Rahman, Leelu Miah and, of course, Luky, who is like a dead person in Abba's arms against the backdrop of her surroundings.

Salena, Mumtaz, Taz and Gully run to Nanu and hug her; their tears dampen a portion of her sari. Nanu in turn pats each of their little heads and tells them that she loves them, also that they'll be missed. She tells Luton to study hard and look after his Amma and sisters, but to Pilton she says, "Give your mum a break and listen to her, and don't be so naughty. And *do not hit Luky*. When she gets better, make sure you treat her nice."

Lastly, she approaches Luky. "Listen to your mum," she says in a whisper, at the same time wiping hair from her eyes. "And listen to what she tells you. I know you are going to grow up to be a good girl and a good doctor."

"Time to go," Abba says, glancing at his watch. He gives his salaam to Nanu and the others and turns to leave. But

Salena won't let go of Nanu's leg. "I love you, Nanu. Won't you come back with us?" Nanu bends at the waist and squeezes her granddaughter. "I'd love to get on a plane with you and see England, but maybe next time, my dear, when you're older, you can take Nanu."

"Okay, Nanu. Next time." Salena smiles. "When I'm older."

"Then it's settled," Nanu agrees.

Sunia goes to Nanu's side.

"Don't cry, my Sunia," Nanu begs. "What are you crying for? You're gonna come back and see me. All of you will." She smiles. "And don't worry about Luky. She'll be fine. You'll see. As soon as you get home, she'll be running around like normal and playing with her sisters and studying her books and—"

"But it might be years before I'm here again," Amma ekes. "It was years since I was here before, and there's always *that* chance."

"Have faith," Nanu says. "Allah grants longevity. You know that. Besides, my grandchildren are growing and they'll probably come and get me one day."

Rahman steps forward and places a hand on his wife's shoulder. "Come on or we'll miss our flight."

"Accha," Amma nods. Then gives Nanu one last squeeze.

"Please take good care of my grandchildren," Nanu says as they go, "and don't ever hit them. Remember, boys need to be naughty once in a while, even though it drives you crazy."

Minutes later, Nanu, Leelu Miah, Heron and Jooshna watch them step onto an airplane. They watch the airplane take off into the air. Then they stare at the blueness of the sky until all that remains is a trail of fluffy white stuff.

—*Nanu? Are you there?* Luky asks.

—*Yes, dear, I am here.*

—*Where did you go?*

—*Nowhere, my child; I am in your heart.*

—*Nanu?*

—*Yes, dear?*

—*Can I ask you something?*

—*Of course.*

—*Does Allah really have a window in heaven that he looks out through and sees all that I do?*

—*Yes, dear. Allah is all-knowing. But do not be afraid, for Allah is ever-merciful and kind.*

"Luky, Luky! Wake up, wake up! Are you all right? Talk to me. How do you feel? Can you move? Do you think you can sit up?"

Luky opens her eyes; white walls surround her and Abba is in a chair in the corner and Amma is next to her bedside, as is an elderly man in white. But where is Nanu?

"You are a very lucky young lady," the elderly man says to her. "No pun intended, of course, but you made it here just in time. Nevertheless, we expect a full recovery."

"Wher—where am I?" she asks.

"St. Luke's Hospital," he says, "and as soon as you're able to hold down some solids and go to the toilet, you'll be able to leave." The doctor steps closer. "I bet you can't wait to sleep in your own room again after being here for a week."

"A week?"

"Yes, and the best advice I can give you right now is to take it easy and rest. A nurse will be in to check on you shortly."

Luky closes her eyes and her parents huddle around her. She is thankful to be on Little Horton Lane again, for the western amenities she'll now be able to enjoy, but she'll forever rue the day she wasn't able to say goodbye to Nanu.

"We were so worried about you," Amma says, interrupting her thoughts. "Day after day, I recited verses from the Quran and ran my fingers through your hair. I blew on your forehead and prayed to Allah to *please make my daughter better, to please take away her fever.* And constantly, I held onto these prayer beads, thumbing through each one, performing dhikr," repeating Allahu Akbar, God is great, over and over again. "And now that you're awake... Oh, Luky, your recovery has been the answer to my prayers, and I'll ever thank Allah for the miracle he has given to me."

"Yes. Masha'Allah," God has willed it, Abba concurs. "God has given you back to us, and if you are feeling up to it, we can go home and eat some of your Amma's special sago pudding."

Luky smiles. She takes a quick bite out of some hospital biscuit and asks Amma to help her to the toilet and she does.

9

Spring. 1981.

A girl of nine and three-quarters sits in her room, listening to songs on her radio. But a knock on the door, the front door, sends Salena, who is sitting next to her, to the front room window to peer through its shades.

"Boro affa! Boro affa!" Salena calls, her feet running from the window to the hall and up the stairs to her room. "Boro affa! Boro affa!"

Luky turns off the radio.

"It's your teacher," Salena says, trying to catch her breath. "He's here, he's here, he's here!"

"What are you talking about?" Luky asks.

"Mr. Andrews!" she exclaims. "He's here!"

"Oh my God! Oh my God!" She runs to the closet and pulls from the hanger her favorite salwar and kameez and changes into it. She goes to the mirror, which is on the wall opposite the closet, and brushes her hair, smiling the entire time that she does it. She dons her best silk and most stylish hijab, pink in color and trimmed with lace. She applies kajol or liner to the top of her lids and a slight hint of rouge to the apples of her cheeks. Lastly, she applies gloss, so shiny and sparkly, to her lips.

"What was he doing when you came up?" she asks.

"Nothing."

"What do you mean, nothing? He must have been doing something."

"Nope," says Salena. "Just knocking."

"You didn't let him in?"

"I wanted to tell you first. I know how you fancy him."

"Salena! You spastic. My God. Is he still down there?" Luky points to the doorway. "Go and let him in! Hurry! What are you still doing here?"

Salena runs.

Mr. Andrews has on a light-blue, buttoned-up long-sleeved shirt, beige slacks, a herringbone patterned tie, a black pair of leather shoes on his feet, and a skinny black belt attached to a silver buckle around his waist.

"Hello," he says to Salena.

"Hello, Mr. Andrews. How are you? Do you remember me? I'm Luky's sister, Salena."

"I certainly do, young lady. And I'm fine. We met at the school on parents' night. And you were with your mummy and daddy, and I still remember that beautiful dress." He loses himself in thought for a moment and Salena giggles. "But how are you today? And how is school going for you?"

"I'm well, Mr. Andrews, thank you. And school is going great. I got my report back and it has all A's."

"You did? That's brilliant! Well done! I'm so glad to hear it. But tell me…is your father home? I'd very much like to have a word with him."

"I'll go and get him for you, Mr. Andrews. Be right back."

She hustles to the dining room where Abba is sitting, savoring a cup of tea. "Abba, Abba!" she says.

Abba looks up from the table and away from his tea.

"Boro affa's teacher, Mr. Andrews, is here, and he is wondering if he can have a word with you."

Abba rises and goes to the door to greet Mr. Andrews and welcome him inside. He ushers him into the front room.

Meanwhile, Luky sneaks downstairs atiptoe and scurries her way to the kitchen where Amma is busily minding her own business.

"Slow down, slow down. I can't understand a single word you are saying," Amma says.

"It's Mr. Andrews," Luky continues, "my teacher. He's here."

Amma looks puzzled. "Who?"

"Mr. Andrews. My English teacher? Don't you remember? You met him at the school on parents' night. Both you and Abba where there. Salena was there and she was wearing that dress. Please tell me you remember."

"Ah, yes…Mr. Andrews." Amma nods. "The young one."

"That's him," Luky says. "And he's in the front room right now. I saw him go in there with Abba."

Salena enters the kitchen.

"Abba said he wants you to make some tea and some snack."

"Anything else?" Luky asks, hoping Salena tells her something good, like news.

"Nope," she says, "that's it," and turns to go.

"What do you mean that's it? They must have said *something* about me."

"Oh yeah," she says, walking away. "You're getting an award, some type of cup."

"The Dennis Stevenson cup?"

"Yeah, that's it. For academic improvement."

"Oh my God! I can't believe it! Really?" But then she starts to think about the house and the smell of the house and wonders where the spray is and the chinaware, "Because we have to serve Mr. Andrews his biscuits and tea on something nice," she says.

"The chinaware's in the top cabinet." Amma points to its location, rolling her eyes. "And the can of aerosol is there." She points to a cupboard beneath the sink.

"Got it," Luky says, making off to greet the air with a bouquet of scented mist. "Can you go and change now?" she asks Amma after spraying. "Pleeease. You can't go wearing that curried rag to see my teacher."

Amma examines her sari, thinks it looks just fine. "But I don't need to see your teacher. I've already met him. Besides, I can't speak good English."

"Who cares? I'm sure he's gonna want to see you. Can't you at least say hello?"

"Accha, accha. I'll be down in two minutes. Just start making the tea."

"Did you put the milk and sugar in already?" Amma asks, coming back.

"Uh-uh," Luky says. "He's shada, remember? He's not like us Bengalis, who lump all the ingredients together all at once. He'll expect everything to be carried in on a tray: the cups, the saucers, the teapot, the creamer, the sugar bowl, even the teabags." Luky pauses and takes a short breath. "Shada people are posh, Amma. High-class. They like to author their own cups of tea."

"Well, that's fine, beti. But you're forgetting the teabags." Amma opens a drawer and selects a handful of number two's.

"I already have them, Amma. The Tetley ones. I'm not serving Mr. Andrews those cheap knockoffs. You can save those things for the Bengali women who come over."

Amma turns away. "Just hurry before your Abba wonders where you are."

Luky picks up the tray and walks from the kitchen to the dining room and makes her way to the hallway. She goes past the stairs and the living room, all the way to the front room door, where she stops for a minute to breathe and clear her throat of an imaginary blockage. Only after all that does she feel brave enough to enter.

"I've brought tea," she says, trying not to look at Mr. Andrews or trip. But when Mr. Andrews looks in her direction, she can't help but look back, nor can she help the burning in her ears. *Oh, Mr. Andrews.* How fascinated she is by his ashy-brown hair, his light colored eyes, the whiteness of his skin.

"Luky, how are you doing?" he asks her. "I was just telling your father how much you've progressed lately and how good you've been doing in…"

But Luky hears nothing more of it. Only plays with her fingers as Mr. Andrews showers her with compliments.

"…such an excellent student too," he says to Abba. "I'm so proud of her." He crosses his legs and folds his hands over his knee. "Her other teachers tell me she is doing just fine as well."

Luky sets the tray on the coffee table, which is right in front of the sofa, upon which sits Mr. Andrews. Abba is in an armless chair across from Mr. Andrews and Salena is on the floor next to Abba with her legs curled beneath her.

Luky takes a saucer and cup from the tray and hands the two items to Mr. Andrews. He says *thank you, Luky* as she puts in the Tetley tea bag and pours, from the mouth of the ceramic pot, a stream of piping hot water that engulfs, completely, the white rectangular bag. When it reaches the cup's brim, she hears him say, "That's enough, love," so she stops. *Oh, Mr. Andrews.* She can hardly believe her eyes, that the love of her life, the man of her dreams, Mr. Andrews, is really, really here.

Amma enters the room.

"Hello, hello," she says, her face partially hidden with her sari. She is proud that her daughter's teacher came for a visit. *She must be a really good student* she thinks. But the look on her husband's face when Mr. Andrews reiterates how Luky will receive the cup from the mayor in the city centre on such and such a day in the future is what contents her heart the most.

"Masha'Allah, masha'Allah," Abba says again and again. He rises to pat his daughter on the back. "You're gonna be something someday, and that's how it should be: you study hard and Allah rewards you." He looks to Salena. "You should all be like Luky because now she's getting the cup." He turns back to his eldest daughter. "I'm very proud of you today, and I know you'll make a great doctor." He smiles a grin as wide as the sky is long.

Later, when the lights go out in Luky's bedroom, which is a longtime after Salena's mutterings have evaporated into snores, Luky rues the fact that Mr. Andrews' visit was so short in duration, and that he couldn't stay a bit longer. Her mind then wanders to the mayor and the cup and the curtsey she'll have to perform before exiting the stage. But the last thing she thinks about is Abba and whether he'll be angry or upset when the mayor takes her hand and kisses it.

A dream: Luky gets the cup.

The mayor grins and kisses her hand and the crowd cheers.

At home, Abba takes the cup to the dining room and places it on the mantelpiece above the fireplace.

—*Why don't you go and check your stupid cup* Saqir says to her. *There's something in it.*

—*What?*

—*Check it.*

She flees to the dining room and runs to the fireplace. She reaches toward the mantelpiece with her fingers. She lowers the cup to the ground. *Eeeewwww. What's in here?*

—*It's piss.* Saqir laughs.

—*Are you for real?*

—*I pissed in your stupid Dennis Stevenson cup. What are you gonna do about it?*

—*I'm gonna tell dad.*

—*Better not.*

—*Watch me.*

She brushes past her brother, but a punishing slug to the arm halts her momentum, and all she can do is reach for the shooting pain and cry, "Abba, Abba!" as Saqir runs away.

—*What's wrong, what's wrong?* Abba comes running.

—*Sootoh bi-shab hit me; he peed in my cup.*

—*Whaaaaaat?*

—*He peed in my trophy.*

—*Where?*

—*In the dining room.*

"Pillllllllton!" he roars. He searches room to room until he finds him. He drags him by the ears to the dining room. "Clean this up," he orders, "and polish it until it's silver."

10

The following day, Luky waits for her teacher to say something untowardly about her house or its contents, but he never does. Only says how nice it was to see her parents again and tell her father about the cup. Still, she couldn't help but feel embarrassed concerning her typical Bengali home and his possible reaction to it: she especially worried about the curried smell, the Christmas decorations in the middle of freaking June, though not because they celebrated Christmas (they didn't), but because Abba was so fond of colored light strings, tinsels, and sparkling bulbs; there was also the tuliped wall paper.

"Luky!" Melanie calls.

Luky sees three girls approaching.

"Is it true?" Melanie asks.

"Is what true?"

"About Mr. Andrews, that he came over to your place the other day?"

"Yeah. He came over."

The girls look to each other's faces, shocked.

"He told my dad I'd be getting the cup."

"Not the—"

"Yep. The Dennis Stevenson cup."

The girls snicker. "We feel bad for next year's winner," they say.

"Why?"

"Because the cup's gonna stink like curry."

The girls howl and walk away. But Luky doesn't move, just stands there thinking about the day a girl named Melanie came over for a visit, back when she was seven and a half.

"Amma, can one of my friends come over?"

"No."

"But Amma, there's this girl named Melanie at my school who keeps telling me how much she wants to come over, so that she can try some of our food. She's *dying* to have curry and rice, so can she?"

The next day, Amma sets the table and calls the girls to dinner. Salena and Mumtaz take their seats at the table and Taz and Gully plop to the floor next to the ottoman. Melanie and Luky are the last to arrive but waste no time in joining Salena and Mumtaz at the table. "Okay," Luky says to Melanie, "time to eat." They begin to eat with their hands, all except Melanie, who was the only one given a fork. "Ugh. You lot eat with your hands?" she says.

Luky looks around, not knowing anything was amiss. "Sometimes," she lies, wishing she had a utensil.

"Does your friend like the food?" Amma inquires. "Ask her if it's too hot?"

Luky turns to Melanie. "My mum wants to know if you like the food and whether it's too hot."

Melanie raises her brows. "Your mum doesn't speak English?"

"Not really, but—"

"You mustn't have lived here for very long, then. I mean your family. Because mine's been here for ages, and we can all speak perfect English just fine."

"It's just—"

"What did she say?" Amma asks.

"She said it's good."

"Not too hot?"

Luky shakes her head. "Just right."

Amma smiles and stuffs another fingerful of rice and curry into Gully's mouth. She goes to replenish Melanie's near empty plate, but Melanie says, "I don't want anymore. I'm full."

Amma blinks. "Ferrotte nee ekta!" she shouts out of nowhere. She's one filthy girl! "Don't her parents own a nail clipper? How come they're so long?"

"Bundoh ho!" Luky says back to her. Be quiet! "Don't say stuff like that. She's right there, Amma. She can hear you."

"Well, she can't speak Bengali, can she? So she's not gonna understand."

"But Amma—"

"Look at those nails," Amma continues. "My God. They're longer than anything. Just look at them!"

"Sooboh!" Luky shouts. "Maithtoe na." Don't talk.

"What is she saying?" Melanie asks.

"Nothing. She was talking about the food."

"...a monster," Amma goes on.

"Sooboh, sooboh!" Luky says.

Salena and Mumtaz make yucky faces at boro affa and then snicker.

"Stop it, you two!"

"What's wrong with them?" Melanie asks.

"They're just being silly, that's all."

"Your family's weird."

Just then, Abba enters the dining room and sits at the table, and Amma proceeds to serve him his food. In one fell swoop, he gathers a clump of rice with his fingers and turns to Melanie and says, "Hello. I'm Luky daddy. How are you?" and shoves the clump into his mouth.

"Very well, thank you."

"You like this kind of food?" he asks her, pointing to the curry and munching.

"Mm-hmm."

Oh God. Luky tries to make herself smaller and disappear and become invisible; her world feels like a toxic wasteland.

She looks to her parents, who are both eating with their fingers, and then to Melanie, who is still holding the fork.

The next day, at recess, she overhears Melanie tell a group of friends, "They eat with their hands, like animals."

"Eeewww, that's gross," the friends say. "Do they wipe their bums with leaves?"

"Probably," Melanie tells them. "I didn't see any toilet paper. But listen, her mum's all covered up and her dad wears this little black cap on his head like the Jews do, and you wouldn't believe it, but they have this big home. I really don't know how they can afford a place like that. My mum says they shouldn't even be allowed in our country, especially since they can't speak the language. Do you know they still have their Christmas decorations up? I mean, don't they know it's bad luck to have them up after Christmas? I guess not, but if you're gonna live in this country, I think it is something you should at least know."

I just wanted to fit in and be like them Luky said to a close confidant years later. *But she thought we were some type of animal, some thing from another planet, or that we were weird or some type of walking germ.*

Needless to say, Melanie never revisited, and the last time she and Luky spoke to one another was that day at Buttershaw Middle, when they spoke about Mr. Andrews and the cup.

The school day ends and Luky boards the bus for home. In the dining room, Abba tells her that he has to leave for work much earlier than his usual shift starting time at the garment factory, and that he needs her to pick up her sisters.

"Just take the main road," Abba says. "You'll be fine."

"How come they can't take the bus?"

Luky exits the house and trots down the stone steps and advances to the sidewalk after pushing through the front gate. She travels along Little Horton Lane south and passes the church across from Park Road. She moves toward the zebra crossing, which spans the width of Little Horton Lane, connecting St. Luke's Hospital (which is on the opposite side of the street) to the parking lot in front of the nurses' residences. She watches the traffic come to a standstill at the zebra crossing as a bevy of nurses walk across it. She hears their voices, sees their smiling faces, sees their feet atop the black and white markings that delineate it, while a small line of vehicles count down the seconds until they are no longer blocking the roadway.

Past the zebra crossing now, the red post box and the green bus stop benches, she advances by the well-landscaped front yard of the hospital, with its many scenic bushes and trees; and on her right is the remainder of the parking lot. But just a little farther ahead, she decides to take an alternate streetway, even though Abba had warned her not to, one that slightly veers to the right called Little Horton Green, as opposed to the more straightforward and more logical route her Abba always takes: that of continuing down Little Horton Lane, past All Saints Church, until reaching Pullan Street and rounding the walk there to the right and following the paved bypath that leads to the front doors of the school, All Saints First School. But that way, Abba's way, is boring; why, besides the imposing tower firmly connected to the southeast corner of the church's nave, the only other attraction of any real interest are the sprawling branches of some genus or other that hang over the dry stone walls with their minions of pullable leaves.

On Little Horton Green, she passes by the church (it's on her left), all the while admiring its pointed arch windows, its pointed arch entryway, which is stationed in the northwest corner of the structure; and as she continues, she passes by a coterie of residential homes that are arranged in the shape of a backwards letter P, all on her right. Now. Straight ahead is Kennion Street; she sees the signpost pop into view. *I'm almost there* she thinks. *Almost to their stupid school.* She wonders about the time, guesses it is close to four.

At the corner of Kennion Street and Little Horton Green, she turns and looks one way and then another, only to turn around again and repeat the whole process. Why? Because something is moving on the other side of that tree. Which tree? The one right next to the stone boundary wall.

"Hey you, I'm talking to you," a man shouts. "You fucking nigg—"

Luky freezes.

"Yeah, you heard me. You brown fucking slag. Come 'ere!"

A zillion and one thoughts zip through her brain like a tidal against an un-leveed riverbank and she wonders if she'll ever be able to...

The man comes closer.

Luky runs.

Though how far she ran and also to where she ran is anybody's thesis. The only thing she remembers is taking off and racing like a motorcar and the way her thighs were burning and the feeling of uncertainty, of whether he was going to...

That aside, her worries hadn't prevented her from running up to the first house she saw and shoving open its gate and rushing up the steps to the door and banging on it.

"What's wrong love?" an elderly woman asks. "What's wrong?"

"He's after me! He's trying to get me!"

"Who is, love?" The woman looks to the gate. "Who is after you?"

"He is!" Luky turns around.

"Don't worry, love," the woman assures her. "He's gone." She sticks an arm out to pat Luky's shoulder.

Gasp.

"There, there," the woman mutters. "Do you know who it was that was chasing you?"

Luky shakes her head.

"Did he do anything to you?"

"He couldn't get me."

The woman looks relieved. "Would you like to come in and sit down for a bit?"

"I can't," Luky says. "I need to pick up my sisters from school." She wipes the sweat from her face. "But I don't know the way."

"It's not far, love," the woman tells her. "You just need to go that way." She points with her finger. "To Kennion Street and turn right."

Luky opens the gate to go.

"But shan't I phone the police, dear?" the woman asks.

Luky shrugs.

"Well, be careful," the woman says in a voice that's grandmotherly. "And don't worry. I'll be right here the whole time."

Luky runs.

"Hey, boro affa," Mumtaz says, standing next to Taz and Gully. "Where's dad?"

"…"

"Boro affa, are you all right?"

"I'm fine," she says to Salena. "Let's go."

On the way home, conversation is kept to a minimum, and never once does Luky tell them about the man; she simply cannot bring herself to speak the words, nor does she want to scare them. Also, the very idea of verbalizing something so shameful makes her feel nauseous.

"Boro affa, what are you looking at?"
"I'm not looking at anything."
"Then why—"
"Just keep walking," she says. "Please."

11

Sunday.

Shortly after fajr. In the fall of nineteen hundred and eighty-three. A twelve year old girl sits in the front room on the floor, her younger sisters beside her, waiting for the instructor's arrival. Other children from the neighborhood are there too, as is the case every Sunday. Why, just take a look on the other side of Luky and you'll see, nervously chewing on the tips of her fingers, Suja, whose mummy they call khallah nee or black lady, though not to her face of course. And look! On the other side of Suja is Fermeeda, the eldest and only child of a man whose stature measures an absurd 1.9 meters; and don't even ask about his wife's posh style of dress either. How she tailors her clothes to accentuate her features. It kills them. But what about the young man next to the window, the one by his three goofy pals? Not Abir; he's still at the university in Manchester, finishing up his studies. Not Saqir either; he's still in Dewsbury, studying to be an imam or prayer leader. No, the young man in question is much younger, closer rather to the age of Rahman's eldest daughter, Luky, who only recently celebrated her twelfth birthday, just before the advent of school. And his looks? Well, on his face he wears glasses that recall to mind the bottom parts of glass bottles, and he is further distinguished among his peers by three distinct moles, or maybe those are birthmarks?—innately arraying different parts of his splotchy face; and in case you are wondering after the boy's name, it is Sheepu, and he never misses a class.

A sound.

From the front entry hall. *Oh no. It's the door.* The main door to their home. And it's Abba. *It must be Abba and his guest,* their teacher, arriving on time and stepping through the doorway.

"Asalaam alaykum," the imam says as he enters the front room. Abba goes to the kitchen.

"Wa alaykum asalaam."

Not paying attention, Luky's eyes start to wander over and across the others in attendance. She watches Sheepu readjust his spectacles, then wipe, with the back of his hand, something icky from his nose. *Ugh* she thinks to herself, *how gross.* At the same time, he smiles in her direction, even eye-kisses her irises, and for whatever odd reason (though later she surmises it was a subconscious effort), she smiles back. Then loosens a portion of her hijab by pretending to scratch, with the tips of her fingers, the place where her hair and the border of her brow meet.

"Luky!"

She looks to the voice.

"Surah Al-Fatiha," the opening chapter, the imam's voice cracks. "Recite it for us, now!"

She recoils like a child at the sight of the bogeyman.

The imam tromps forward.

She butchers the text with her tongue.

"Enough!" he thunders.

The others make no sound.

The imam treads closer. Luky flinches.

The imam walks behind her. She can feel his offensive breath on her neck when he squats.

"Last week," he begins, "when I was here, I asked everyone to be ready. Did I not?" He impatiently waits for an answer. "Well...did I?"

Luky nods.

The imam rises and raises his cane high above the kufi covering his bald spot.

Luky closes her eyes and pictures his yellow breath.

Allahu Akbar, he shouts. Then forces the instrument of penance on her shoulder.

Whack.

Allahu Akbar, he calls.

Whack.

Allahu Akbar.

Whack, whack, whack.

At night, she remembers how these days used to be when Pilton accepted the brunt of the canings, and for the first time ever, she wishes he were here.

It is half past seven on the morning of a school day and Abba gets off the bus at the bus stop, happy to be off work, and walks along Little Horton Lane for home. *Whoa! Looking good* he says, entering the dining room. *Are you lot ready for school today?* his smile growing brighter and more lucid. *Don't forget your crisp money.*

They hold out their hands.

"Ten pence each," he says.

They thank him.

"You're welcome." He sinks into his chair.

"School-o jai ram gi," Luky says, rising. I'm going to school now.

Abba looks to his daughter. "Thik acche. Allah hafiz."

"Allah hafiz, Abba."

At the bus stop, Luky remembers how Abba used to hug her in the morning, but when the bus driver beeps his horn, the memory starts to fade.

In her seat, she sees her hijab, along with the preapproved slacks Abba had purchased for her, poking out of her book bag. Without hesitation, she crams them under some notebooks. Though a part of her feels guilty for doing it, what other choice does she have? Which is why, after leaving for school every morning, she first goes to the rear of the church across from Park Road, which is a mere baseball toss from her home, and removes her Islamic gear and crams it into her book bag. Only then, after all that hassle, does she make her way to the benches.

Looking out the window, she pictures Abba walking her sisters to the bus stop, her sisters, Salena, Mumtaz and Taz catching a ride to Priestman Middle, the school that they go to, which is nearly two kilometers away on the south side of Thornton Lane. She pictures Abba leaving the bus stop with Gully after that and walking to All Saints First School, the school that Gully goes to, and then going home. But of all the things she pictures…

Eyeing her skirt now, the whiteness of her knee-highs, she smiles. God, she looks good. She pulls out eyeliner from her book bag and outlines the contours of her eyes. She pulls out lipstick, which resembles the hue of a light-pink rose, and covers the fleshy parts of her lips. She brushes her lengthy black tresses and gathers them into a bundle and cinches them very close to the base of her skull, using a barrette. Lastly, she looks into a mirror.

At the zebra crossing, passengers fiddle in their seats while pedestrians crisscross the lane. She stares at the nurses' residences and sees two nurses in white skirts and navy blue capes approaching. She rushes to another seat on the far side of the bus and watches some more enter the hospital's entrance. She watches them disappear.

The bus moves forward.

Toward Buttershaw Upper.

To Reevy Road West.

It drives.

At school, Luky makes her way to the far side of the building to where, hidden amongst the trees and against an unwindowed wall, her shada friends are waiting, smoking. She dislikes this part of the morning, but there isn't any other way around it. *I'm already different* she thinks to herself. *I don't wanna be seen as too different.* She remembers the first time she had tried smoking; it was when Abba threw down one of his cigarettes, and that was months ago. Now she just nicks them from Abba's stash; and whenever Abba leaves one unattended (a lit one), she helps herself to a couple of drags.

"Boro affa," she remembers her sister saying, "you can't keep smoking dad's cigarettes like that. He always wonders why they're half gone."

"I have to. I need to get better."

"Why?"

"You wouldn't understand."

"Try me."

"My friends..." Luky looks away. "They..." she sighs. "Never mind."

"Luky, Luky!" Her friends wave.

Luky runs.

(Her friends are all English, all white. And she, the only Bengali in the group).

Caroline speaks first. "Let's ask Luky," she says.

"Yeah, let's ask her. Let's find out what *she* did this weekend."

"Ooh, yeah. And don't leave out the details either."

"Especially if it's about *that* guy."

Luky swallows, wonders how to respond. "Umm, well, I..." She stutters, pauses. Takes a breath and tries to deflect the question. "I have an idea," she says. "Why don't you lot go first?" She looks to the others, one by one. "We'll save the best story for last." She points to herself. "Mine."

"Fine," the others say.

"Ooh, wanna hear what I did?" Justine says.

The girls nod. "What, what?"

"Well, actually, it was what somebody else did to me."

"Oh my gosh, Justine! Who?"

"Tell us!"

"Yeah. Tell us what he did?"

"It was Gary Leyland," Justine continues.

"Ooh, you went out with Gary?"

"Mm-hmm."

"He's so fit!"

"And hot too!"

"I love Gary," Hazel replies. "He's so dreamy."

"Where did you go?"

"The rink," she giggles.

"How was it?"

"Good, but do you wanna hear the best part?"

"Tell us!"

"Yeah, hurry!"

"Get on with it!"

"Please!"

The girls step closer.

"He led me to a corner…"

"Yeah, yeah?" they say.

"…and pressed me to a wall."

"Yeah, yeah?" they say. Their eyes like the moon.

"…and kissed me."

"And, and?" they say.

"I let him feel my knockers."

Luky pictures Gary Leyland touching Justine's breasts.

The girls explode.

"Why, you little tart!"

"He's a ripe one, isn't he?"

"But did you 'do it' with him?" Caroline asks.

"Yeah," Hazel wants to know. "Did you have sex with him?"

"Maybe," Justine replies.

"You trollop! You did, didn't you?"

"Oh my God, she did! Look at her face!"

"Sod off! You lot are just jealous."

"Are not," Caroline says. "But listen to this." She grabs Hazel and Hazel reddens. "This little cow's mum said she can go on the pill when she turns thirteen. You know what that means?"

"Yeah," the girls say. "It means she can get shagged all day and night and not worry about babies."

The girls howl.

"Here," Kimberly lights a cigarette and passes it to Luky, "have a fag," but when Luky touches the butt of it to her lips, she coughs.

"Now tell us what you did," they say to Luky. "We haven't much time."

"What do you mean?" Luky asks, passing the ciggy to Hazel.

"Over the weekend? You said you were gonna save the best story for last and all that crap, remember?"

"Yeah, yeah," Hazel adds. "The bell's gonna ring any second, so hurry."

"Well, I..." she pauses, takes a breath. "I..." She thinks about the last two days and the activities in which she participated, the prayers, the chores, the prayers. "I went to the movies," she swallows.

"With who?"

"With him."

"Oh my God! Where did you sit?"

"In the back."

"Was it dark?"

"Yeah," she nods.

"Did he put his arm round you?"

"Or hold your hand?"

"Or buy you food?"

"Or snog you?"

"He…"

The bell rings.

"Shit! We gotta go! Come on, run!"

In the hall, they see Mr. Wosencraft, his tight slacks and shirt, and they can barely move. Oh God, they are so mesmerized by his shoulders, his blonde hair, and legs.

"Look at his bum," Hazel says. "Oh my gosh! He's so fit."

"What about his shoulders?" Caroline asks. "And his hair? Wouldn't you just love to run your fingers through it?"

Mr. Wosencraft changes direction.

The girls giggle.

"Hey, Mr. Wosencraft," they say, blushing with embarrassment.

"Hey girls," Mr. Wosencraft replies, running his hand through his hair.

"He said 'hi' to us," Hazel says.

"Yeah. He must like us," Kimberly adds.

"You know," Luky butts in, "Mr. Butler," the swimming coach, "taught me how to do the backstroke the other day. He held me here." She reaches for the small of her back. "And here." She touches her nape.

"Oh my gosh," Hazel giggles. "Really?"

"Yeah."

"I can't believe it. He really likes you."

"I know." Luky smiles back.

Just then, Justine, Caroline and Kimberly turn a corner and say goodbye. They run up the stairs to their homerooms.

"Come on," Hazel says. "We don't wanna be late."

They enter the classroom, which is at the very end of the hall, and when the door closes, the final bell rings and class begins.

Lunchtime.

"Luky!" Kimberly calls from the hall. "Come 'ere."

Luky runs. "What is it? Aren't you gonna eat?"

"No. Wanna go?"

"To where?"

"Anywhere."

"But—"

"What?"

"I don't know."

"Come on. It'll be fun. We'll be back before school lets out. I promise."

"Okay."

They sneak past Mrs. Cooper's class and Misses Sykes' class (Misses Sykes was the teacher who lost her temper one day and threw an eraser at a kid named Clifton), and at the end of the hall they turn left and bolt through the double doors and sprint down the walk to the street, at which point they cross over and cut through the park to the following avenue, which is where they wait for the bus at the bus stop.

"We're here," Kimberly tells her, rising from her seat.

"The pub?" Luky asks, looking to the thing occupying the corner.

"My house." Kimberly points to the second story. "The pub's on bottom."

"Oh."

They walk to the back of the building and enter through a wooden door. "This way," Kimberly says.

Luky follows.

They walk up a flight of steps. "Wait! I almost forgot!" Kimberly says. "I have to show you something."

They walk back down.

"Here, help me move this barrel," she says. "But be quiet or they'll hear us."

"Who will?"

"Just help me."

The girls push.

"Okay," Kimberly says, pointing to a hole in the wall where the barrel used to be. "Take a look."

Luky peers through the opening and sees numerous tables and chairs, high stools decked around a crowded bar and people talking, holding onto their glasses, sipping beer and smoking. Against one wall are wooden barrels; against another a dartboard.

"Ever been inside?" Luky asks.

"Lots of times," Kimberly says.

They cover the hole with the barrel.

"Come on. We gotta get money from my dad."

"Why aren't you lot in school right now?" Kimberly's father asks.

"We, umm," Kimberly clears her throat, "got out early."

"I see." His eyes penetrate their faces and his mouth takes another swig of his beer. "Well?" he asks, waiting for an answer, his voice upraised.

Kimberly looks to Luky and then back to her father. "We were hoping we could go to the city centre," she says. "I need a new blouse for school."

"How much?" he wants to know.

"Twenty quid."

"Flippin hell!" Twenty bucks. "That's a bloody expensive blouse, innit?" He pulls from his pocket a wad of bills and hands her a twenty and a tener. "The tener's for your friend here." He smiles at Luky. "Maybe she can buy some chippies or something."

"Thanks, Mr. Tully," Luky says.

"Anytime, love." The man winks. "Anytime."

When they reach the city centre eighteen minutes later, the first thing they do is purchase ice cream and candy.

"Ooh, Crunchie bars," Luky says. "I'll take five, please."

"And I'll take seven of these," Kimberly says, pointing to the bin of Curly Wurlys. And within ten minutes, they are broke.

"Luky!" Kimberly shouts.

"What?"

"What's wrong with you?"

"Nothing."

"Then how come you didn't answer?"

"Sorry. I was…"

"Come on," Kimberly says to her. "Never mind."

They walk past the museum and the arcade, then stray to the cinema and its walls, where, for ages or so it seems, they stare at the posters and wonder aloud whether their own lives will be as glamourful when they are older. They go to Sunwin House Department Store after that, a place they would later refer to as the place where their journey came to an end. But for now, they try on sparkling jewelry and odd looking hats.

"Oh my gosh," Luky says, looking at the clock. "The time!"

They hurry to the exit.

At the exit, Kimberly pulls something from her skirt.

"Wanna see what I got?" she asks.

"What?"

"This."

"Oh my God! You took that?"

"Yeah! I nicked it."

They step through the double doors.

"Just where do you think you two are going?" the guards say.

"To home."

"Good one," they laugh. "Now step back inside, please."

Kimberly looks to Luky and Luky looks to Kimberly, and all they can think of to say is "Shit."

But as luck or fate would have it, they are let go with only a warning; not even their parents are called.

"See ya tomorrow," Luky says.

"Yeah, see ya."

The bus stops near the green benches on Little Horton Lane and Luky gets off.

"Tell your parents the bus was late getting back," Kimberly yells to her. "It always works for me."

"I will."

At the church, Luky slips into her slacks and hijab and breathes.

"Where have you been, boro affa?" Salena asks, opening the door, wishing her sister had a key. "Mum's been looking for you?"

"She has?"

"Yeah. She wants to know if you wanna write something to Nanu. She's sending her a letter."

"Where is she?"

"In the living room."

"Luky!" Amma calls. "Oh, there you are." She races from the living room to where Luky is standing. "I'm sending your Nanu a letter," she says. "Would you like to write something in it?"

She hands Luky the letter and Luky takes it.

"I'll have Abba post it when you're done."

Relieved that she is not in any trouble, Luky starts up the stairs to her room. Tromp, tromp, tromp. She walks through the doorway and tosses her bag to the floor and grabs a pencil from the top part of her dresser and a small pillow from the closet and sits at the edge of her bed, the pillow on her lap, the letter on top of the pillow, and thinks about Nanu in her white sari, the mark of a widow, and wishes she had one in color.

She wonders about her grandfather, her Nana. Wonders what he was like. Wishes she could have met him. Wonders if Amma wishes the same.

Dear Nanu, she writes. *I miss you more and more with each passing day, with each rising and setting of the sun, and I hope at least one of your bags is always packed and ready to go because, sooner or later, we're coming back to get you, and you'll always be home with us, in England, in Bradford, and even when we visit London.*

Nanu, I still have the Tagore book you gave me (remember the one you snuck in my bag when I was sick?), and I read its pages daily, or at least every other day, anyway. I love when the poet says, 'the dawn sleeps behind the shadowy hills...the stars hold their breath counting the hours...and there is only your own pair of wings and the pathless sky.' Oh, if only I were a bird, Nanu. Then I could soar to your very door, and you could ride on my wings to London town, and we could make the am achar (pickled mangoes) *on the rooftops of the queen's palaces and eat with our hands till we burst! But I do hope to see you soon, Nanu. The sooner the better, actually.*

Please give my salaam to all the uncles and aunties, and give my prayers to all the cousins. And please pray for me, Nanu. I wish you were here. Love, your growing granddaughter, Luky.

She folds the letter and tosses the pencil on the dresser and the pillow she tosses to the closet. She exits the room. On the staircase, she squeezes the letter to her heart even tighter and hastens to the dining room, wondering who it was that just screamed out loud like that, and sees Abba holding a torn envelope and Amma at his feet, sobbing.

"What's happened to my mother?" Amma screams. "Please tell me what's wrong with her. Is she alive? Please tell me. Please, please, please."

"I don't know how to say this," Abba begins. "But—" he kneels down and holds her— "she's gone."

The girls run in and Amma crumbles in Abba's arms. "Oh, Allah," she screams. "Why? I've already lost one brother and now my mother's gone too." She looks up but can't see. "I'm an orphanage now," she cries, "an orphanage." Her voice loses strength and falters, and for a moment all she does is shiver.

"Someone get water," Abba says.

"Oh, Allah," Amma starts up again after a lengthy bout of sobbing. "Why, why, why?" She clenches Abba's leg when he tries to back away for the water. "Please send me back," she begs him, "to Bangladesh. Please. I wanna go back and put her in the grave."

"But they've already buried her," he tells her. "The letter came this morning, but it was dated over a week ago."

"Nooooo!" Amma cries, her body shaking and shaking. "I don't have my mother!" She reaches for Luky's arm. "What am I gonna do without my mother?" she asks her. "What am I gonna do without my mum?" and for a certain amount of time after that, even though all the girls and Abba are around her, no one makes a noise.

That night. A dream.

—*You gotta take care of your mum because something really bad happened.*

—*What happened?*

—*Your mum's not gonna take this very well, but your Nanu passed.*

—*When did she pass?*

—*A few days ago, after fajr. She went to the da'h* (a curved, raised blade attached to a piece of wood) *to slice all the fishes, to prepare everything for the lunch; and as she was telling your cousins about the fishes and something else no one can remember, she fell over the blade, and that was it. She died right then and there. She was gone.*

Life is never the same again on Little Horton Lane and the girls don't know what to do about it. Most days Amma spends reading the Quran. Sometimes she reads non-stop, barely sleeping a wink. Other times she reads here or there, napping odd hours. She is seeking that inner peace, but has yet to find it. And more and more and more, Amma is in a daze and Abba doesn't know what to do about it. And sometimes, when Amma cooks, her tears fall into the curry.

The girls know things will not get better anytime soon, which is why they never complain when they are told to do something, which is why they never ask to play outside with their friends anymore, which is why they...

And why would they do any of these things? It would only upset their mum.

Oh, how they loved their beloved Nanu! Oh, how they loved her to death! Luky remembers the final time she spoke with her grandmother. It was over the phone. Nanu said to her, "Don't cry, my Luky. What are you crying for? You're gonna come back and see me. You're gonna come back and see Nanu, and then we'll make the am achar."

12

One year later.

In the fall of nineteen hundred and eighty-four. A red and white double-decker bus winds its way to a screeching halt and a stunning girl of thirteen emerges from it. Her hair flows in a warm September breeze and the black shades on her face shield her eyes from the bright thing in the heavens. Gloss sparkles on her mouthparts and her white teeth glisten like ivory as they chew on bubblegum. Her dark gray school skirt hangs slightly above her knees and her long white socks stretch far above her two calves. Her clothes, all tailored, have been taken in at the sides, revealing a waist that is curvy.

Rozina and her brother, Zaheed, and another of Luky's friends, Ruxana, follow Luky down the walk after stepping off the bus. Zaheed reaches for Luky's hand and Luky turns and pushes up her shades to the top of her forehead and closes her eyes as Zaheed pulls her close and kisses her. They stay that way for some time, then hug and go their separate ways: he towards Pullan Street and she towards home.

At the rear of the church, she sets her bag on the ground and jumps when someone or something touches her shoulder.

"You forgot this," Zaheed says, smiling.

"What?" Luky asks, looking.

"This."

He plants a wet one on her lips and her body burns and it melts. He tells her to call him later and she says *I will*. After, he runs toward his sister and his sister's friend, toward Pullan Street and beyond, while Luky changes into her slacks and covers her head and wipes the glossy stuff from her lips. Also saliva. Then, after tucking away her shades, she casually heads for home.

Oh God. She ponders Zaheed's kiss and the image causes a swell of emotions to ebb and flow through her body. She remembers the first time she had kissed a boy. It was shortly after Nanu's death on a Sunday after the imam and all the Sunday school guests had left for the day. She remembers telling her parents, "Me and Salena are going to the shop," and leaving, and how, after, they had really gone to the park. "To meet somebody," she had said to Salena at the swings. "Just a friend. So stay here and wait." And Salena didn't know what was going on. How could she? There was no way she could know what boro affa was up to. So she stayed by the swings while boro affa disappeared behind a stone wall. Now. On the other side of that stone wall stood Sheepu, and when Luky saw him, she darted to his presence and told him that she liked him, which was all part of her ruse (she wanted to learn how to kiss, okay. It wasn't like she liked the boy or anything. He wasn't even her type!). And grabbed him. And kissed him. Then he grabbed her and kissed her! She didn't even know he knew how to kiss. But he did! He even used his tongue and she thought, "Well, that's it…this is the French kiss they always talk about." But she didn't like it. All she could feel was this big fat spongy thing. Not to mention the sense of bugs on her body. But maybe that's how it was supposed to feel? Maybe you *were* supposed to feel suffocated and all grossed-out? *But why is he squeezing the bottom part of my bum?* she wondered. *Is this still part of the French kiss?* Apparently not, because after that Luky shoved him. She had to. She just couldn't breathe anymore, and she was pretty darn sure the bum squeeze thing had nothing to do with the French kiss.

She remembers some weeks later when Salena came up to her and asked, "Why are you always avoiding Sheepu?" and how she had finally confessed her wrongdoing that day in the park. "Remember when we said we were going to the shop to buy sweets?"

"Eeeewwww, gross," Salena had said. "You kissed the three spotted boy? Yuck, boro affa. How could you? Did you touch those black spots on his face too? I hope you washed with Zamzam water." Holy water from Mecca.

Looking back, her first kiss wasn't all that, but how could it have been, when it was with the likes of Sheepu? No, she wasn't happy she had relegated herself to the three spotted boy, wishes it would have been with a real stud like Zaheed. Nevertheless, she was grateful for the opportunity; at least she got to kiss a real person. Anyway, she knew deep down that if the real deal ever presented itself, she'd be able to hold her own with flying colors. In the end, she was proud she got to practice the much talked about and famous French kiss.

At night, she readies her clothes for the morning and jumps into bed. With isha already in the bag, she pictures Abba saying goodbye to Amma and catching a bus to his workplace. She pictures him at a break table, all alone, sipping tea and smoking.

She rolls to her side.

"Shaub namaz for so-ni?" Amma asks, walking up the stairs. Have you all done your namaz?

"Oy," they say, then turn out the light.

Amma drifts to her room.

Later. Unable to sleep. Luky thinks about Zaheed and his smile and his cute adorable face. His shoulders so broad. His arms so firm. She thinks about his eyes and how, whenever she is near him, he stands transfixed concerning her every move. Yes, she fancies him. Can't picture life without him. *It's amazing* she thinks, *how it all began as an innocent crush. We'd talk. Give each other the eyes. But now it is much more than that.* Now all she thinks about is his touch. On her body. *Oh God.* She presses her fingers to her belly and glides them to the innocence of her knickers, where she…

Burns: her entire body is aflame and her fingers are the soothing ice.

3am and Luky is still asleep and dreaming. Of boro bi-shab. Her big brother. Luton. She sees him walk through the door with Jahvid, one of his friends, and watches them remove their shoes and make their way up the stairs to Luton's room and slam shut the door.

Luky feels Salena by her side. They eye each other a moment and then follow their brother's trail. At the door, Salena knocks.

What is it? Luton asks. *What do you want?*

Salena asks whether he and Jahvid would like something to drink.

Yeah he says, *a couple of lilts would be nice. And tell mum to make some kabobs.*

In the kitchen, Salena searches for a tray while Luky goes to the fridge for the lilts. Both of them tell Amma to make the kabobs.

"Here, Salena," Luky says, handing her the lilts. "Take these on the tray and I'll wait for the kabobs."

Knock, knock. "Are you there, bi-shab?" Salena asks. "I've your lilts and biscuits for you."

"I'm here," Luton says, opening the door. "Thanks."

Salena goes to the kitchen.

"Did you see him?" Luky asks her. "What was he doing? Did he smile at you? What did he say about me?"

"Who?" Salena asks.

"Jahvid?"

"Jahvid's not in there, boro affa. Only boro bi-shab and Shamsheed."

"Who?"

"Boro bi-shab and Shamsheed."

"Who's Shamsheed?"

"Boro bi-shab's friend."

"Oh." Luky tries to picture him, wonders if he looks like Zaheed. "Is he hot?" she asks.

"Oh my God, boro affa! He's so cute."

Both girls giggle.

"And his hair's all flicked back with lots of gel and really spiked up, and just before I left he smiled and asked me what we were doing."

"Really?"

"Yeah!"

The girls crack up and grab each other. Just then, Amma comes out of nowhere with the kabobs. "Here," she says, wondering what they are up to, "give these to your brother," then leaves.

The girls start up the stairs, kabobs in hand, but when they see Luton and his friend coming down, they stop.

"Hi, Luky," Shamsheed says.

"Hi, Shamsheed," Luky says back.

"Ooh, kabobs," Shamsheed says. "I'll take one."

Luton takes two.

"Bye, Luky," Shamsheed says.

"Bye, Shamsheed," Luky says back.

They watch the boys descend to the bottom and slip on their shoes.

Oh God. Luky's body burns and it roasts, but then, like thunder, a voice is heard behind her and she turns.

No one is there.

She turns back. Salena isn't there either. Just some wall. Some familiar looking wall: it looks like a wall from her school.

She hears the voice again and her body trembles, but she doesn't know what to do about it. Bam. Her body hits the wall; her head follows. She feels a slap on the side of her cheek. Wipes her lip. Looks up and sees Pilton grinning. "You want me to kick your head in?" he asks. "Stupid cow. Wearing a skirt like that? Where's your trousers?" He turns away. "English hoisos," he says. You think you're an English. He turns back. "Just wait till I get home and tell Abba. Just wait until he finds out."

Luky stays silent. She has to at this juncture; well, that and flee.

"Just where do you think you're going?" he asks.

None of your business, asshole she wishes she could say, but a statement like that would only heighten his anger. So she stays quiet. Her gaze pointed downward. Her feet moving.

Farther away now, his voice still rings in the distance. "You mess around with boys," he says, "and I'll kick your face in. You hear me? I'll beat you up. I'll kill you."

But Luky never looks back. Knows her brother wouldn't hesitate for a second to hit if he caught her. Which is why she keeps moving.

Oh God. She remembers the raggedy jeans he used to wear on his legs. The Mohawk he used to wear on his head. The single stud in his left ear. *Such a punk he was. What took him so long to change?* God...he was so hyper. The neighborhood bully. The Bradford wild child. The type who would toss a stone through a person's window or knock on a neighbor's door and run or tear plants from a neighbor's garden and laugh. He'd come home from school with black eyes times two and bruised knuckles times ten (though we always wondered what the other guys looked like). He'd get suspended and expelled, caned every Sunday. *Oh God.* Dad and mum were rarely ever shocked by his behavior. Such a rascal, that Saqir. Always cocky and rude. The supreme bully of the school. Always thought he was the shit, wearing those boots and torn up jeans, and such scruffy jeans they were!

Along with those muscle shirts that showcased his muscles. God...he was just one big fat watchdog for dad.

The dream ends, but Luky's zzz's continue.

Saturday.

5:12am. *Knock, knock, knock.* "Time for namaz," Abba says to Luky's door. He says it again and walks away.

Oh God. Luky opens her eyes, feels like screaming.

"Boro affa, time to get up," Salena says. "Time to do namaz."

"Salena," Luky yells, burying her head beneath the pillow. "It's only five."

"But boro affa—"

"Turn the light off!"

"Be quiet or dad's gonna hear you."

"For fucks sake, Salena...will you just turn the light off and let me get back to sleep? I'll do my namaz later."

Salena flicks the switch and grabs her jai namaz and prays.

"Boro affa, boro affa, boro affa! Time to get up." Salena says a bit later, jumping on the bed. "Wake up, wake up."

Luky opens her eyes. "What do you want? Didn't I tell you to turn the light off?" She covers her face with the blankets.

"But boro affa...it's morning."

"Oh..." Luky says, rubbing her face and yawning. "Did you already do your namaz?"

Salena nods. "Did you do yours?"

"I need to shower first. What time is it?"

"Almost ten," Salena says. "But don't worry, I told mum you were doing homework."

"Thanks. But could you get off me now?"

Salena nods.

"And could you bring me something to eat? I'm starving."

Salena leaves.

Luky dresses and goes to the bathroom. She sits on the toilet and pees. But when she goes to rinse off her privates, she notices icky brown blood floating around the toilet bowl, and when she reaches for her knickers, she notices even more of it stuck to the fabric. *But how? I'm not even bleeding. Can it be coming from my?* Yet she shrugs away the idea because her only wish right now is to shower and put on clean clothes.

"Here's your food, Boro affa," Salena says. "Boro affa? Are you feeling okay? What's wrong?"

Luky glances to her groin and sees that the blueness of her salwar has been discolored. Without thinking, she sticks her hand down there and pulls it out again and sees redness. *Oh God. I have to tell my mum.*

Don't worry, Amma says when Luky tells her. *All girls get this. Once a month, in fact. It's called a period.*

"But why is it that color?" Luky asks.

Don't worry, Amma says. *It'll change as you become regular. But listen...you're growing up now. You're not a young girl anymore; you're a woman. So you have to be careful. You have to stay away from boys. It's gunah* (sin) *to even be around them. You can get pregnant you know, and sometimes it can even get stuck.*

"What can get stuck?" Luky asks.

The man's danda Amma replies, *his thingy.* She gestures to her privates with her finger. *And when that happens, Allah*

149

will never forgive you, and it'll be a disgrace to the family; the entire community will know. Amma steps closer. *Haven't I ever told you about the girl who began messing around with boys as a teen?*

Luky shakes her head.

No? Amma asks. *Then I must tell you. This girl began committing sin with a boy from a nearby village, and one day they both got stuck and nobody could separate them: not the wise men, not the strong men. And the young girl's family cried. Especially when they had to abandon their daughter and disown her. God, the shame of it all. It caused them so much grief and despair. But the worst part came when the girl had to be taken to the city hospital in Dhaka and cut away from the boy with razors. Are you listening to me, Luky?* Amma asks.

In the bathroom, Amma continues. "Every so often this pad gets wet, a little bloody. That's when you need to change it. But don't just throw it away. You need to wrap it in something first, like tissue paper. You don't want anyone to see it. It's embarrassing. And this is where I keep the new ones." She points to a bottom cabinet. "In a box. The rest are hidden in my armoire beneath some saris. And this is how you change them."

Luky feels disgusted.

"Oh, and another thing," Amma continues. "You're not allowed to touch the Quran or pray during this time, understand? It's forbidden."

The day ends and the sun sinks behind the horizon and hides its warmth and light from the shadows and quietness of night, but fajr namaz comes and goes without any warning so Luky sleeps. When she wakes, she deems it strange that Abba didn't knock or tell her to do namaz. *How odd* she thinks. *Abba always raps on my door every Sunday as a reminder. But not today?* And when the imam arrives, same thing. Abba doesn't call her down. Not that she is complaining. She is more than tickled to remain in bed and listen to her radio. Besides, the imam's stupid cane and Sheepu's ugly face aren't exactly sights worth rushing off to. But there must be a reason for Abba's lapse in procedure. How come he doesn't ask her to pray or recite from the Quran? Why doesn't he seem to be the least bit curious as to the state of her faith? There must be a reason. There has to be a reason...but who holds the answer?

Wait. "Isn't it haram to pray while bleeding?" Yes, it is. She answers her own question. Amma told her as much yesterday. But Abba wasn't there for that conversation, was he? "No, he wasn't." And he doesn't know about the bleeding. Does he?

Or maybe he does.

She stamps to the kitchen. "You told him, didn't you?" She crosses her arms. "You told dad."

Silence.

"You did, didn't you?!" She points to Amma. "Look at your face. You told him!"

"So what?" Amma replies. She shrugs her shoulders and continues chopping onions. "Kitchu hoi-boh ni?" Does it matter?

13

They arrive to the residence of King George today and his widow is the only one home. The house seems cold and barren without the man they once knew as uncle, without his wonderful rhymes, his songs. But their visits to his house are regular and his widow appreciates them greatly. She and Amma usually spend the bulk of their time in the living room, downstairs, sipping tea and yakking about curry dishes and dal dishes, about unnamed relatives and boring news from Bangladesh. They gossip and chat about neighbors and speak of gatherings and saris. They mull over forgotten photos and long lost memories, some fond though some not so, and then they cry and sometimes they laugh. Sometimes they are quiet, while at other times they stare blankly at the Hindi film playing on the telly. But Luky and Salena always run upstairs, as do their younger sisters. It's where they talk about boys and cool pop bands, where they goof off and play games like hide-and-seek. It's also where they once found a pile of dirty magazines in an otherwise empty room. Luky remembers stumbling onto the stash: "I went in there to hide, and there they were, all stacked on top of each other in a closet, and when I picked up an issue, I saw two naked women on the cover, and when I flipped to a random page, three more with a man." She also remembers how she felt after opening the forbidden pages for the very first time: "I loved it! I couldn't tear myself away. It was different, and at the time I remember thinking, 'When I get older, will my thingy look like that?' Then I tried holding the pages at different angles to capture a better perspective, but the view made no difference; I wanted more, but the photos had nothing more to give."

"Boro affa, what are you looking at?"

"Salena, come here."

"What is it?" Salena asks, going to the closet.

"Look." Luky points to the page.

"Eeewww, nasty!" Salena says. "We're not supposed to—"

"Shut up and stand over there, then, while I look through these," Luky tells her. "And make sure no one comes up the stairs."

That was months ago. Since then, things have evolved. Why, take last week for example, when Luky couldn't remove her eyes from the body of a girl who was changing in the school locker room. And the boys? Well, they're a different story altogether. But what about that friend of Luky's, the one they call Fermeeda? What's her story?

Why, yes, Fermeeda. I remember. She's the one who lives just up the lane on the opposite side of the street. She's of the same age and goes to the same school. They've known each other for ages, a number of years, I think. But no, Luky couldn't always go to her house whenever she wanted to. She couldn't just say to her mum, "Oh, I'm going over to Fermeeda's." No, she couldn't say that. Instead, she had to plan it out in advance and beg. "Is it okay if I go to Fermeeda's house? Is it okay, huh? Is it okay?" Otherwise, Amma might be apt to issue a negative decision, which is how things normally went for the eldest daughter at eighty-eight Little Horton Lane. Only once in a while would Amma reply in the affirmative. Yet even on such grand occasions, she would usually follow it up with a particular detail, a specific stipulation to which she demanded adherence: "Well, only for an hour, and then you'll have to come back." Of course, after such terms were stated, Luky knew quite well what to expect thereafter: first, Amma would phone Fermeeda's mum to let her know of her coming; second, Amma would rush to the front room window and stay looking out the window until Fermeeda's mum ushered her inside. Only then, after all that hassle, would Amma close the curtain and drift to the kitchen.

What did Luky and Fermeeda do on their playdate?

Watched movies, shows like *Little House on the Prairie*. Talked about school and boys and hot teachers. Pretended to be members of a pop group. Sang. Danced. Fermeeda was Cyndi Lauper and Luky Madonna. Sometimes Luky would pretend to be some girl and Fermeeda some guy, and Fermeeda would say, "Well, if I'm the guy, I have to be on top, and if you're the girl, you have to be on bottom." Then they'd practice, and Fermeeda would be on top and Luky on bottom, and one time they even touched lips, and it felt good.

Friday.

Some weeks later.

Luky comes home from school.

"Boro affa, run!" Salena hollers. "Dad's got friends here. Mum too."

"Oh God." Luky panics and darts for the stairs, but Abba's loud voice brings the soles of her feet to a standstill.

"Luky!" he calls.

Crap. He wants me to make some tea. Slowly, she labors to the kitchen.

"Luky!" Amma calls.

For fuck's sake.

Salena runs to the bedroom and hides.

Stupid cow Luky thinks.

"Luky!" Amma calls again. "The guests need tea, so hurry while I entertain."

In the kitchen, Luky makes tea.

Abba comes in and carries out four cups on a silver tray. Amma comes in after and grabs three. Eight minutes later, Abba storms back. "What did you do, pour a whole tub of sugar in there?"

"Next time, I'll dump in salt," she mutters low enough so Abba can't hear. Abba leaves and Amma enters.

"What's this? Pond water?" Amma asks.

"You're lucky it's not piss," Luky says loudly, though not meaning to.

"Forgive your dirty mouth," Amma shoots back. "You're not allowed to say stuff like that. Ittah farayni." It's not permitted. She steps closer and wags her finger. "Allah forbid your dirty lips."

Luky rolls her eyes.

"Dur'ho!" Amma says, pointing to the door. Get lost!

Luky leaves.

Upstairs, she finds Taz and Salena relaxing on Salena's mattress, flipping through a magazine. Mumtaz is sitting in a chair in the corner and Gully is scribbling on a notebook with some markers, and they're all listening to the radio. The DJ says something about Cyndi Lauper *coming up next.*

The girls smile. Then grab hairbrushes for microphones. While Gully cranks up the volume.

I come home in the morning light, Cyndi begins.

Luky closes her eyes.

Her mind sees Cyndi dance across an English street, a pink dress on her body, a black hat on her head, and spin and turn and kick her legs to the air. *Wicked* she says when Cyndi twists and rattles her head around, her red locks like a whirlwind. *Cool* she says when Cyndi wrenches her father's arm and jerks it to a position slightly above the small of his back, just like a police officer would a criminal. *Wow* she says when Cyndi phones all of her friends. But her favorite part is when Cyndi and her mates try on spiffy new shades and dance between two rows of buff looking gents. And to think, she only saw the music video one time, at Hazel's home, just a few short months ago. She recollects the day clearly:

After cutting class, Hazel and I stepped outside, and I could feel the warmth and heat from the sun on my body. The sky was blue and the clouds in the sky fluttered like breezy ghosts. We walked real slow to the bus stop, waited for the bus to pull up to the bus stop, and when it arrived, we boarded. When we reached Hazel's flat, we entered through the main door, and the first thing I saw was her mum on the sofa, smoking, and her dad right next to her mum, with his arm draped over her shoulders, chugging a can of beer. I couldn't believe it. I mean, there's her mother, a female, relaxing on the couch in the middle of the day, in plain view of her children, in plain view of a guest no less, just hanging out, blowing puffs of smoke through her lips and watching the telly. And no one's in the kitchen. It's empty. And no one's slaving over the stovetop, cooking curry or dried fish, or telling the kids to make tea or do namaz. 'That's such a disgrace,' Amma would say, though I kinda thought it looked cool. But even cooler was the packet of fish and chips on the coffee table and the half-eaten pizza right next to it. I thought, 'God, they have this big fat pizza and all these fish and chips. If only we could eat that stuff for dinner each night.' I mean, their lives seemed so easy. There didn't seem to be any difference between the man and the woman; it felt like the mother was the same as the father. And their walls! If only you could have seen their walls. So plain. Their entire house was steeped in neutral colors. It wasn't like our house at all, how it resembled a Moroccan carnival. Gosh, I was so ashamed of Abba's decorations, all those bright colors and lights.

'Do you want some chippies and pizza?' Hazel's dad offered. Delighted, I stuffed my whole face while watching the telly as Hazel sat by my side. Her mum then got up to change the channel, and all of a sudden Cyndi Lauper's video came on; it was about girls having fun. And would you believe it? Not once did Hazel's parents tell us to switch the channel; not once did they say, 'Look at those bay-deen,' those disbelievers, 'you shouldn't be watching stuff like that, they're shaking their khumbols,' their asses, 'they're shaking their boonies,' their titties, 'and they're shaking it right in front of your face!' No, *things like that were normal at Hazel's house, Kimberly's house, Caroline's house; at ours we were restricted in what we could watch. Romantic scenes were simply out of the question, as were any channels that showed moving hips or tight-fitting clothing or dancing. 'Change that, change that,' was all we would hear, or 'Change that fat filthy channel!' Guess they felt we would be influenced, so they tried to keep us on a tight leash, guess they thought if we weren't exposed to such things, then we wouldn't want to do them. If only they knew how much I wanted to do them!*

When Hazel led me to her room, I saw her wardrobe, chock full of short skirts and tight fitting tops, and her walls, plastered with posters from movies, though some were of musicians. I remember wishing I had posters like that in my room, posters of Rob Lowe or Madonna. Or of Prince. I really loved his long hair. But I knew Amma would have called him a lamba suilie, a long headed dirt bag, and she would have wanted to know, 'Why doesn't that guy get a haircut?' But things like that weren't allowed in our rooms, and it didn't matter if they were famous or not, or whether they were guys or girls; if I wanted anything like that in my room, I'd have to sneak it in and hope my mum didn't see. God, if she ever caught me. 'Take that thing down,' she would say. 'It's haram! You can't do your namaz when there's a picture of any human.' Maybe she thought it would provoke us to do bad things? I don't know, but secretly I'd admire my friends for having them in their rooms, especially Hazel. And I always wondered why her mum never hassled her about taking them down. It was weird. But since I didn't want to look like a total idiot, I didn't say anything. I didn't want her to think, 'Oh my God, where is this girl from? Why is she so different?' It was hard enough trying to blend in with the white people here, but then for me to ask questions like, 'Doesn't your mom cook?' or 'It is normal for you lot to smoke and have beer in your hands?' or 'You mean to say you're allowed to have pictures of people?' Gosh, I didn't want to make it seem so obvious, did I? I was trying to blend in here!

Luky opens her eyes. Then come the words to the second verse: *My mother says when you gonna live your life right?*

And that's the moment all five of Abba's daughters decide to jump on Luky's bed and move their bodies to the beat. They boogie and spin like drunken dervishes, swing and jitter like Mr. Bojangles Robinson on candy and caffeine. From one bed to the other they leap; from Salena's bed they hop to the floor, only to repeat the whole process until the voice of Cyndi fades to the background.

Just then, a pounding knock on the door, like the butting knock of a ram, interrupts the silence between songs and a voice most unsavory screams with the force of ten lungs, "Open this door!"

Quickly, Mumtaz turns off the radio.

"Bay-deen jadth!" Amma howls, bursting through like an explosion. You rowdy caste of disbelievers! "You're bringing the ceiling down! What are you lot doing up here, anyway? The whole floor's gonna fall on our heads." Amma points to the ground. Then to her daughters. "Shaytan dorsay shopti." The devil has all of you. She points to walls. "And take those pictures down, those forbidden pictures of men! They're haram," forbidden. "The good fairista," the good angels, "won't come in here during prayers."

Luky rolls her eyes. She hates this house and her life, wishes she were Hazel or Caroline or another of her shada friends. "I can't do anything in this place!" she screams. And the sight of her Amma's belly makes her nauseous. *Probably another girl* she thinks to herself, *another goddamned stupid girl.*

Later that night, she thinks about the morrow and the many chores awaiting her fate. She thinks about Janet and Caroline and Hazel and the party that they're having over the weekend and how, if at all, she'll be able to attend; and as the lights change from on to off and as Amma lies down to sleep, Luky smiles, for she thinks she has found a way.

14

Saturday. The next day.

Luky helps Amma make breakfast. After, she helps her sisters with the housework but is adamant about not cleaning the kitchen.

When all the housework is finished, she watches the telly, but every so often, especially when Amma is busy or tangled with other affairs, she sneaks to the hall to make phone calls to Zaheed, though sometimes she calls Kimberly or Hazel; at other times she calls Maqbull or Ruxana, but mostly she calls Zaheed.

1:30pm.

Zuhoor namaz is finished; as usual, Amma lies down for a ghum, a nap, while Abba, after praying and eating, sits in front of the telly, while Luky, up to no good, sits in her room, upstairs, whispering to Salena.

"Okay, boro affa. I got it. I wait here by the window, and when I see your signal, I run down to let you in."

Luky nods. "And if dad calls, make sure you go running."

"Okay, boro affa, I—"

Both girls look to the doorway as a noise interrupts their scheme. They see Mumtaz and Taz, standing shoulder to shoulder.

Luky casts a death stare in their direction.

"You can't sneak out like that, boro affa," Mumtaz says real prissy, "or mum and dad are gonna shout."

Luky makes a fist. "Who asked you, *Mumtaz?*" she says, rising. "Why don't you shut your face?" She steps closer, baring her knuckles. "Besides, I hate spies." She crashes her hand into her palm, not once, but twice.

Mumtaz inches backwards and Taz apes her.

"And what's your problem?" Luky says to Taz. "You want me to kick your head in too?"

Taz doesn't move.

"Come here," Luky orders, reaching for the two eavesdroppers. She drags them to the closet and stuffs them inside. She hears Taz whimper a bit and say, "Mumtaz, it's dark in here. I'm scared." And Mumtaz say, "Here, Taz, give me your hand. Here, take my hand and hold it." So she kicks the door and threatens them; she tells them that if they try to get out or hit the door in any way or make any noise whatsoever, she'll beat 'em up bad, she'll knock their blocks off. "I'd better not hear a peep out of you two, you hear me? Or I'll kick your heads in, I'll beat you up! And if I find out you told mum or dad, I'll kill you."

"Okay, boro affa," they squeak out.

Good. But just to be sure they understand she re-kicks the door.

Great. More gasps.

Satisfied, she walks away, her mind picturing two scaredy cats.

From the hall, Luky closes the bedroom door and scurries atiptoe to the stairway, her barefeet making no sound. Salena follows. They carry their shoes in their arms and sneak down while holding onto their breaths. They open the front door, but slowly, for fear of making a creak.

Luky slides through.

"Make sure you don't make a noise," she says to Salena.

"Okay, boro affa."

"And remember...stay by the window; if you have to leave for any reason, just keep checking back. I won't be long."

On the street, Luky stots like a gazelle to Caroline's home. She loves being out here, the feeling of being free, and the thrill of visiting a friend's.

At the party, Zaheed opens the door.

"What are you doing here?" Luky asks him.

"Oh, your mates told me about the party and I thought I'd surprise ya."

"Well, you have," Luky smiles. "You have."

Minutes later, they leave and walk to an abandoned home. Inside, they kiss and he tries to take off her clothes. But she doesn't let him. Okay, maybe she lets him take off her top as she is just fine with him touching her breasts. After all, wasn't it good for Justine?

He sets her down on a table and kisses her mouth and tongues her. He pulls off her underwear. Then, suddenly, everything becomes more passionate, more heated, and they begin to lose themselves and all traces of time. His hands drop to her skirt and the material rises to her waist. He unclasps his belt and his pants drop to his ankles. He places his hands on her hips. He pulls her closer. He lifts her bum, gently, and moves forward to…

"Oh my God!" Luky says. "I think it's sliding in!" She shoves him away.

Zaheed gasps, a look of fear in his eyes. "I didn't do it! I didn't do anything to you!"

"You did! It almost went in. I felt it!"

"It was just near your thingy," he says. "The tip just kinda touched it." *But what did I know? I was only thirteen and wet. So I put my clothes on and told him I wanted to go home. But he got mad with me because I screamed. And you're never gonna believe what happened, but he dumped me! He didn't even wanna talk to me anymore. Eventually, I stopped talking to Rozina and Ruxana. The entire situation was awkward. But, yeah, that was one horrible incident that I never forgot.*

Sometime later, she arrives home, her cheeks still stinging from tears. She throws pebbles at the bedroom window and peeks through the letterbox. *Where the fuck is she? She'd better get her ass down here.* She tosses another stone. Finally, Salena waves.

"Boro affa, hurry, run! Mums awake," Salena says, grabbing her sister by the arm and pulling her inside.

"Where is she?"

"In the living room, doing asr."

Luky bounds up the steps and Salena follows. Together, they hear Amma.

"Shit. Mum's calling," Luky says.

"But she doesn't know you left, and neither does dad. He's been gone the whole time, at the masjid."

"Oh shit. Quick! Give me the jai namaz. Mum's coming."

Salena gives it, and when Amma comes in and sees Luky so devout, so earnest in her prayers, and Salena reading an Islamic book no less, she leaves.

Yes!

After, Salena tells Luky, "I'm going downstairs to watch the telly and get something to eat. Do you want anything?"

"No," Luky says, watching her leave, the drama in the abandoned home still bothering her.

"Boro affa?"

"Who's there?" Luky asks, looking to the closet, bewildered.

"Me."

"And me."

Oh shit. I forgot about you guys. She opens the door. "If either of you tell mum or dad, I'll bust your heads in, I'll give each of you a fist sandwich." She punches Mumtaz in the arm just to make a point, while Taz reaches for Mumtaz's hand and holds it. "Next time, I'll put you in the kitchen cupboard."

On Monday, everyone thinks that she did it, and by the middle of the afternoon her mood switches from downright despondent to totally fucked up. And to make matters worse, whenever she sees another couple talking or kissing or holding hands, she feels like dying. Why, take Gary Leyland and his bird for example. Just look at them eyeing each other's every bend and sway.

"Jennifer," he calls her name.

That fucking slag.

She watches them carry their lunches outdoors and sit next to a tree. She watches them eat and stare into each other's eyes. She watches them say I love you and I love you too, then rise and go into the building, hand in hand.

Disgusting.

She wishes she had someone to look at her like that, to be the object of someone's devotion. She remembers the day, nearly eight months ago, when Gary Leyland wrote her a note asking her to go on a date; she thinks maybe to the movies. The note said to circle either yes or no. She had, of course, after reading its contents, circled no, but then proceeded to playfully circle yes and or. But such antics fomented a pang of deep regret in her heart and for that reason alone she wrote a reply at the bottom clarifying her romantic availability and calling attention to her prior weekend plans: *Gary, I am so sorry, but I am already spoken for, and this weekend my boyfriend is taking me out to the city centre. We're going to the arcade and then to the movies, but I am flattered by your interest, Luky.*

Yeah, right she thinks. *Me, spoken for? That's funny. Because the only thing keeping me comfy this weekend is Mr. cleaning supplies and maybe Mr. dirty plates.*

Luky blinks and Gary and Jennifer are gone.

A cold breeze. Luky folds her arms across her body and presses them to her chest. Her left hand is on her right bicep. Her right hand is on her left. She wishes she were home in bed beneath the covers right now, listening to music and staring into the poster of Rob Lowe's eyes. Or downstairs, in the living room, next to the fireplace, absorbing the warmth and dreaming of her future prince, the one Nanu said she'd marry.

The wind starts up again and Luky squeezes herself even tighter. She thinks about Amma and the many shawls she made for her and her sisters over the years and how Amma had begged, pleaded with her even, for her to wear one to school. *'I'll freeze to death,' I said, 'but I'm not gonna wear one of those ugly sweaters.' Hell no, what would my friends think of me? I've a reputation to consider here. Which is why the corner church became my clothes bin.*

But she wishes she had one on right now.

Luky decides to slam the last two classes of the day and walk to the bus stop. She thinks maybe she'll visit the shada people's shop before going home, the one on Park Road at the end of Elizabeth Street. *Yeah, definitely the shada people's shop* she thinks. *They always have better candy than our corner store has, which is run by cheap ass Indians.* She laughs when she remembers what Amma said about them the other day, how their food was always ancient and kept on the shelves way beyond the expiration date. *To make more money* Amma had said. Of course it was always easier to nick things from *their* corner store as there was usually only one person on duty, some elderly lady. And most times, after hearing the door open, she would just pop out long enough to see who it was and then disappear again to the back. *Yippee!* Because that's when Luky would fill her pockets with candies and munchies and only purchase the goods Amma had actually requested.

Crossing through the park to the bus stop, she decides to make her way to the swings. Sitting on one, she pulls backwards on the chains and kicks her legs and feet forward, then pushes on the chains and pulls her legs and feet back. She's swinging and feels like a kid again. But a voice, actually a group of voices, catches her attention. So she stops swinging. Gets off and straightens her dress out. Then walks over to where the voices are.

Kids. Some her age, some not. All from her school. Eight or nine in total, some from both sexes. All standing in a circle. Listening to music from an old boom box, sort of like the kind the khallah bandors carry on their shoulders in America. Watching a boy. Actually, watching two boys, breakdancing. One does a headstand, the other, Ebrakhan, a flare. Though now he's moon-walking.

He's cute Luky thinks. 16. In the last year of upper school. Like Zaheed, he's Paki. Tall with light skin. Black hair. Broad shoulders. Muscles. Lips. A smile and two eyes like the sun on a cloudless day.

The song ends and they top off their act with a high five. Slowly, the crowd disperses. Luky along with it.

Until...

Someone touches her shoulder. She turns.

"Hey," Ebrakhan says, smiling. "I saw you watching me."

"Everyone was watching you."

"But you were the only one *looking*." He winks. "What's your name?" he asks.

"Luky." She clears her throat. "What's yours?" although she already knows it.

"Ebrakhan."

On her way home, she stops by the shada people's shop, her heart racing wildly. She walks in, giggling, not even aware of the shada beta in his mid-fifties, slightly balding, slightly obese, donning a bit of white hair on either side of his head, sitting behind the counter, keeping a sharp eye on her every twitch and move. But Luky, in a world of her own, can only think about the park and Ebrakhan, his lips on her lips, and how the memory of her ex is...is...just a memory.

She folds some candies in her waistband, grabs a Flake bar from the top shelf of one of the aisles and takes it up to the counter and places it just in front of the man and smiles. But the man just stares back, peering into her pupils, eyeing the deepest portions of her conscience.

"I believe you've other stuff to pay for, love," he says.

"No," Luky shakes her head, "just the Flake bar." But the man bats another question to her. "Are ya sure, love? You do know stealing is not good."

"I'm sure." But the man continues his line of questioning.

"Now ya don't want me to tell your parents, now do ya?"

Luky says no, that she doesn't want him to tell her parents.

The portly man leans in closer. "Are ya sure, love? Are ya sure?" He raises his brows and Luky thinks his eye may pop out. *And that's when I realized, 'Oh shit, he definitely knows.' So I pulled out the candies and shook my head no when he asked me if I wanted to pay for those too, because I didn't have any money. Which is why I ran outta there. I didn't even buy the Flake bar. And for the longest time after that, I stayed away from that place. But wouldn't you know it, my mum sent me back there. But instead of me going in, I sent Salena while I waited on the sidewalk where it was safe. So Salena went in and bought all the stuff, and the only time I ever went in there again was when the old man wasn't working. But I never stole from there again. It was just so much easier to steal from the Indian store.*

Luky bolts from the store and crosses the street and runs in between a row of brick-walled houses. She turns slightly to her left onto Little Horton Lane, runs across the street to the church, changes out back of the church, and heads for home.

15

Almost maghrib time. So Abba leaves for the masjid.

"Turn off the telly and do your wudu," Amma says to the girls. "It's time for namaz."

The girls obey.

In the bathroom, they perform wudu. All except Luky, who remains downstairs, washing in the kitchen sink. After, she goes to the dining room, where she rushes her namaz and hurriedly searches for Abba's jacket. *But where is it? Isn't it supposed to be hanging on the back of the door?* Yes, but then she remembers he took it with him to the masjid. "Because sometimes he gets cold," she mutters. So instead, she looks to the mantle where rests an old biscuit tin. Blue in color. The one with the tiny slit in the top, the one that Abba usually sticks all his loose change in. When it's full, he donates the entire sum to the orphanage in Rajanpur.

Luky tries to open it; she shakes the thing upside down and smacks it, but only one or two pennies flop to the floor. Wait. There's more loose change in the ashtray. Not much, though. But enough. She counts out thirty pence, laughs. It's plenty. *Abba usually gave us ten or twenty pence each week, but since I was the eldest, I usually got more—sometimes as much as fifty. But that was our crisp money, and I couldn't use my crisp money to make phone calls. That was for the crisps! So I had to take money out of the ashtray or Abba's pocket or out of the charity can for the needy.*

"Did you already do your namaz?" Amma asks Luky, coming into the room.

"Oy, Amma," Luky replies. "Now I've got a test to study for."

"Thik acche," Amma says. "That's fine." She walks out and goes to the living room. Luky's sisters come down from the bathroom and go in with her.

When Luky feels they are busy at namaz, she races to the front entry hall and reaches for the payphone (yes, the payphone. You see, Abba had this crazy idea that his daughters might one day grow up to call boys and he figured a payphone was the best way to prevent them). Frantically, she begins dialing numbers. But a voice, the operator's voice, slows her momentum.

Please deposit ten pence the woman says. *If you would like to proceed with your call, please deposit ten pence for two minutes.*

Luky drops a coin in the coin slot and hears the line ring.

"Hello?" Hazel asks. "Who's this?"

"Me."

"Luky, is that you?"

"Yeah," Luky says. "What are you doing?"

"Oh, I'm going to see my boyfriend later. He's taking me for chippies and then we're going to the cinema."

"Really? What are you going to see?"

"I dunno. I was hoping we could just snog."

Luky pictures Hazel kissing.

"…and he stayed over last night too."

"Who did?"

"My boyfriend," Hazel says.

"He stayed over?" Luky asks. "Your mum let him?" She can't believe what she is hearing.

"Yeah," Hazel says. "Why wouldn't she?" as if shocked by the query. "We're going steady, remember?"

Click. Time's up. The line goes dead. She dials Maqbull's number, but no one answers. Then Rozina's, but hangs up before it rings. Because of *him*, Zaheed. Finally, she calls Ebrakhan.

It's ringing.

He picks up, says "Hello."

They talk.

"Who is it?" Amma demands, coming up behind her.

"No one," Luky says, shooing her away. "Just one of my friends."

But Amma isn't so bent on moving away from the phone until she knows the sex of the caller, so she reaches for the receiver. "Who is it? Who is it?" she demands, without even taking a breath.

"No one."

Luky tries to push her away, but that's when Amma gets this gut feeling that her daughter is probably speaking to a guy. "Rakh, rakh!" she screams. Hang up, hang up. But Luky tells her, "No. Get away," then tells Ebrakhan, "Look, listen, I gotta go. I can't talk to you right now," and hangs up.

"Who were you talking with?" Amma asks.

"Maqbull," she lies.

"Why do you spend so much time talking to that girl for?"

"I don't spend so much time talking to that girl for. God. What the heck do you want me to do around here, clean all day? I can't do anything."

"You can help me in the kitchen," Amma says, walking toward it. She holds the door open and waits for Luky to follow.

Inside, Amma lets her have it. *Girls aren't supposed to talk on the phone you know, they're supposed to—*

What can we do then?

Amma grabs a knife and severs the leafy stem from a pepper and gives Luky a really bad glare. *You can start by being a really good Muslim you know, and by performing your womanly duties—*

Luky cuts her off. *We can't do anything, can we? We can't do anything except make babies. I hate it here. I wish I was dead.*

Oh no, that's a sin. Don't say things like that. Read your surahs. Girls aren't supposed to raise their voices. Read your surahs. It'll calm you down.

I don't wanna calm myself down.

You need to calm yourself down.

I don't wanna smell like you.

Before going to bed, Luky asks Amma, "Tomorrow, after I get home, can I go to Maqbull's? We're doing a project for school and—"

"No." Amma shakes her head.

"But—"

"No," she says without thinking.

"But—"

"No!" Amma snarls, a threatening look in her eyes. "Why do you hang out with that kit kita mangi?" That dried pussy girl. Amma shakes her head, steps closer and sighs through the whiteness of her teeth. "That girl's like a skinny tree."

"Her name's not kit kita mangi, Amma. It's Maqbull."

"Don't they feed that girl?" Amma asks. "Don't they have any food in their house, any bhat?"

"They don't eat rice," Luky says. "They eat chapattis."

Amma rolls her eyes. "That's why, then. That's why they're not nice and juicy like our girls are, because chapattis are dry."

Luky goes to say something but doesn't.

"Tomorrow, after you come home," Amma tells her, "you can take your sister with you to the library, and that kit kita mangi," that dried coochie girl, "can meet you there. I don't want you going to a Paki home."

"Fine!" Luky walks away all pissed off and storms up the stairs to her room and yells, "Turn the fucking light off, Salena!" and goes to sleep.

In the morning, long before Amma begins to stir, Luky pulls from her schoolbag a small box of hair dye and rushes to the bathroom. Thirty minutes later, for that's what the directions state, she begins rinsing the concoction from her hair and drying it with an oversized towel. Afterwards, she peers into the mirror fully expecting to see blonde locks, but instead sees orange. The goddamned color orange. Reflecting its way back to her eyes. "Oh shit," she mutters. "Dad's gonna kill me. What the fuck did I do?"

Behind the church, she does her usual Clark Kent to Superman switcheroo, becoming Luky hottie, and goes to the bus benches like a starlet.

At school, she shows off to her friends.

"Too much peroxide?" Caroline says a bit sarcastically.

"Yeah, well, fucking get lost," Luky says with a smile.

Caroline laughs. "Oh, you know that we love it."

"Come over to my house tonight," Kimberly says to Luky. "I'm gonna have Caroline over and Hazel and Janet and…"

Luky smiles. She already cannot wait.

Near the end of the school day, Luky decides to slam her last class, mathematics, and hang out with Ebrakhan at the park, the one next to her school. They take turns pushing each other on the swings. Then lie on the grass facing each other and kiss and speak of fond memories from their youth. Ebrakhan tells her about his grandmother, who still resides in Pakistan, and his father, who was shot in the head by a couple of punks in some alleyway, and the time he and his brother played ball at the school and his brother fell down and broke his ankle. Luky tells him about Abba and the park he used to take her to and how his hands were always so callused from the factory that he worked in and how he used to drape her knickers over the heater on cold wintry nights, so that they'd be warm on her body after a bath. The memory makes them both giddy and they hug. She also says something about Nanu and the rooftop. Oh, the magic of it all, she tells him. Just her and Nanu and nobody else.

After going home, Luky takes Salena to library. But leaves as soon as she gets there. First stop: Maqbull's. Second stop:

Hazel's. Then it's back to the library again, where she meets up with Salena and boards the bus for home.

At home, Amma sees an orange tuft of hair. "What did you do?" she asks Luky, yanking the scarf off.

Abba sees a pumpkin.

"Rabbisher jadth!" he shouts. "Whoonga rabbish!" he bellows, meaning you belong to a caste of rubbish, you damn trashy bastard. Without warning, he drags her to the bathroom and puts his black hair dye on her head, giving her jet-jet hair.

"Aah," he says. "Look at it. Doesn't it look so nice?" But Luky doesn't think so, thinks she looks even more fucking Bengali than before.

At Kimberly's house, Janet asks, "What happened to your orange hair?"

"Oh, I didn't like it. So I dyed it back."

Three weeks later. At lunchtime in the cafeteria. Luky scoffs her food in a flash, then leaves. She cavorts to the gymnasium, where she watches Ebrakhan in his shorts. He notices her standing there in a daze, just staring, so he approaches. Says *hi* and plants a few measured kisses on her lips, to which she responds in kind.

Afterwards, she meets up with Suja in biology and together they decide to cut class. Luky likes Suja but isn't too keen on hanging with her at school because she doesn't want any of her white friends thinking that she is now best buds with darkies, especially Bengali darkies who have village-minded parents with nonnative tongues. So they decide it best to first meet in the restroom before cutting.

Luky is the first to arrive. She stands before the sink, the mirror, and fixes her eyeliner, her lipstick. But in through the door waltzes Nasrin, also known as Scarface (you see, her Pakistani uncle slashed her face with a knife for looking at another boy), a fourth year student who should have graduated a year ago. And she's marching across an invisible path, one that's leading straight to Luky's face.

"What the fuck do you think you're doing, you fucking tart, seeing Ebrakhan like that? You're not a fucking Paki. You're just a whore." She pushes Luky and Luky crashes into the sink.

"You shouldn't be with him," Nasrin continues. "You little slut." Again, another shove.

Luky's feet get tripped up and she falls.

Nasrin steps closer, reaches for Luky's hair. But Luky whacks her in the mouth.

"Fucking cow, get off me!" Luky snarls.

Suddenly, in walks Ruxana, Nasrin's sister. "Stop it, Nasrin! Just leave her alone! Go and pick on someone your own size."

Still swearing, Nasrin stammers to the hall.

"Are you okay?" Ruxana asks Luky, holding out her hand.

"I'm fine." Luky brushes herself off and stands without assistance.

"Well, don't worry about it," Ruxana says. "My sister's just a bitch like that. You know how she fancies Ebrakhan, and it pisses her off that he likes you. She's just jealous."

"Sod off."

Ruxana leaves and Luky goes back to fixing her eyeliner.

Suja walks in.

"That bitch Nasrin just attacked me," Luky tells her.

Suja's jaw drops. "Oh my God. That girl's such a fucking whore. Let's go."

They sneak to the bus stop and catch a ride to the city centre. Their first stop: Market Street, for that's the location of Rackham's department store. Inside, they traipse through the aisles, surveying, with their fingers, a multitude of goods and wares (in other words, they steal shit, not to mention get caught).

What's going on? Luky says when some guy grabs them.

Please come with me the man says. *You can sit in these seats.*

Luky shits her pants. But for some strange reason, she and Suja start cracking up. Every time they look at each other, they think *what the fuck did we do? I can't believe we got caught* then crack up, and this despite the fact they are both so worried.

Not long after, the police come and take them to the police station and call their parents, and guess who comes? Luky's brother (and not the nice one either), along with her dad and Suja's brother. Oh God. That night, did Luky get the worst fucking beating of her life or what? She got beat by her dad. *I didn't give birth to a thief!* Whack. *You're not my daughter.* Whack. *None of my daughters steal!* Whack. Then by her brother. Whack. Who put too many bruises on her face and body, causing her to miss a week of school. But Suja didn't get beat. No, her brother only told her *you can't see Luky anymore,* and that's it.

16

Springtime. April. 1985.

Luky comes home from school and says *hi* to Salena and takes off her shoes and hears some noise in the front room and goes to investigate. Inside, she sees Amma by the window.

"Come here!" Amma says, waving her arms. "Hurry!"

Luky goes to the window, Salena with her, and looks out while shielding her body with the curtains. They see their street, Little Horton Lane, but nothing further.

"What?" Luky asks Amma. "What do you want us to look at? There's nothing out there."

Amma points to a position about a meter or so from their front steps.

Luky sees a ginger headed woman wearing a pair of cutoff denim shorts and a tight fitting v-neck top, minus any sleeves, smoking. She watches the woman suck on her cigarette and blow a dirty smoke ring to the skyline, coloring the air a ghostly gray.

"Who is she?" Luky asks.

"Sylvia. King George's first wife," Amma says. "She rents a house a few units down." Amma motions with her head, indicating the direction.

"Oh my gosh," Salena yips. "Is that really his first wife?"

Amma nods. "He married a shada beti you know." A white lady.

Luky can't stop looking. Nor can she fathom how this harlot could've landed King George. Surely, Amma must be mistaken. Or confused. But she isn't. Because King George, after immigrating to England, married a white lady named Sylvia, with whom he had three children, all girls, and then, in his old age, went back to Bangladesh to marry a girl half his years. By that time, the kids from the white lady were all grown and said to be very pretty, with light skin and dark eyes, though somewhat tall with a slender build. *Mum said King George was probably the first Bengali to have married a white lady and to have fathered kids by one. Which is why he was the king of the Bengalis. She also said Sylvia drank a lot and was going around with different men while they were married, which is why he decided to dump her ass in the first place and marry one of his own. Anyway, King George is a legend. He was there in Bradford before any other Bengalis were and he was also the kindest man on earth.*

The woman throws her cigarette and begins walking northward along Little Horton Lane toward Woodville Terrace and disappears completely from view. The girls strain their eyes to capture one last glimpse.

Luky blinks and wonders how Sylvia could have behaved so treacherously toward King George. The mere thought sickens her insides to such a degree that they feel like wrenching. But then she wonders if what happened to them could ever happen to her and—

"Luky, are you listening to me?" Amma says.

Luky snaps out of it.

"I need you to—"

"I can't do it!" Luky snips. Ami farr tam na. She crosses her arms.

"Khaynay farr tay na?" Amma shouts. Why can't you do it?

"Khaynay farr tay na?" Luky mimics her.

"Go and do it or I'll tell your father!" Amma warns. So Luky goes and does it. Otherwise, well, you know what would happen if she didn't.

Today was a day of flashing lights and sirens, of doctors and anesthesia, of women reading surahs, of needles and stretchers. A day of cutting and maneuvering, of pulling a baby girl from a pregnant woman's belly. They named her Shanaz but called her Shanu for short. She was eight pounds two ounces, baby number eight, the last of Rahman's children.

Nine days later, Amma is released from the hospital, but remains bedridden, upstairs, in the throes of her condition. Another week passes, and not once since the birth of Shanu has Luky attended school; not once has she spoken on the phone to any of her friends, and not once has she been out to see Ebrakhan. Amma is simply too weak from having the baby and much too drained. She's been told by the doctor to take it easy, and, as such, somebody has to watch and care for the baby, and that somebody has to cook and help Abba in the kitchen, and that somebody has to make tea for the guests and make sure all the rooms are tidy and neat, and that somebody has to... Well, you get the picture; somebody has to do all the things that Amma usually does, and that somebody is the eldest daughter of Rahman, Luky.

But lately, Luky's nights and days are rather joyless and morose, not to mention sleepless and dour, for Amma's utter dependence on her and her alone is shackling. Why, every time the baby cries, she changes another nappy. When the baby cries, she runs to the kitchen for a bottle. When the baby cries, she reaches for a dummy. When the baby cries, she sings it a lullaby. When the baby sleeps, she can't do a damn thing but wonder when the baby is going to wake. It is an endless nightmare, a never-ending incubus attack, this rigmarole of caring for her sister, and she wonders, "When will it all end? All I do is feed her. I'm up in the night. I'm up in the day. I look after her. I change her nappies. I'm so unhappy. Abba is unhappy. I think he wanted a boy."

All is quiet now, and all is calm; and the eldest daughter of Rahman is asleep in her room, and Amma is asleep in her room, and everything is...

A mess.

Everything is in shatters, and Luky can't take it anymore, the crying. And when she goes to Amma's room, she picks up the baby and shakes it. "I can't stand this stupid kid!" she yells. "I hate it. It won't shut up. I'm gonna kill it. I'm sick of it!"

"Dur'ho, dur'ho!" Amma cries, barely able to stand. Get lost! Slap. "That's a sin to say things like that." Farayni. "God forbid your dirty mouth." Slap. She grabs the baby from Luky's hands.

"She's just a stupid girl," Luky says. "Why does it matter?"

Slap. "What about you then, when you cried, I didn't wanna strangle you, did I? Or when I changed your nappies? I didn't wanna kill you."

"But khali baby ho-wow." You keep making babies. "You keep giving birth to babies, and I can't do anything because of this baby!"

Today, which is Wednesday, is the first day of a new hairstyle at Luky's school. A fringe cut or so they call it.

"Cool," Luky thinks, wishing she could get a trim like that.

"What do you think of mine?" someone asks. "Do you like it?"

"It's nice."

Hazel comes running.

"I'm gonna have Kimberly, Caroline, Justine and Janet over to my house later," she tells Luky, all quiet like it's some sort of state secret, "and we're gonna give ourselves fringe cuts. Wanna come?"

"Oh, I don't know if I can get out tonight."

"That's okay. Maybe next time?"

Luky senses her feeling of being let down. "Well, let me go home first and ask my mum. If I can talk her into it, I'll come later."

Hazel smiles. "Can't wait."

The final bell rings and Luky's friends take a bus to Hazel's, while Luky takes a bus for home.

In the dining room, Luky sees Amma on her ottoman, sipping tea. "Asalaam alaykum," she says, walking to the kitchen.

"Wa alaykum asalaam."

Luky swipes a biscuit from the counter, a samosa from the fridge, and prepares a fresh cup of tea while nibbling on the biscuit. Then it's back to the dining room again, but Amma is no longer on the ottoman; she is tidying up the room, straightening up the chairs. So Luky says, "Here, let me do that for you, Amma. Why don't you sit down and have another cup of cha?"

"I'd love to," Amma says, taking the cup and saucer from Luky's hand and revisiting the ottoman with a smile.

Luky straightens up the chairs and grabs the vacuum.

"There. All finished," Luky says, moving to the door. "I've got homework to do now, so please don't bother me. I really gotta get it done."

"Don't worry," Amma says. "I won't."

Upstairs, Salena tells Luky that Abba is in his bedroom snoring.

"Well, at least he won't hear me when I leave."

"I just hope he doesn't hear you when you come back."

They sneak their way to the front door and Salena opens it.

"What time is asr today?" Luky asks, stepping outside.

"Six forty-three, why?"

"I just need to know what time to be back before dad gets home from the masjid."

"Oh." Salena thinks of another question. "But what should I tell mum if she asks for you?"

"Don't worry. I did some favors for her and told her I'd be doing homework and not to bother me, so I think we're good."

"Then see ya before seven."

"Yeah, see ya."

The door closes and Luky catches a bus to Hazel's.

At Hazel's, they give each other fringe cuts in Hazel's bathroom. Afterwards, they jibe Luky in a playful sort of manner concerning the spelling and rendition of her name.

"What was your dad trying to be, cool or something?" they ask.

"Yeah, why'd he leave off the c?"

Luky thinks about the real reason, which is that her father couldn't spell, and says, "He just wanted it to look more like a name, that's all."

"Wouldn't it be cool to visit Luky's someday?" Janet asks.

Luky blinks and wonders what such a scenario might look like. She pictures a multitude of bad things happening to them, agonizing things, each one of them involving Amma's purple sari, but what she pictures most is...

Another blink. "Oh my gosh, I gotta go!" she bleeps, looking at the clock.

When she reaches home, she throws a little stone at the window. Salena's not there. So she tosses another one. Finally, Salena appears at the window and mouths the words "I'll be right down." But what's taking so long? Minutes pass and still no Salena. Luky wonders what she should she do? Maybe toss another stone? "No," she answers, ruling against it. Opting instead to peek through the letterbox, but when she peeks through the letterbox, she...

Shits her pants. Symbolically, of course. Because that's when Abba opens the door, scaring the fuck out of her. Trying to step through the doorway, a bunch of his friends right behind him.

"Where did you go?" he asks, trying to stay calm with his friends there.

"To the shop," she says. "I had to get something for mum." But Abba knows better, which is why he gives her the eyes. And yes, she understands their translation. Clearly, they can only mean one thing: "When I get home, you're dead."

Well, Luky thinks to herself, *at least he didn't see my hair.*

After asr, Abba comes home and marches up the steps to Luky's room. He knocks on the door and Luky opens it with fingers atremble. Amma appears directly and stands by his side. Which is the same moment Luky remembers her hijab, that it is no longer on her head.

"What's this?" Amma yells, reaching for Luky's hair. "What are you trying to be, a shada fourie?" A white girl. "Girls aren't supposed to cut their hair. It's a sin."

"Only rubbish cut their hair," Abba chimes in. "Beauty lies in a woman's long hair, and I will not have any of my daughters looking like those trashy shada fouries who cut their hair short and look like boys."

"I didn't cut it," Luky says. "It got burned." But Abba doesn't buy it, and neither does Amma, and if there had been a person standing there after she had said that, that person would have heard a smack, then a scream.

17

Lunchtime. The beginning of June—the day of her and Ebrakhan's anniversary. They've been together now eight months, and she cannot wait to see him, which is why she runs to the gym.

"Hi Luky," his friends say.

"Where is he?" she asks.

"Slamming the rest of the day," they say. "We thought he was with you."

"I heard him say he was going to the park," adds another.

But Luky wonders why he would leave without her? *Maybe it's a surprise* she thinks. *After all, it is a special day.*

A smile. A brightening of the face.

She cuts school and goes to the park. No one is there. She checks by the swings. No one is there either. She checks by the bus stop, and sitting on the bus stop bench, holding hands and kissing, are Nasrin and a boy, a familiar looking boy, though she can't quite tell his features as her vantage point isn't the most advantageous. But now that the boy turns, his profile becomes clear. Oh God, it's Ebrakhan. And she can hardly believe it. She runs and only stops again when her legs can't carry her any farther. All alone, she wishes her life wasn't her life. Wishes it were somebody else's. *It's probably because I can't go out more often* she mutters. *That's probably the main reason why he's with her and not with me. If only my mum were a little more lenient. If only my dad were a little more understanding. If only they were more white.* Suddenly, she thinks about King George, his parka cold and snowy and the stiffness of his body from head to toe, but then it starts to rain so she goes home. Only she's late getting back, really late, and she hopes that Salena is still at the window. But when she flings some stones at it, no one responds. So she casts more stones and peeks through the letter box and casts more stones and waits. *Where the fuck is she?* she wonders, but she doesn't have to wonder for long as Salena appears at the window, her face somber and grim. But why? And who is that sidling up next to her? And whose hand is that on the windowpane?

Luky's heart sinks.

A few minutes later, a crazy man drags his teenage daughter inside.

—*Now where are you?*
—*In the library.*
—*How come?*
—*My boyfriend.*
—*Your boyfriend?*
—*Yeah, he drives a black car.*

—*What kind of car?*

—*I don't know what kind of car.*

—*Is he Paki?*

—*Yeah, he's Paki.*

—*Where did you meet him?*

—*At school; he was picking up his sister.*

—*How old is he?*

—*Eighteen.*

—*How old are you?*

—*Fourteen; I turned fourteen in August.*

—*Is he cute?*

—*All my friends think so.*

—*So why the library?*

—*It's where he studies.*

—*Your Amma lets you?*

—*I have to take Salena.*

—*Is Salena here with you right now?*

—*She's downstairs where I left her. I'm on the fourth floor.*

—*Can you tell me about the first time you met your boyfriend at the library?*

—*We spoke for a while at a carrel.*

—*About?*

—*I can't remember what about. I think I asked him how often he came to the library and he said he always came to the library, so that's why I started going to the library too, to see him.*

—*Where is he now?*

—*In the girl's bathroom.*

—*In the girl's bathroom?*

—*Yeah, it's where we make out.*

—*Who's calling you? I hear someone.*

—*That's him.*

—*Do you have to go?*

—*I have to go.*

—*To the bathroom?*

—*To the bathroom.*

—*To make out?*

—*To make out.*

Luky leaves, only to return twenty-five minutes later with runny makeup and tears.

—*What happened? Did you meet him?*

—*Yes.*

—*And?*

—*He pulled out a condom and put it on his thingy, and I was looking at him. 'What the heck is he doing?' That's the first time I ever saw a real dick. It was hard. I got scared. I was shivering. 'What the heck is he doing?' He told me he wanted me to sit on it, but I said, 'No, I'm not gonna sit on it,' and he said, 'Sit on it, slowly,' and I said, 'No, I'm not gonna sit on it, slowly. I'm scared.' 'But there's nothing to be scared about,' he said. 'Really. It's not going to hurt at all because your thingy's moist inside.' 'Really?' I whispered, so I thought I'd give it a go, but when he grabbed me, I started crying. 'I can't do it, I can't do it,' and that was it. I ran out of there and came to you.*

—*Will you ever go back?*

—*I can't say. Can anyone?*

—*Now where are you?*

—*In the house.*

—*How come?*

—*Because of my mum.*

—*What does your mum have to do with this?*

—*Everything.*

—*Can you be more precise?*

—*A short while ago, I started seeing a new guy.*

—*A new guy?*

—*Yeah, Idris. He's two years older than me.*

—*Is he Paki?*

—*Yeah, he's Paki.*

—*How did you meet him?*

—*We bumped into each other at the library, in the exchange. That's where all the students kinda go after school, where they go to hang out, where they go to talk and play games. I asked him who he was and he smiled.*

—*And your Amma was okay with this?*

—*Are you kidding me? She didn't even like me going to the library. I had to get a note from school saying how beneficial it was for students to be there.*

—*And it worked?*

—*Yeah, my parents even praised me for giving the extra effort when it came to my studies.*

—*But you weren't really studying?*

—*Hell no. I barely even went to school. I'd take attendance and then leave. I'd goof off and spend the entire day with Idris at the library or at the city centre.*

—*Idris wasn't in school then?*

—*No, he was already done with upper school; he was sixteen.*

—*What about a job?*

—*Once in a while he would work at his uncle's shop, but mostly he'd spend his time with me.*

—*I see.*

—*And that was the life, and the more I goofed off school, the more my grades fell. I went from A's to C's.*

—*And what did your parents say when they got your report?*

—*Who knows? I was with Idris.*

—*Well, what did they say when you got back?*

—*'Where were you?'*

—*And you said?*

—*'I was in school.'*

—*But obviously they didn't believe you.*

—*Hell no. 'You weren't in school,' my dad said. 'You weren't in school.' Slap! Right on the face, and I started crying. 'Where were you? Where were you?' he asked. Whack, whack. Then he pulled out his belt and beat me till I told him where I was. He beat me really bad. I had red marks all over my body. Then he grabbed me by the hair and hauled me to off to the living room and shut the door and beat me again till I told him what I was doing. 'Who were you with?' he asked. 'Were you with any boys? Why were you in the city centre?' 'No, no,' I said, 'I wasn't with any boys, just with a few of my friends from school. We were just going around to the stores.' Then my mum came in with the deywah—an oversized wooden spoon—and said, 'Deshi neeyah beeyah deemo,' meaning, if you don't settle down, we're gonna take you to Bangladesh and get you married. But I was too angry to care. So I shouted. Then my mum said, 'Girls aren't supposed to raise their voices like that. They're supposed to speak in subdued whispers.'*

—*And did you?*

—*What?*

—*Speak in subdued whispers?*

—Hell no. Of course not. I yelled at the top of lungs, 'I don't care! I'll raise my voice whenever I want to!' And then she said, 'That's haram,' forbidden for a woman to do that. She said a woman should be very delicate in all her movements, and that her presence should be completely veiled, especially when she's married.

—And you said?

—'I'm never gonna get married.'

—And then?

—'Life's not everything you think it is, beti. You're living a life of fun right now, but you're not realizing it. Though later on you will. Once you're married, it's a hard life.' But I told her I would never go to that country and get married. Never. But what did I know? How was I supposed to know my life was gonna end up in that shithole, whereas none of my sisters did?

—You sound bitter.

—Is that a question?

—An observation.

—Well, I'm glad you're so observant.

—Listen—

—Why don't we just take a break?

—But Mrs.—

—Luky. It's just Luky.

—We don't have much time.

—I see.

—So if we could continue.

—Fine.

—Tell me about Salena.

—What about her?

—Wasn't she your partner in crime?

—For the most part.

—Well, didn't she ever get hit?

—None of my sisters got beat the way I did. Once in a while they'd get hit, but that was only because they couldn't get an answer out of me. But otherwise, no, not really.

—So you're saying you always got the brunt of it?

—Always.

—How did that make you feel?

—Pretty goddamned shitty. How do you think it would make me feel?

—My opinion is irrelevant. I'm trying to determine—

—Yeah, like I said, 'Shitty,' with a goddamned in front of it.

—I heard you the first time.

—Well, how was I supposed to feel? You tell me. I wasn't allowed any space. What do you think somebody in my position would do? I couldn't move. They counted my footsteps. Thank God though for those goddamned ugly shawls my mum made for me. Without them, the beatings would have been horrendous.

—And Saqir?

—Well, let's put it this way. Here's me. Knock, knock, knock. And here's him, 'Where the fuck did you go?' and here's me, 'I went to the store,' and here's him, 'You didn't go to the store, you're lying, you don't have anything in your hands. Who sent you to the store, anyway?' Then he would yell for mum. 'Amma? Did you send her to the store?' I dreaded getting caught by that bastard. I couldn't stand it. He made such a big deal out of everything. He'd tell my mum. He'd tell my dad. Then my mum would say, 'Where did you go? Why did you go out without telling anyone?' and blah,

blah, blah. And then my brother would slap me. 'Where did you go? Tell me? Tell me, where did you go? You'd better tell me now before I tell dad or beat you up.' So I'd tell him, 'Oh, I went to Maqbull's,' and he'd say, 'Why did you go there for? Why did you go to that fucking Paki home? You'd better not be lying to me.' Slap, slap, slap.

—Okay, let's get back to Idris now. Besides the library, where else did you two meet before going to the city centre?

—The park; sometimes at Maqbull's.

—Maqbull's?

—Yeah, her mum was always away in Pakistan and her dad was always working.

—What did you guys do there?

—Make out, of course. We'd go to Idris' too.

—Idris'?

—Yeah.

—His parents were okay with that?

—Yeah. He even introduced me to them and everything, and they even let us go in his bedroom.

—Unbelievable. Though it must have been shocking. I mean, his parents' behavior, especially when you take into account the views of your own parents, who come from a similar background and culture but who remain at the opposite end of the spectrum.

—It was. I couldn't believe it. They even let him close the bedroom door.

—Now, at the beginning of this segment, you said you were stuck in the house because of your mum.

—That's right.

—So obviously it's because they caught on about Idris.

—Obviously.

—*But tell me, how exactly did we get to where we are today?*

—*If you insist.*

—*I do.*

—*Well, my parents hated it that I was gone so much. They hated my friends, my grades. They hated everything I was doing, and after a while they wouldn't even let me go anywhere, not even to Fermeeda's, and she lived right across the street! Mum said, 'You're not allowed to go out. Girls don't go out.' But I'd beg her. I'd say, 'Pleeease, can I go to a friend's?' But no, the answer was always no. God, they became so fucking strict at the end. Then my brother, I don't know how, but he heard I was seeing someone.*

—*Idris.*

—*You catch on fast.*

—*What did he do about it?*

—*What do you think he did about it? Beat me up, then told my mum and dad I was seeing some boy, and my dad got really mad with me and hit me and told me I couldn't go out anymore, and that I was a disgrace.*

—*And you said?*

—*'I wasn't with boys. I've never been with boys.'*

—*And?*

—*Nothing. There's nothing.*

—*Just a little more and we'll be done with this.*

—*I'll never be done with this.*

—*Just tell me what happened.*

—*My parents kept a close watch over me. They knew I was seeing someone. They just didn't know who.*

—*Did Idris ever call you?*

—Several times. My mum even heard his voice once, but then she heard a click.

—So Saqir was home at this time? or just for weekends and holidays?

—My brother? Oh, I almost forgot to tell you.

—What?

—About his madrasah.

—His what?

—The Islamic school that he went to. He was studying to be an imam, remember?

—Ah, yes, in Dewsbury, I believe.

—Yes, in Dewsbury.

—And what is it that you have to tell me?

—That he got kicked out. He had some conflict with the big imam there and they got into it really bad. I guess Pilton whacked him a few times with a cane.

—A cane?

—Yeah, you know my brother and his temper. But the weird part was that he was so gung ho about the madrasah when he first got there.

—So he came back home?

—Yep, which was shitty news to my ears.

—How did your parents react?

—They were devastated. How do you think they would feel? It was such a big thing in our home having a son at the madrasah. When my mum first found out he was going there, she said, 'Oh, my prayers have been answered. Masha'Allah, he's come into God's ways. He's following God's path. He's walking in God's footsteps.' And I remember my dad being happy too. 'That's my son! He's coming into civilization. God's answered our prayers. My son just wants to go to the *madrasah and become a mullah or an imam.' 'Yeah, right,' I thought. 'Bullshit. He's just going through some sort of phase and you lot don't even know it. You lot don't even know that he's trying to pull a slick one,' but I knew. First it was all that punk crap with the mohawk, then it was this whole Arabic thing.*

—*So he never finished?*

—*Nope. He came home one day and never left.*

—*So besides the hittings, what was so bad about lodgerbob...er, I mean, Pilton, being home?*

—*Well, besides the fact I had a 24/7 police escort, I always seemed to be on the wrong end of one of his mood swings.*

—*But at what point did everything seem to come to a head?*

—*Oh, I don't know. Maybe the day Idris gave me a hickey? Not sure. Actually, no, that's wrong. That day had nothing to do with it; it was actually the following day when I brought my dad some tea. 'What do you think I am?' he said. 'Don't you dare serve me tea with those haram hands. Do you think I was born yesterday? You think I don't understand what's going on? What's that on your neck?!' And I jumped backwards. 'It's nothing. It's nothing,' I said, but I guess he could still see it, even though it was covered with foundation. 'I've lived in this country for so many years,' he said, 'and you think I don't understand what's going on?' Whack, whack. He was just going off. Then he said he was gonna take me to Bangladesh. So I ran to my room. I couldn't stop crying. Then my mum came in. 'If you're gonna disgrace the family like this, were gonna marry you off.' So I called Idris and said, 'Listen, I can't see you for a while. My parents found out and my dad hit me. They even threatened to take me to Bangladesh.'*

—*And he said?*

—*That we need to play it low. He knew how bad it was getting for me in the house, and that's when he started talking about marriage. He said we could run away together and get married in Pakistan. That nobody would know.*

—*And what did you think of that whole scenario?*

—*'Yeah, let's do it,' I said. 'When should we get outta here?'*

—*When did you?*

—*I'm stuck in the house right now, remember? I can't go anywhere or see anybody, not Idris, not Maqbull, not Justine, not Kimberly, not Hazel, not—*

—*Okay, I get the picture. And I think that's enough for today. You've done quite well for yourself, and I'm very proud of your progress. I'll now begin counting backwards from three to one—ready?*

—*Ready.*

—*Okay, here we go—three, two, one.*

Part III. Death, Or Forced Marriage to an Old Guy. Goodbye England. Life in the Village. Thank God for America. 1986—2008.

1

The house was her prison, and she its only inmate. But the plan, like all plans involving detainees striving for their freedom, was simple: to leave and never come back.

Today is the tenth day of August, and summer is nearing an end. The year is nineteen hundred and eighty-six. Yesterday was a day of scheming and planning, of tying up loose ends, while tonight begins the first day of tomorrow.

Luky is ready, as are both bags. Inside are clothes and makeup. She won't be in need of anything else. For now, the bags are hidden beneath the bed, just as they have been since yesterday.

Amma is presently in the shower and will be for some time. Abba isn't home. Who knows where he is? Not Luky, and why should she wonder? *Now's the time to leave* she thinks. So she gathers her bags and makes her way to the front room, walks into the front room and carefully sets her bags down, not wishing to make a sound, and goes to the front room window and pushes aside the shades and sees Idris pulling up to the curb. She watches the passenger door open. That's her cue. So, with belongings in hand, she exits the guest room and makes her way to the front door, destiny's brink. One more obstacle now and she's free. With her right hand, she unlocks it; with the same she gives the handle a turn. With mouse-like ability, she opens the door and sets her items on the stone steps and then she closes the door with scarcely a squeak and begins her descension. At the gate now, only a few more meters to go.

From the passenger seat, she closes the passenger door; the bags are in the back and her face smiles from the front. *We did it* she exclaims, but their success, at least in her own mind, is rather hard to believe. Excitement and fear course through her body, her veins. She swallows. Silently, she prays that they make it. But soon paranoia takes over and her pumping organ misses a beat. She scans all directions for Saqir and his shadow. But no one is there. Driving off, they leave eighty-eight Little Horton Lane to the darkness, and all they can see in the rear-view mirror are streetlights and carlights.

Luky sighs; a piece of her will miss her old life, especially the good times she had with Abba when she was little. But those days are long gone. A new life, far away from parents and problems, awaits.

Years later, Luky would remember the moment she absconded her life as a happy one. *I was so glad to get out of there, really. I remember looking at Idris and couldn't believe he was there and everything was really happening. We were gonna live the fairy tale life for God's sake. Happily ever after.*

The light turns red and the car croons to a standstill. Idris and Luky giggle, then hug. The light turns green and the wheels start to roll. Idris takes Luky to a friend's. *It's only for the time being* he says. *Just for the time being.* They walk inside. The only two inhabitants are a man and a woman, both in their twenties, both smokers. The man shows her to an empty room. The woman carries a blanket and tosses it to the floor. "Here's your bed," she says dryly. "I hope it's not too soft." The man laughs and says something to Idris in Urdu. Idris nods and replies to the man in the same tongue.

"Don't we have any food in this house?" Luky interrupts. "I'm starving."

"I'll bring you something tomorrow," Idris says to her, "when I come back."

"You're leaving?"

"Just for tonight."

"But I thought you were staying?"

"I have to go."

"But—"

"Look," Idris says, "I'll be back tomorrow." He reaches for the door. "Goodbye." The door opens and Idris steps through. The door closes and he's gone.

Morning comes and Luky rises from the blanket and the floorboards. The man and woman are out, and there is no food in the house, and neither is there a phone. Her only saving grace is the telly (at least it's in color), and for the next several hours it is the only thing that keeps her together.

Around suppertime, the man arrives home followed by the woman. They have fish and chips but never offer any to

Luky, and Luky's intestines can only growl at the lack of nourishment inside her belly.

Later, Idris comes over with leftover chippies and a slice of cold pizza.

The following day is a Tuesday, and at three in the afternoon the man comes home and tosses a newspaper onto the table. He begins to close all the shades and curtains, one by one, and the light in the room dims. Though not once does he speak to Luky about anything, just goes about his business as if she is non-existent. An hour or so later, the woman arrives home. She too, like the man, carries a newspaper. She throws it on the sofa and tells Luky to pick it up. "They're looking for you, you know."

"Who is?"

"The police. You're officially a missing person."

Around eight o'clock pm, Idris comes over empty handed and takes Luky to a darkened room so they can kiss. Wednesday through Friday comes and goes like the twilight, and Saturday is the same as Friday. Today is Sunday, the middle of the afternoon, and Luky, all alone, falls asleep.

—What did you think was going to happen?

—I thought I was gonna have all this freedom. I thought we were gonna get married and go to the cinema every single day. I thought we were gonna have a jolly good time, me and him, snogging in back alleys, behind corner shops, eating pizzas and chippies the live long day. I thought I was gonna land on a magic fucking wand and everything I ever wanted was gonna happen out of nowhere, and I thought it was gonna feel so good. 'Whoooo-whooo! I'm out of my dad's house now! I can go out and do whatever I want, whenever I want. I can

be like the English.' But then reality hit me when I got stored away in that little flat, and all I did all day was wait for him to bring me food. I couldn't even open the curtains or touch the shades. They thought the police might come through and get me or something. I fucking hated it there.

—Did you tell Idris how you felt?

—Of course I did. 'When are we gonna leave?' I said. 'When are we gonna get the fuck outta here and get married? What are we waiting for?'

—And?

—He said he was gonna get me out.

—You must have been going crazy?

—Is that your stab at irony?

—Of course not.

—Because the situation was a disaster. I lived it. I breathed it. My heart was emptied out because of it.

—I didn't mean to—

—Why apologize?

—Shall we continue?

—Let's.

—I was curious as to whether you were homesick or missed your mum during this time?

—By the ninth day, all I wanted was out. I didn't feel stable. I couldn't shower. I didn't have my breakfast. I hardly had any food whatsoever. 'When are we gonna leave,' I asked him. 'When are we gonna leave?'

—And?

—He said, 'Don't worry, we'll leave.' But when? I really wanted to know. I was finally free, finally able to come and go as I wanted, but where the fuck was I? Stowed away like some *bandit. That's not the kind of freedom I signed on for, and if he couldn't take care of me for nine days, then—*

—What?

—Well, how could he take care of me for the rest of my life? Where was his plan? He didn't even get me a birthday present for fuck's sake. He said, 'I bought you something but left it on the bus by mistake.' Yeah, right. So he comes over and we make out, but helloooo! I'm dying here, and kissing doesn't squelch hunger pains, now does it? But my mum's cooking does, and 'If this is freedom,' I thought, 'I don't want it.' I missed my mum's food and was ready to go home.

—Luky? Oh, there you are, I thought I lost you.

—You didn't.

—You had me worried.

—You shouldn't've been.

—I'll keep that in mind.

—Please do.

—Are you ready?

—As I'll ever be.

—Then let's get started. What are you doing?

—I'm in the cellar.

—What are you doing in the cellar?

—I snuck out last night; I'm trying to sneak back in.

—Wait, I thought you were at Idris' friend's house? Are you not there anymore?

—No, the incident I'm speaking of took place over a year ago.

—Oh, well, where did you go?

—To see Ebrakhan.

—*I remember him. He was that snake in the grass you caught with Nasrin.*

—*Scarface, you mean.*

—*How could I forget?*

—*Apparently, you can.*

—*Well, that can be debated, but getting back to the question before us.*

—*Which is?*

—*Why are you still in the basement?*

—*I'm trying to get back inside.*

—*But you said you snuck out yesterday evening, which means today is the following day, which means you've been in the cellar all night.*

—*Again, such an observationist.*

—*I do have my moments.*

—*Don't we all?*

—*Back to the basement.*

—*Well, let me tell you about our basement. It's dark, scary. Try picturing a medieval dungeon. Now try picturing one of Dante's hell circles. Our cellar is more akin to one of the circles. It's wet, damp. Dank often comes to mind. Mice run rampant and slugs make love to the walls.*

—*Not too cozy, then?*

—*For pests, maybe, and people like you.*

—*Now getting back to what you said earlier, you stated that you've been there all night, so how come you can't get back in?*

—*Because the door leading to the house is locked. My mum must have locked it before she went to bed, or maybe my dad did before he went to work.*

—*Then how did you get into the basement in the first place, from the outside I mean? Didn't your mum or dad lock that door too?*

—*No, they would have had to go down into the basement to check that one.*

—*That's the door that leads to the back garden, correct?*

—*That's right.*

—*And where is Salena? Isn't she your savior?*

—*Good question, and yes to the second one.*

—*So you're waiting?*

—*Yeah.*

—*For her?*

—*For her.*

—*Did you try throwing stones at the window?*

—*I did.*

—*And?*

—*Nothing.*

—*How odd.*

—*Not very.*

—*Why's that?*

—*Because she's probably sleeping.*

—*Can you blame her?*

—*Of course I can blame her.*

—*But it isn't even yet lauds.*

—*We're not Catholic.*

—*I was referring to the time.*

—*Oh.*

—*Just tell me, when did you first realize your predicament was so dire?*

—*When I couldn't get into the house; I would have thought that evident even to you.*

—*Yes, well*—

—*Wait. I hear something.*

—*Luky, are you there?*

—*I'm here.*

—*What happened?*

—*It was Salena.*

—*How did you know?*

—*Who else would it be at that hour? She's always downstairs in the morning. So I tapped on the door and said, 'Salena,' and she said, 'Boro affa, is that you? Are you still down there?' and I said, 'Yeah, I'm still down here. The door's locked. Dad must have locked it. You were supposed to let me in.'*

—*And her reply?*

—*'Oh, I fell asleep.' 'Well, I didn't fall asleep,' I said, 'I had to stay awake all night in this freaking basement, and it's cold down here, and there's mice,' and she said, 'I'm so sorry, boro affa, I fell asleep.'*

—*So you were afraid?*

—*Hell yeah, I was afraid. You could see the mice running in and out of boxes and tiny holes underneath the stairwell, which is why I stayed at the very top of the staircase all night, with my head and shoulder against the doorside. I was afraid they were gonna come and get my feet or something, and I hated the look of those slugs, with their fat slimy bodies. I thought they were gonna crawl up my legs. It was the most horrific feeling, and the entire time I was thinking, 'When that fucking bitch Salena wakes up in the morning, I'm gonna kill her for not staying awake.'*

—*So Salena said, 'Boro affa, is that you?'*

—Yeah, and I said, 'Who the fuck do you think it is? Of course it's me,' and she gasped, 'You're still out there?' and I said, 'Yeah, I've been out here all night. Dad must have locked the door,' and when she opened it, I could see she was scared.

—And then?

—I pushed her out of the way and hit her. I was so mad. 'I'm sorry for not staying awake, boro affa,' she said. 'I'm sorry.' But then I called her a stupid cow. 'Where the heck were you?' I said. 'I told you to watch out for me.' But the worst part was that I couldn't even go upstairs and lay down.

—Why not?

—Because I had to go to school, and I knew my mum would be up and my dad would be coming home from work soon, so I had no other choice than to drag my ass upstairs and get ready. Man, I tell ya, I only wanted to see Ebrakhan for an hour or two, but ended up getting stuck in the basement for the whole fucking night.

—Did your parents ever catch you down there?

—Of course. Many times.

—An example?

—One time my mum opened the door and saw me coming up the stairs and pulled me by the hair and said, 'Where did you go, where did you go? Tell me, tell me?' and I said, 'I didn't go anywhere,' and she said, 'You did. You left. I checked upstairs. I checked downstairs. I checked everywhichwhere and you were gone.' Another time, my dad opened the door and saw me. 'What are you doing down here?' he said, and I said, 'Oh, I was just getting something from the basement.' Then whack, right across the face.

—How did that make you feel?

—*Not too goddamn good. I tell ya, I just wanted to lay in bed and sulk, but my mum wouldn't let me. Instead, she followed me upstairs and told me not to do it again what I did or otherwise my dad, she said he was gonna hit me. She told me to do my prayers. She tried to get me to come down and help her in the kitchen, but I said I didn't want to. She told my sisters to ask me if I needed anything, but I said, 'Get away,' when they came in because I didn't wanna talk to them anymore, and it made me even more mad to see them trying to be so good, thinking that they were gonna get it next if they didn't behave. Man, I tell ya, I just wanted a little bit of freedom.*

—*Did Salena ever put up a fight when you asked her to aid you in your escapades?*

—*When didn't she put up a fight? 'Why do I always have to do this, boro affa?' she'd say. 'Why do I always have to do this?' 'Just fucking shut up and do it!' I'd say, but she would always resist. 'Dad's gonna kill us,' she'd say, or 'He's gonna beat the hell outta me because of you.'*

—*And your reply?*

—*'Yeah, right. Dad barely touches you, and even if he did, so what? Do it anyways.' Eventually, though, my dad put a big fat padlock on the cellar door.*

Awake. Luky opens her eyes. She sees Idris kneeling beside her, smiling. "What time is it?" she asks.

"Nearly seven o'clock."

"In the morning?"

He shakes his head. "In the evening."

"Did you bring me any food?"

"Some crisps and fish fingers."

"Thanks, Idris," Luky says. "Thanks."

Later on, during the witching hours, Luky lies awake. *I can't wait to leave this fucking place* she thinks. *I can't wait to leave.*

Now today is Tuesday, and Idris and Luky are seated on the sofa, having it out. "When are we gonna leave?" Luky asks. "How much longer do I have to stay?"

"We'll leave. Don't worry. These things take time."

"But when? I'm like a prisoner here. I've been here for nine days, and not once have we done anything fun."

"How about tomorrow then?"

"Tomorrow?"

"Yeah, tomorrow we'll go to the city centre. We'll hit the cinema, the museum. We'll go to the arcade...we'll hang out."

Luky smiles. "Tomorrow."

2

Wednesday. Idris comes over and they go to the city centre.
*We were just getting on with our regular lives. It was the first
time in ten days we'd been out, and then, like something out
of a dream, I saw my dad out of the corner of my eye. Oh my
God, he was right there across the street. I looked at him and
he looked at me. I dropped my bags and stood there, just stood
there. I got scared and didn't move a muscle. Which way was I
going to 'Run!' I told Idris. Then I saw my dad chase him with
a pocketknife. He had a pocketknife! 'Oh my God, I can't
believe this is happening.' But he got away, thank God. Then
my dad came back. 'Chull!' he said. Come with me. So I went
with him to the bus and got on. But we had to go to the police
station first because I was still classified as a missing person.*

*The whole ride there, I just put my head down and didn't
say a word. I felt so worthless. My dad's head was down too,
and I knew he was sad. It was like his father had died or*

something. Or like the sky had fallen on him. 'What am I gonna do?' he said. 'What am I gonna do? My ijudth is gone,' my prestige. 'It's ruined. It takes years to build it up and two seconds to fall. What are people gonna say? Oh, Rahman. What happened to your daughter? She was in the newspaper. Did she run away? Oh, Allah. There's no point in living anymore. My face is ruined. I can't go to the masjid. I might as well die.' I knew I had embarrassed him. I felt like I did the worst thing in the world, like I ruined his whole life. He looked like the losing side of a battle. He was so upset. Tears were in his eyes. I think it was the first time I ever saw my dad cry. And I'll never forget the way he kept shaking his head like he was going to prison and how he wouldn't even look at me. I remember feeling really sad that I did that to him, that everything he was feeling was because of me.

At the police station, my dad said, 'I found her on Lumb Lane.' And I didn't know anything about Lumb Lane at the time, but that's supposedly where all the hookers went to. Then the police started asking me questions: 'What were you doing on Lumb Lane?' and 'Who were you with on Lumb Lane?' and I said, 'I wasn't with anybody on Lumb Lane,' and they said, 'Yeah, you were. You were with somebody,' and I said, 'No, I wasn't with anybody. I ran off on my own.' Then, finally, they let me go. But I thought, 'Shit. Now I'm gonna get such a good bloody beating. I'm gonna get such a good bloody beating.'

At home, the hittings begin before Luky removes her footwear. Whack. "Where did you go?" Whack, whack. "Who were you with?" Whack. "Where did you go?"—*and they were yelling and screaming, and Amma was crying and tugging at Luky's hair and swatting at her face, and Luky was crying, and then, finally, the mishmash of fists and slaps, the tussling of tired bodies, the yanking of black hair and pieces of disheveled clothing, dwindled to a gradual cessation, but the drama of that ill-fated day had only yet begun...*

"Now get in the kitchen and help me wash the dishes," Amma says. "Do what a woman's supposed to do."

Abba and Saqir walk to the dining room in disgust.

"I don't wanna do what a woman's supposed to do," Luky snaps. "I'm not a woman!"

Amma steps closer and points a finger at her daughter's face. "You won't act this way when you're married."

Luky pushes Amma's finger. "I never wanna fucking get married! If I get married, I'll kill him!"

Slap. "God forbid your dirty mouth!" Slap. "God forbid. You seem to be forgetting your role in this world, beti. You're a woman, and a woman has no value unless she is married, and once she is married, she has to obey her husband. That's it, that's your fate. You stay in the kitchen and you work."

"Well, I don't wanna be in the kitchen all day sweating behind that stove for hours and hours. I don't wanna wear a sari and spend all my time cutting onions and vegetables. I don't wanna grow up and be like you!"

"One day you'll regret it, mark my words. When you're married, your mother-in-law's gonna say, 'Your parents never taught you anything. They never taught you the duties of being a woman; they never taught you how to cook. What kind of girl are you, and what kind of parents are they?' and it's gonna be a hell for you and a disgrace on us. It's gonna be a shame."

Luky shakes her head. "I won't have a mother-in-law to tell me how to do anything because I'm never gonna get married, so I don't need to learn how to cook. I can eat fish and chips all day for the rest of my life."

"Humph." Amma steps back. "Have you taken a look in the mirror, lately? You're a woman, a fifteen year old woman. You're not a kid anymore. I was married to your Abba at fifteen." Amma shakes her head. "You think you're living a fairy tale life, don't you? You think you're a storybook? You're not, beti. You're not. And there aren't any magic wands or lamps."

Luky rolls her eyes.

"But one day," Amma continues, "you'll be married, and more likely than not you'll have a nagging mother-in-law on your back all day like a neck ache, and then you'll realize what I said."

"No, I won't! I'll kill myself before then." Luky takes the rag off her head and throws it to the ground. "I hate my life! I hate this culture. I can't go anywhere. Or do any damn thing. I hate it so freaking much!" She kicks the rag with her foot. "And you won't let me go to a friend's."

"Which friends? the bay-deens? the Pakistanis? Or let me guess, the half-naked shada fouries with short skirts, baring their fat elephant thighs? Do you really want to walk around with those huge filthy girls, those disbelieving butchers?"

"Yeah, it's better than walking around here with your purple sari." She says it pissy too, then adds, "I hate living here. I hate it so fucking much! I'd rather kill myself than live like a prisoner. I wanna live like my friends do. Their lives are so much better than mine. They get to do this and that, and they can go out whenever they want and see their friends and have boyfriends. *Their* parents understand. *Their* parents are white."

"You want boyfriends? You know what happens when you have boyfriends? You get gunah," sin, "and Allah will never forgive you, and you'll burn in hell forever." Amma points to the wall. "Those friends of yours are the bay-deens, and this life is all that they have; they won't have a plot in the hereafter, but if we obey Allah and pass all of his tests and live a good life, then we'll be rewarded with blessings and paradise, we'll be assured a spot in the world to come. This life is short, beti. Remember that. So there's no point in enjoying it. You may not wake up tomorrow."

"I don't care! I don't want the kind of life you talk about when I'm dead. I'm sick of it!"

"Well, if your itch is so bad, we'll take you to Bangladesh and get you married. How do you like the sound of that?"

"I don't care! It's better than being here." *It was hard when the outside world was in front of my eyes, when my friends were out doing fun things and I wasn't. On top of that, my mum made it seem like my life meant nothing, that we were all gonna die and live forever, so which would we rather choose: this life or the next? 'Don't be like the bay-deen,' she would say. 'They've gone astray. Instead, live for the life to come.'*

"Okay, fine. You'll see what it's like when you get there; you'll see what it's like when you're suffering. Just don't come crying to me." Amma takes a breath. "I don't know, maybe it's for the best, maybe this situation was supposed to happen. You've embarrassed us and given us a bad name, and now your Abba can't show his face to the community. His reputation is like a sinking ship."

"Maybe I don't give a dam about his name. It's always what the people say. What about me? Don't you lot ever think about me?"

"Of course we do. But you gotta keep your Abba's reputation intact. You gotta think. You gotta be more like so and so's daughters. They're good girls. They always wear their hijabs. Why can't you be more like them? They don't do any—"

"Yeah, they do! You just don't know it. You lot are never around. Sure, they wear their hijabs, but as soon as they step off the bus, they tear 'em off and make out with boys. At least I don't do that, at least I'm not as bad as those girls are. Those girls are worse."

"Forget about those girls, then. You're the one who—"

"If you'd just cut me a little slack, then I wouldn't have to sneak around and do stuff!"

Smack. Amma can't take it anymore. "Dur'ho!" she says. "Get out of my face!" Smack. "I don't wanna see you right now."

"Don't worry. You'll never see me again!" Luky rushes to the stairs and Amma reaches for an arm.

"Get away from me!" Luky screams. "I hate you!"

"Get down here!"

"Leave me alone." *All they care about is shame and prestige. For once it would be nice if all they cared about was me.*

—*Then what happened?*

—*I went to my dad's room. I felt so ashamed. I was angry. And the more I thought about it, the more I wanted to end it. So I went to where the pills were, some kind of pain meds, and started swallowing. But I can't remember if I knocked something over or if something fell. 'What's this ringing in my ears?' I wondered. The next thing I knew, I was on the floor, and I remember everything being hazy.*

—And then?

—Someone said, 'Call the ambulance!' but I don't know who said that or who dialed the numbers. My mum said, 'Call your dad!' (obviously, she was talking to my brother). Then the ambulance came and I heard my mum say, 'She's dying!' So they took me to the hospital and wheeled me through a set of double doors. 'Where am I? What's these white lights?' I could feel something going down my throat. 'Stop being such a baby,' someone said. God, that made me so mad. I couldn't believe she was so mean. Fucking bitch. How could she be a nurse? I've always wanted to be a nurse, but I wouldn't be a fucking nurse like that cow, no way. I wanted to punch her in the stomach. The next day, my parents came to take me home, but nobody really said anything. I think my dad said, 'How ya feeling?' or 'How ya doing?' It's really too hard to remember.

—What happened after you got home?

—'What the hell is going on?' I wondered. 'How come no one is giving me a beating? They're actually treating me kinda nice for a change.' I mean, my brother just ignored me and my dad only said, 'You know what you did was wrong,' then told me I could go back to school in a day or two, and when I went back to school, everybody knew I had run away because it was in the papers. I was famous, and from then on it wasn't too bad in the house. My parents eased up. They even let me have friends over. Can you believe it? They said it was fine. My mum even overlooked Idris' phone calls. 'Wow, the family's really changed,' I thought. But the real shock came when she

said, 'You can go see him at his home if you'd like.' 'What the hell is going on?' I wondered. So I went to see Idris at his place on a Saturday after my dad called me a cab. 'Wicked,' I thought. 'This is cool. I can't believe it.' The next day, I told Idris, 'Oh my God, my dad, I think he's okay with it. I think he's okay with us seeing each other,' and he said, 'Yeah, I think your dad spoke to my dad,' and I screamed, 'Really? What did they talk about?' and he said, 'Oh, I don't know what they talked about, but it must have been really good.' And Salena didn't talk to me much during this time, and I didn't feel like talking to her anyway, so it wasn't that big a deal, but Salena did say that dad was really upset when I was gone, which made me feel even worse than the day he brought me home from the police station, and it made me wanna help my parents and be there for them, and I desperately wanted to win back my dad's affection and regain that connection I had lost. I realized I had hurt my dad's feelings. I knew that as well as anyone, and I knew I had embarrassed him when I ran away.

—Which explains why you were so willing to escort your mum back to Bangladesh.

—I only wanted to make my dad happy, that's all, and after ruining his reputation I thought it was the least I could do. Anyway, it was only supposed to be for two weeks.

—Where was Luton at this time?

—I can't remember if he was in Manchester or London, but he was rarely ever at home.

—Now tell me about the telegram.

—The telegram?

—The one your father received.

—Oh, about three weeks after I ran away, a telegram arrived at our house saying that my uncle, Leelu Miah, was on his deathbed. So my mum starts wailing at the top of her breath. 'What am I gonna do? My brother's gonna die. My mother just died three years ago and my other brother died [so many years ago], and this is my last brother,' and my dad said, 'Well, you know, you can't go by yourself to Bangladesh, you can't speak good English, you might get lost on the plane. So I guess either Pilton or Luky, one of the two, can go with you, but only for a week or two. You can't stay too long,' and my mum said, 'Okay, that's fine. A week or two is fine, and if Luky could come with me, I'd feel better,' and my dad said, 'Well, Luky would be the best choice. She'd even get two weeks off school, which I don't think she'd have a problem with.'

—And in your head you were thinking?

—About my Nanu, mostly. I was thinking how my mum wanted to go back and bury her but never got to, and I didn't want to be the one to stop her from going this time, even if it was to see Leelu, and to complicate matters further, my parents had been really nice to me over the previous three weeks, so I thought, 'What the heck? Why not? Fine. I'll go for two weeks. What does it matter?' So I phoned Idris and said, 'My uncle's on his deathbed, so I have to go to Bangladesh with my mum, but I'm only gonna be gone for two weeks,' and I told him I was sorry I wasn't gonna be there for his birthday (I think it was around September seventeenth, though now I'm not too sure), but I'd certainly get him a fantastic present. So just before I left, I told Salena, because my parents gave me the money to buy him a cassette player, and she said, 'Fine,' that she would give it to him, so yeah, that was it, and when the time came for me to go, I said goodbye and told him not to worry, that I'd only be gone for two weeks. 'I'll write to you every day,' I said, then kissed him and went to the airport.

—So they played it?

—Excuse me?

—They played it.

—Played what?

—You, your mum and dad. They took advantage of your emotions and the angst you felt over your wrongdoings and made plans behind your back. They led you to believe one thing, but really intended for another, which is when they worked their magic.

3

The plane lands at the airport in Dhaka and Luky and Amma and Luky's sister depart through the exit doors and tote their baggage along the passenger boarding bridge. They lumber past the airport terminal gate, Amma balancing Shanu on her hip and Luky inching behind. They hand over their passports to the officials manning the makeshift booth labeled immigration and wait for them to be stamped. A minute later, they are given passage through a set of featureless doors, and a few seconds after that they are standing face to face with a throng.

Luky covers her nose; the entrails of the terminal stink to high heaven and the beggars, some with grayed-out eyes and malformed limbs, are undernourished, underbathed. And the scenery, dare anyone mention the scenery? Horrific. Utterly contemptible and eeewww. The moldy walls, unclean floors. The eyes of many strangers, staring.

"Who's picking us up, Amma?" Luky asks, a gleam of worry in her eyes.

"No one. We're getting on another plane, remember? We're going to Sylhet." Amma wipes a stream of milky froth from Shanu's lips with her sari.

"It's just that it's been a really long time," Luky says, thinking that the last time they were here, Nanu was still—

"Luky?" Amma calls.

"What?"

"Hurry or we'll miss our flight."

They board a small plane by walking up a detached staircase that is leaning against the side of the craft. They find their seats in the middle of the vessel. God, they're squished in. So Amma positions Shanu on her lap to make more room. The overhead bins are crammed full with other people's belongings, so where do they put their stuff? "Beneath the seats," the stewardess says. "And if there is no room there, then on top of your legs."

Luky scans the interior with her eyes: men rove the center aisle and women chat over seat tops; the aisle resembles a logjam. Finally, one of the female flight attendants instructs everyone to be seated. "If you wish this flight to depart on time, then please return to your seats."

Luky marvels as the menfolk hasten to their appropriate places. Why, the last thing they desire is delay.

"Fasten your seatbelts," a voice says over the loudspeaker.

The riders do as they're told.

The plane taxis from the apron to the runway, then down the runway it speeds...building steam, finally tilting its nose toward the heavens and receding to the clouds with a whoosh. Forty-five minutes later, the plane begins its descension.

Luky peers out the window after leaning across a napping old lady and sees that the aircraft is flying below the clouds. *Are those cows?* she wonders. But wait. What's that? *Trees and bushes? Swampy water and ratty old boats? Nasty. What the hell is this place?* God. She doesn't remember the likes of this place being so uncivil. How dare her mother say, "Don't worry, Luky, everything will be really good there and you'll like it. You'll see all of your cousins, and it'll be really nice. Bangladesh is so much more modern than it used to be."

The plane greets the earth with an uncouth first impression and the passengers release a pent up sigh of relief as the craft stammers to a bumpy and nerve wracking halt. Thud, thud, thud. Over the unpaved strip it skids. Amma and Luky collect their possessions and schlep to the side exit door. They deplane to the ground with the aid of some stairs and enter the airport after walking across the apron. But Luky is aghast at her new surroundings and wonders whether they've entered a whole new universe altogether. The word hectic comes to mind. She hears shouts, disrupted screams. Muffled announcements cackle through an unseen loudspeaker and the squalid, rundown terminal is damp and fetid to each nostril. On top of that, she has to go pee but decides against using the toilet because everything is simply too disgusting, and God, she isn't about to let anything in this place touch her thingy.

To the left and right, she sees trampy lounge furniture, wall stains, and rustic villagers waiting for a hand out. It seems as though everything is humming at the same time. But how to get out of here? How to maneuver to the nearest exit area? *Oh God.* How to move one inch? But you can't move one inch. Not with these people. Some elbowroom would be nice right now. Or maybe safe passage to the nearest getaway apparatus. But nope, that is asking too much. Way too much. Who are these people, these malnourished beggars? Creepy. Their protruding eyes bulging. How to stand it? What the hell do they want? These zombies, like the zombies from *Thriller*. Shit. Can't breathe. Now what? All crammed up. Their arms outstretched for the Londoni girl. They're hungry. Their hands cupped for alms. No escape. Luky feels encircled. Are they aliens? Or just starving Ethiopians who've wandered too far east? Who knows? Does anybody? Disgusting.

"Why are you holding onto me like that?" Amma asks. "I'm trying to hold onto your sister. Look for your uncle."

"Which uncle?" Luky asks.

"Akrum Khalu, my sister's husband."

"But they all look the same, Amma," Luky says. "Dark and ugly."

"Just look for him," Amma breathes.

"But I don't know who he is! I can't remember his face."

"Sister!" Akrum shouts.

"There he is!" Amma points.

Luky watches Akrum Khalu and his goons disperse the people with their hands and feet. Punch. Kick. Like snow plows. "Get out of the way, you fucking bastors!" they shout. "Get lost!" Amma watches them toss a human to the side. "Move it or I'll slap your teeth out!" One guy gets smacked in the face. "Get outta here!" So the beggars part and Moses…er, that is, Akrum Khalu, leads them to the exit on the other side.

Outdoors now, Luky has to hide her gaze from the sun. Behind her, the airport terminal façade is rain-stained and hooded by crow droppings. The sight of it nearly causes her to barf. On the street, which can hardly be called a street, Akrum and his men load the vehicle with baggage and wait for Luky and Amma (and Shanu) to climb in. Suddenly, the beggars converge with single-minded desperation (they want money). To Luky, they resemble locusts, ready to chomp on anything that is green. *Oh God. How did that Thriller video end again?*

"Watch out!" Akrum says. "These kids are thieves. They'll steal the taste from your tongue. Don't let 'em fool ya."

Some kid, maybe six or seven, approaches the car window. Others next to him. Like tiny little kids, four or five years old. Some without limbs. "Please, Londoni affa," they say. "We've no money for food. Can you give us some takas, please?" *Some were blind. It was horrible. And then Akrum got out and tossed one like a sack of trash. 'Get out of here!' he yelled. 'You mother fuckers! Get out of here!' and the kids kept hitting the glass with their hands. God, the whole scene was beyond my imagination, and the driver kept beeping his horn.*

"So, how are you?" Akrum asks Luky as the car leaves the beggars to their misery.

"Fine."

"How was your flight?"

"Long."

The car chugs forward, and two hours later it arrives at Akrum's.

"How was the ride?" Rabiya asks Luky as she takes Shanu from Amma.

Bumpy. The car kept jerking every time it hit a pothole. At times, the men had to push it from behind just to get it moving again. And muddy puddles were everywhere. All over the place. Like busted shanties. Shit. Like raw dirt. All nasty and smelly. Like sewer. When are we gonna get to Akrum's? Are you kidding me? This is it?? We're here???

"Kita?" Rabiya asks Luky. "You were saying?"

"Fine, Khala. Just fine."

Rabiya smiles and hugs her niece. "Welcome home," she says. "Welcome home."

But tons of people keep coming. From where though, who can tell? They're supposed to be relatives, but how can they have so many relatives? It's a never-ending line waiting to see the Londonis. But this isn't Buckingham Palace, and neither sits here the Queen. So why all this fuss, this big to-do?

But that's how it is in Bangladesh.

Though all Luky can think about is changing her light-pink salwar and matching kameez, the one with the gold stripes down the sides, into something more comfortable. But with the amount of plebs still lurking around Akrum Khalu's property, waiting to stare at the Londonis with an awe usually reserved for stone Gods and movie stars, no relief is foreseeable. Shit. But Amma loves the attention. So does Shanu. See how they absorb the compliments like a double sponge? Amma in her beige colored sari, Shanu smiling from her lap.

Amma grins.

"Oh, Sunia, you look so pretty!"

Another lady appears from the side. "Oh my gosh, is that Luky? She's grown so big!" Another lady drags Shanu out of Amma's arms. "Is this the baby? She's so cute!"

Sweat drips from Luky's brow and someone brings her water and snack. But nothing tastes right—not the water, not the snack. And that smell! What's that smell? How revolting! And the people, how come they won't leave? Luky wipes the frustration from her eyes, but the undesirable malady of her condition remains, just like the people do. Ugh! And there's so many of them too, just staring.

"Aah, such nice skin you have!" Luky hears someone say. "So beautiful!" adds another. "So fair. So shada like the bhat." But this rigmarole weakens her constitution, so much so that she cringes within her skeleton and belts out a silent scream. Finally, Akrum shoos everyone away with a flash of his biceps. "Now get out, you sons of bitches! You'll see 'em again tomorrow morning." Which sets Luky to thinking, "They're gonna come back tomorrow?"

They lock the main door and Luky switches her clothes in another room and readies herself for nighttime. But where to sleep?

Rabiya explains the arrangements.

"I can't sleep here," Luky says. "It doesn't have a proper mattress." So Rabiya goes and gets a comforter and lays it on top of the mattress to make it more comfy.

"There, that should be better. Enjoy."

But it doesn't matter, Luky feels itchy and can't get comfy and feels like bugs are crawling all over her face.

In the morning, Luky eats eggs, parathas and sliced papayas. After, Amma tells her to take a bath, but Luky replies, "Where am I gonna take a bath?" Because last night, when she used the bathroom, it was ugh! disgusting! nothing more than a small room devoid of windows. At its base was a concrete floor, crude to the soles in texture and concaved to a certain degree in character, so as to allow the easy gravitation of liquids to its central, sieve-covered drain, where, supposedly, everything and anything, in a calculated display of civil engineering at its most quixotic, funnels away to the darkness. *But it smells like piss in there!* Nevertheless, Amma tells her, "Where you took the piss last night, that's where you're going to take the bath."

"What? I took a piss there last night! And now you want me to take a bath there too? That's not a bathtub! It's a floor covered in piss!"

"Well, I'll boil hot water and wash the floor. Don't worry. I'll clean it." So Amma boils hot water and washes the floor. Eventually, Luky goes in there with her Bata sandals on her feet and two towels on her body (you didn't expect her to step in there barefeet where everybody peed all night, did you?). So with two buckets of water, one hot, one cold, Amma helps her daughter bathe in the place where urine succumbs to the pressure of a full bladder. *And that's when I knew I wanted to come back to England.*

"Are we gonna go back in exactly two weeks?" Luky asks Amma, just to be sure.

"Yeah, don't worry. We'll go back."

What a liar.

On the following day, they set out for Rangarchur after eating a hearty lunch, items that Luky mostly hates. She winces at the thought of going to the village where the food and everything else is sure to be far worse than the worst thing at Khalu's. But she tries not to complain, really. She knows they are here to visit Leelu before he passes, and besides, in two weeks she'll be back in luxury, and what, in the grand contrivance of all things, is two weeks?

They take a ricksha to the launch, their goodbyes previously stated. When they reach the river and its waters, they remove their footwear and navigate down a muddy bank, Luky holding onto Akrum's arm, Amma holding onto a cousin's, and Shanu holding onto her dummy.

From the riverside, they embark across what appears to be a wooden rampway, then enter, along with many others, the heart of the ferry; from there, a man directs them to the woman's quarters, a tiny private room, closed in, with only two small windows in the walls.

The boat sails.

But the air is stifling in this closet. *Well, it can't get any worse than this* she thinks. But the mugginess is overwhelming, like a suffocating pillow, and the heat is encasing, closing in from every angle. What's worse, the boat moves slowly.

Luky's black salwar and kameez is sticking to her body like an unwelcome houseguest, oblivious to the oppression its fabric is causing. Water grumbles and churns beneath the hull and the craft's outdated engine sputters and clanks, giving her nerves the willies. Women sit and stare and the humidity is like a harsh mistress with a whip, when all that's needed is a fan.

Luky peers through one of the tiny windows and sees numerous villagers going about their daily lives: old men in dirty punjabis smoking hookahs on hand-woven mats; young children running totally naked and shrieking at the top of their lungs; women washing clothes in their saris on the riverbanks and sun-burnt men tending cattle against the backdrop of a lonely tree. *What kind of fucking world is this place? Thank God I'm leaving in two weeks (little did I know).*

Sweat drips from Luky's nose and a pang of hunger rips through her belly. She hears a rappa-tap-tap on the door and then silence as the voices in the room go dim. The door pushes open and a canon-like voice furnishes the room with fear. "Want anything to eat?" Akrum bellows after wiping his sweaty face. "Yeah," Luky and Amma say. "Well, here," Akrum says. "What are those?" Luky asks. "Chickpeas," Akrum says. "And here's some fruit on a stick."

"How much longer is it gonna be?" Luky asks Amma. "Are we even close yet?"

"Yeah, yeah, we're close. It shouldn't be too much longer." *But I was in total shock. I didn't know it was gonna be like this. When I was younger, visiting Bangladesh seemed so magical. Spending time with my Nanu on the rooftop and all that. Back then, she was my world. Now my world had no world.*

Thirty minutes go by. Another knock.

"We're pretty close to the village now," Akrum tells them. "Should be there in ten to fifteen minutes."

"Accha," Amma replies. "Ten to fifteen minutes." She turns to Luky and smiles. "Masha'Allah, masha'Allah! We're almost there! Thank Allah." She motions to Luky's feet. "Get your shoes on—hurry!"

4

The boat reaches the river-landing place after a three hour jaunt and the gangplank is lowered to the mud. Passengers debark and curious villagers mass along the unsilent bank. Luky walks slowly, nearly vomiting at the sight of the commotion, then gets swept up by the mass. *I felt like a celebrity; everybody wanted to touch us and carry our baggage. 'Look how good you look,' they said. 'So fair.' But I couldn't stand all that crap. I was thirsty and dying to get to my uncle's. I was sick and tired of walking, and that forty-five minute hike from the river just pissed me off even more.*

Tears fall as Amma stands face to face with her birthplace. Leelu Miah stands in front of the house, resting his weight on a cane, awaiting their arrival. A black and white checked lungi is wrapped around his waist and a forest green shawl is draped over his shoulders; beneath the shawl is a white genji.

When Luky sees the yard and the house, her mind jogs distant memories. She remembers playing underneath that tree when she was a little girl, the one to the right of the house. She remembers playing within its branches and spitting on the heads of her younger sisters and them yelping and shrieking in disgust. She also remembers the large jute mat they used to have spread out on the grass there, opposite the tree, in the month of April, and how, for hours on end, she and Nanu would sit near the edge of it and wait (Nanu holding a lengthy bamboo pole and she two smaller sticks, one in each hand), hoping some gutsy chicken would scratch its way to their position and tempt fate by pecking at one of the rice-grains, and to this day she can still hear Nanu's voice whispering through a naughty grin: *"Shhh...be quiet. It's coming."*

Cluck, cluck, cluuuuuck...

"There it is! Whack it! Use your stick."

Whack.

Whack.

The chicken squeals and hobbles away to the skirt of the unseen distance and ruffles its feathers in disdain.

Luky laughs.

Nanu blinks.

The vision is gone.

So to Nanu's house they go, but Nanu is no longer there.

But the crazy lady who lives next door is, the one who yells all night and day, screaming dirty phrases at the neighbors and anyone within an earshot of hearing. Luky recalls the lady's face straightaway, but not her name, as it has been misplaced with the passage of time.

"Oh, there's your brother," someone says to Amma. "He's waiting beneath the eaves."

"And there's your sister-in-law, coming to greet you with a kiss."

Leelu's wife trots from the doorway to the place where they are standing, a baby boy on her hip and three more little ones, resembling her husband, shadowing her.

Amma sheds more tears as they embrace, and even more as she hugs her brother. Luky feels bad that her uncle is about to die but can't stop thinking about Nanu.

"Come inside," Leelu's wife says, motioning to the door.

Luky and Amma follow.

The squareness of the small mud hut and its lack of accoutrements disquiets Luky's eyes. Why, everything is colored in the same plain hue except for the door and the unknown world that it leads to. Above her is a roof made of tin; below her is a slice of grassless earth. Decorating one of the room's corners is a solitary bed; decorating one of the others is emptiness mingled with colorless air. Surprisingly, a few embroidered handicrafts deck the door. These include a sequined long-billed snipe foraging for food among reeds near a pond and a long-tailed cuckoo supping on insects from its tree limb perch. Windows are nonexistent, but other openings and holes do exist. The bathtub is without (in Bangladesh they call it a pond) and the shitter is at the edge of the yard. A hole is there and you simply squat over the opening and go. *God, it might as well be on another planet. What is this place? How do people live?*

That night, as they lie down to sleep, thunder rolls and the heavens release their rains. The droplets bob the tin roof like ten-thousand tapping fingers and their dissonance knells within Luky's heart the sirens of misgiving.

Leelu's family and Leelu sleep on the ground atop woven mats constructed of bamboo and share one pillow and one quilt made from old saris. The saris are colorful but none too warm or comforting. Luky and Amma and Shanu sleep in Leelu's bed. *Thank God, because I didn't wanna sleep on that grubby ground. No way. Are you kidding me? I was afraid to sleep there because I thought rats and mice would come and get me, and I wanted to go home. Let's get outta here! I was scared.*

'Where's the bathroom?' I asked my mum when we first got there, because I looked and couldn't find it. Did they move it? And she said it was outside, but I didn't wanna go outside. No way—not alone anyway. So I held it. Then I remember my mum telling me to get ready for namaz. 'But where am I gonna do my wudu?' I asked. 'In the pond,' she said, but I didn't wanna do it in the pond. Are you kidding me? So I skipped that part of it. Later, I asked, 'Where am I gonna sleep? And what am I gonna have for breakfast?' But most importantly, I asked, 'Where am I gonna take a shit?'

'Don't worry, don't worry,' I told myself after hearing the answer. 'You're gonna be out of here soon. You can manage another week, week and a half. You'll be all right. Just hold it together.' So we slept on my uncle's bed.

—*With its tiny little mattress.*

—*Thin as anything too.*

But I was still reluctant.

'Just be grateful you're not where they are,' Amma said to me as she pointed to her bhaiya and his family in the dead hours of night.'

240

Well, you know what? I wasn't grateful.

—I couldn't sleep.

—It was hot.

—My mum had to fan me.

—And when I woke, it was early as hell.

—There were roosters.

—And voices.

—And the lady next door was screaming.

The sun rises and they eat breakfast.

"Isn't uncle supposed to be really sick?" Luky asks Amma after wondering about it since yesterday. "Isn't he supposed to be dying?"

"Yes," Amma replies, "but when he heard we were coming, he got better."

"What was wrong with him?"

"Some gastric something or other," Amma says. "His intestines were aching." *But he looked okay to me. Just walking around on his cane like normal. He asked me how I liked it here and I said it was okay because I knew I was gonna go back home soon, and he smiled. Then I said to my mum, 'How long do we have to stay here for? It sucks. I hate it.' And my mum said, 'Not too long, not too long.' But then it got close to two weeks, and I said, 'When are we gonna go back?' and my uncle heard me and said, 'Why are you dying to go back so soon for? You've come to Bangladesh after so many years, after such a long, long time, so why don't you stay for a while?' God, he pissed me off. I walked away. It was the first time I gave him an attitude. I said to my mum, 'What the fuck is he talking about, we've come from England after such a long, long time, so why don't we stay for a while? Who the heck does he think he is? I don't wanna stay here for a while.*

*When are we gonna go? What's going on with the tickets?'
And that's when my mum told me there's some confusion with
the tickets, some problem. But I didn't understand what the
problem was; I thought maybe the flight got delayed or
canceled. 'Yeah, the flight's kinda delayed,' she said. So now
I'm getting worried cuz it's been over two weeks, and I knew
Idris would be upset about it, so I wrote to him and gave the
letter to my mum to give to Heron bi-shab to mail.*

In the meantime, Luky and Amma and Shanu go visiting.
They frequent the houses of

—Neighbors living around Leelu Miah.

—Relatives living near and far, though mostly nearer
than farther.

—Friends and acquaintances of Abba's, Leelu's, and
Akrum's.

—Various bari women (village women) and their
children, mainly friends of Amma's.

Though sometimes they play host to

—All of the above.

—But mainly to women whom Luky cannot stand. You
know the type, the spur of the moment drop-ins, the
habitual non-invitees who keep inviting them themselves
without an invite, and when you open the door, there they
are on your doorstep like the reaper when you're not ready
for death, and you have no other choice but to let them in
and suffer the consequences.

But no matter what their locale, they eat

—Papayas.

—Bels, the pulp mainly…mixed into a vessel with
tamarind.

—Lychees (and these are Luky's favorite); they are what grapes would be if someone colored them white and made them sweet.

—Papadums, mere wafers really, thin and flaky pieces of flatbread, made from potatoes or black gram (in this case, both), and topped with a smattering of chopped onions, chili and salt. When it's all said and done, each individual papadum is dried in the open air and cooked over an open flame.

—Jalebis, fried mishtis really, pretz-otic and bow-tied in shape; their orange sugary varnish brings pleasure to each taste bud.

Upsetting though, especially to Luky, is the untethered line of questioning, continuously batted toward her direction.

—How is it in London? What do you lot do there?

Well, we...

—Do you lot have those things you can cook on?

Stoves?

—Do you lot clean your floors?

Yeah, we clean our floors. We have washing machines too.

—Inside your house?

Yeah, we...

—Really big houses?

Ours is kinda...

—We hear men and women smoke and drink there.

I wouldn't...

—And that they go around nude, and that you can't tell them apart; that women do the same jobs as men do and men do the same jobs as women do.

...

—What's it like in London? Tell us what we wish to know.

???

For they've heard the stories.

They're just curious to know more.

At a later hour, the neighbor girls ask Luky if they can do her hair and if she wants to play games like hopscotch and skipping ropes.

*The end of the third week.

Everything still smells broken down needs repairs roofs falling off bamboo mud huts squished in dirt hate it.

Where the fuck are we?

5

Akrum handles negotiations. Leelu has candidates of his own. Even Polash pokes his snaky head in and out the bari. As to why though, who can tell? Visitors come and go more frequently than before, as do people of the male persuasion. But Luky is oblivious to these occurrences. Instead, she spends her time hanging with Ruthna, her cousin, the meju or middle daughter of Leelu Miah, who, at the age of fourteen, is only one year removed from her own.

Watch them! Look at them! Ruthna leads Luky across the village, one arm pressing a kolshi to her hip, the other balancing one on her crown; fetching water at the tube well is one of their favorite jaunts. Luky recalls the day she first accompanied Ruthna to the tube well. She had been lollygagging near the side of the hut, sweating, watching a trio of young boys gun chickens with their slingshots; she remembers thinking that the rocks were witches and brooms instead of rocks when a voice, a female voice, arrested her attention.

"Wanna come?" Ruthna asked.

"Yeah," Luky nodded.

Then later, at the tube well, Ruthna had pointed to a nearby home.

"There's a really cute guy who lives there," she said. "He's really nice too."

"Really?"

"Yeah, and he goes to college."

"To college?"

"Yeah, in the city." *I enjoyed hanging out with Ruthna now she tells me that but she's afraid to tell me cuz she knows her parents Leelu will beat her up but she understands Bengali better than I do so she tells me I don't think you're gonna go back anytime soon.*

Why? We only came cuz your dad was ill.

Yeah he was ill but all these guys u saw coming to the house these mad rush of guys they're all coming to check u out.

No they're not.

Yeah they are they're all coming to check u out to see if they u might get married (as if it's a good thing).

But I took it as a joke yeah right what are u talking about? and she just giggled it off.

*The end of the fourth week.

Enter nutty lady, who is sitting at the edge of Leelu's yard on her haunches like a gorilla, eating freshly picked flowers and grasses. Mud decorates her face instead of makeup (or is that shit?) and tiny twigs, like miniature barrettes, disparage her hair.

"Hey sundori!" Hey beautiful, she calls to Luky from her grassy perch. "Come here." She waves her arms with sweeping agitation.

im not going over to u, ur crazy.

(crazy lady laughing) u don't know what's going on do u? ur done. ur a done deal. ur gonna be left here forever. ha ha ha ha! ur gonna get it (smiling). She makes a circle with her left forefinger and thumb and shoves her right forefinger into it. She rams the finger in and out of the hole repeatedly, all the while laughing. ha ha ha! ur a done deal. forever. they're gonna leave u here forever. ha ha ha ha!

ur crazy. ur just a crazy old hag. ur barmy mad. that's why ur husband drugs u all the time, to keep u quiet. that's why he beats ur crazy ass all the time. ur mad.

The crazy lady blinks, and for a split second remains speechless, lost in thought, but only for a second. im not crazy. ur crazy! and stupid! dur'ho she yells. *dur'ho!* ha ha ha ha ha!

Luky backs away from the yelling crazy and the yelling crazy rushes home, only to reemerge to the yard a minute later, carrying a bowl of am achar and a log.

u don't know what's going on do u? they're gonna marry u off! she throws the am achar to the heavens. ha ha ha! and chases Luky with the log.

Luky runs. But the lady trips and falls, chipping a tooth on the log.

"Stay away from that woman," Amma tells Luky. "She's crazy. She doesn't know what she's talking about. She can kill you. That's why her husband keeps her medicated all the time, that's why he gives her so many doses of drugs—to knock her out so she can sleep."

Four days later, Amma gives Luky a bath in the yard because Luky won't go to the pond again after catching sight of those snakes. Can you blame her? And she can't stand the dirt either, its brownness, its pervasiveness. Its everywhereness.

And the aggravations keep mounting, building, rising like a fuming volcano at the edge of its sanity, ready to spout. "When are we gonna go back?" Luky keeps asking Amma, but Amma's answer is never so sure. "Soon, my dear. We'll be leaving soon. Don't worry." But Luky can't take it, and how come Amma always wants her extra clad? Doesn't she already wear the hijab as it is? And how come she has to be covered from head to heel now, unlike Ruthna and the other bari girls? "Because you're a woman," Amma tells her. "And women have to hide their boonies."

So five weeks have come and gone. Now six weeks have gone by. *And we were sitting on Leelu's bed, and oh my God, I got pissed. 'Are we gonna go back now or what?'*

'No, we're not gonna go back yet.'

'Why? You said we'd only be gone two weeks. You lied. I told Idris two weeks! He probably thinks I abandoned him.'

'You abandoned him?' Amma asks, sarcastically. 'You write to him almost every day. You wait for his letters and you're constantly bugging your cousin as soon as he comes back from the market about the mail (every day I'd ask Heron bi-shab if there were any letters for me. I'd ask him how long it takes for a letter to reach England. 'About a week,' he said. 'Are you sure you're posting them in the right place?' 'Yeah, there's only one post in the market.'). So obviously he doesn't want you,' Amma went on. 'He hasn't responded to any of your letters. He's a Paki, remember? and they're all the same.

As soon as you turn your back, they're with somebody else. Have you forgotten that their fathers are from '71? You should be thankful that Allah saved you from a terrible fate.'

At Akrum's, I asked to talk to Salena on the phone. I asked about Idris. 'Did he get the present? Did you call him and tell him about my letters?' and she made it sound like he wasn't interested anymore. 'Whaat?' I asked her. 'What are you talking about?' and that he doesn't return his calls, only gives her the cold shoulder when he sees her, and that he's getting married to his cousin.

'Well, what did you expect from him?' Amma said. 'That's what dogs do. They sleep with other dogs and bite their own tails. And now that you're older (trying to give me this motherly talk), and since we're here in Bangladesh, and since I'm here... We all have to get married one day.'

'What are you talking about?'

'I got married when I was your age, and if you get married here you'll find a good guy and he'll respect you,' and that's when it hit what Ruthna had said about 'those guys checking you out.' What I thought was a joke wasn't a joke. So I stood and grabbed my mum's throat. I squeezed real hard and she couldn't breathe. 'Bhabhi!' she yelled for uncle's wife. Sister-in-law! Then grabbed my hair and pulled my hands. But I was so pissed off. Blinded by rage. That I pressed my fingers even harder. Then Leelu's wife came in and yelled for the neighbors. Even the crazy lady came running. After a brief struggle, they pried my hands and threw me to the ground. Where I huffed and fumed. I could barely see straight. I thought about Idris and how to get home. Then some woman came. 'You're all grown up now,' she said. 'You don't do that stuff to your mother. How could you do that stuff to your

mother? We all have to get married one day. We're women. That's what we do.' Shit. That's not what I do. Then I saw my mum crying and felt sorta bad for her, but never said, 'Sorry.' Didn't even talk to her when she made me those kabobs either, just went to bed hungry. 'Luky affa,' Ruthna said, 'you haven't eaten anything, you can't go to bed on an empty stomach,' but I told her, 'Get away from me,' then went to sleep angry, and for about three or four days after that I didn't speak to anyone and barely ate anything at all. Then, finally, my mum said, 'You have to eat. You have to.' So I finally ate, but I still wondered about going home.

The next day, Leelu Miah drags Luky to a small plate of rice that is resting on the ground, and next to the rice is a bowl of dal. "Here...eat," he says. "You're all skin and bones."

Whack. Luky cracks Leelu's paw with a right hook and with a foot she scatters the rice and dal to the crawlies. Leelu clenches his teeth and both his and Luky's eyes greet one another in vile dissonance. Luky runs, or tries to, through a door. But Leelu holds her back (he's so strong). Then Luky says, "Let go of me, I wanna go home! I don't wanna be here anymore. I fucking hate it here! I hate it here so fucking much!"

Amma and some other women come running and hold her in place.

"What kind of a daughter did you raise?" they ask Amma. "So disrespectful!"

Leelu slaps Luky in the jaw. "Calm down, you. Calm down! Girls aren't supposed to have so much anger." *But that got me even more pissed off. God, I was almost to the door, but where the heck was I gonna go?*

Four or five days later, she locks herself in a neighbor's shed. *I tried to run away.*

A bolt locks the door from within and no one can enter.

"Do you want something to eat?" someone asks. "Aren't you hungry?"

"No, I don't want anything to eat. I hate it here. I wanna go!" But each rappa-rap-tap of their knuckles is more obstinate in nature than the one before it, though eventually their insistence fades, as do the night hours, and Amma goes to sleep. In the morning, Jooshna takes her place.

"Luky, come on, you can't stay in there forever. You gotta get something to eat."

But how long was the girl in there for? Hours? Days?

Who knows? Who was counting?

Now the sun lowers his head and bows to the oncoming darkness with deference, ending one day and beginning another. Still, no sign of Luky's emergence.

But what brought about this scene in the first place? What made her seek refuge in the shed?

'Sit down, sit down,' Leelu ordered. 'Have your rice.' 'No, I'm not going to have my rice! I'm never gonna have my rice!' Whack, right across the mouth. 'Sit down,' Amma said. 'Why won't you eat?' 'Cuz I don't wanna eat. I can't stand it here. I hate it here. I wanna go!' and that's when I couldn't take it anymore, so I ran. And my mum couldn't catch me. No one could. 'Open this door, goddammit!' Leelu said. But no way was I going to open that door, never. Though, eventually, I kinda gave in because, as hurt as I was, my mum still wanted to get me married.

Night showers the countryside with blackness and bleakness enters the shed dancing in shadows with light. Ill-famed creatures bleep noisome remarks from the forest and Luky's heart bleats a sorrowful tune. But is anyone listening?

"Come on, Luky affa. It's me, Ruthna. Won't you open the door?"

Shit. *What is that crawling scata-scat-scat next to my foot? Oh my God! It just touched my toe.* A scream.

She hates the dark.

In a flash, she pulls the flag of surrender from her bosom and exits the shed. Outside, Ruthna leads her across the darkness toward home.

"Here, drink this." Amma gives something to Luky in a cup.

"What is it?"

"Blessed water. It's to calm you down a bit. Allay your nerves. It was blessed by a hafiz." A holy man.

"I'm not gonna drink that."

Jooshna grabs the cup from Amma's fingers and Luky by the hair. "You gotta drink this! You have to."

More women swarm about, adding their own two cents, sometimes three. "It'll help make you calm."

The villagers had been saying stuff, said they've never seen a girl act like that before, said I was mentally brokendamaged, that there was something physically wrong with me on the inside.

Why are you doing this? Amma kept asking me, everybody's saying that there's something wrong with you.

6

"So are you gonna stay here with me?" Luky asks Amma.

"Yeah. I'll stay until…"

It was then I realized she was leaving.

"But I only have one year of school left. Why can't I finish? I told my friends I'd be back in two weeks."

"Don't worry," Amma tells her. "You can finish school later. You just have to get married first."

I thought about Idris then and wondered why he hadn't written.

"So as soon as I get engaged, I can go back to school and study?"

"Oh yeah, sure. Many people have gotten engaged and gone back to study. Nowadays, even women with kids go back and study."

"But I wanted to graduate with my friends."

Amma places a reassuring hand on her daughter's shoulder. "Your friends will always be there, Luky," she says. "So don't worry."

Amma and Luky go to Akrum's via the launch and Ruthna tags along for support.

Now I realize that the guys who come over are coming to see me, to check me out, to give my mum a proposal.

"I can't cook, Ruthna," Luky whispers to her cousin. "I don't know how to do anything here."

"Don't worry, affa, you're gonna go back to London, remember? You won't need to learn how to cook."

Sounds good to me, but I'm panicking here, and my mum keeps telling me, 'Oh, don't worry about it, you're not gonna live here for very long, you're gonna go back to London.'

Akrum had the passports.

Never heard a thing from Idris, even though I told him in a letter that I didn't have my passport anymore, and that my mum was planning to marry me off.

Did it even get delivered?

"You gotta be dressed decent," Amma says, "and if someone talks to you, you gotta talk politely back."

—*Why didn't you just tell 'em off?*

—*Because I figured I'd be stuck in Bangladesh forever, and I sure as hell didn't wish that. I mean, who in their right mind would choose to live in Bangladesh over England?*

—*Fair enough, but can you tell me your first impressions of the men?*

—*They were goofy looking, with pock-marks staining their faces and skinny twig bodies in between their heads and thigh bones. Just all greasy wrinkleworn oldskinmen, with hair the color of darkness times tar, worn like a fakyesque helmet. Is that a toupee? With huskythick waistlines and topsyturvey gaits, all slumpydumpy looking. Is that a birdchest? Cocky as hell too, with untethered overhanging toenails and uninterrupted growth strands uncut in their nostrils.*

—*That bad, huh?*

—*Worse than hell.*

—*Now you mentioned earlier something about your dad's brother, Polash. Do you remember?*

—*I remember.*

—*So what part did he play in this drama?*

—*Not a goddamned memorable one. Why?*

—*Now, now, there's no need for hostilities. We're only here to—*

—*Help. Yes, I know that. It says so on your brochure.*

—*Then let me do my job.*

—*Fine.*

—*Then proceed with the answer.*

—*To what question?*

—*The one about Polash.*

—*Well, it was no secret that my uncle wanted me to marry his son, Tajir, though I don't recall any formal arrangements, but it was expected because he was the eldest son of my dad's brother and I the eldest daughter of my dad. It was just one of those things decreed by tradition, but my dad didn't wanna go through with it because Tajir didn't have an education. In other words, he didn't qualify.*

—*And you heard this from?*

—*My parents.*

—*An example?*

—*My mum told Rabiya, 'He's even more pissed now because he couldn't get Luky for his son. Can you believe it? First he wanted our land, then our daughter. Well, you know what? That man can eat shit and die. He owes us, not the other way around.'*

The last candidate bids adieu and crosses the premises to a ricksha. Amma watches from the doorjamb as the horseless carriage retires to the starry night and fades to the unseen distance of obscurity. Minutes later, oblivion swallows rider and puller and Sunia's attention wanes from their position to that of her sister's face, but Sunia doesn't find the situation so jovial.

"What's so funny?" she asks Rabiya, putting her hands on her hips.

"You, big sister. What were you thinking? Are you blind or just crazy in inviting those beasts?"

"Oh, Allah," Sunia says. "I just want to find the right candidate for the girl. Someone decent, that's all. Is it really too much for me to ask?"

"But they were monstrous," Rabiya says, "and probably looked even far worse to her."

Amma sighs. "I know our sole purpose in bringing her here was to marry her off as soon as possible, but the last thing we had in mind was this freakshow. Oh, Allah, how did it ever come to this?" She sits on the floor. "What a nightmare."

Rabiya sits next to her.

Amma turns to face her. "What exactly didn't you like about them?" she asks after a spout of silence. "What was so—?"

"Do I have to spell it out for you? Remember the third guy?"

Amma nods.

"He looked like a whale without flippers. And the one right after him?"

"The portly one?"

"Yeah. He looked like a bideshi shickarr." A foreign pig. "But instead of pink, he was black. And the last one?" She motions with her head to the door. "Do I even need to remind you about him?"

"I guess not," Amma sighs.

"And the two short guys?"

"Okay, I get the picture. Then help me find someone more suitable, someone with nice sharp features, educated. A kind man. We don't want her taking off on the wedding day."

Oh, we have someone in mind.

"Not too far away from us, in Arpin Nagore, is a guy who's got his master's, but he doesn't stay here all the time because he teaches in a different city."

"Really?" Amma asks.

Rabiya verified his character.

"...and I've seen him around here since he's been a little kid, and he's never been in any trouble."

It was true. They all knew about the guy, Hash'nuq, and his mother, Aziboon, that she was a little strict, a little greedy, but figured, 'Hey, well, she's not gonna be here forever. So it's okay for her to marry her son.' They were just concerned about finding a half-decent guy, that's all, and according to them he was.

So my mum and Rabiya and Akrum's mum went to meet his mum at their home, but I didn't go. I stayed at Akrum's, and I guess they got treated like queens there. Only she showed them a picture of the second son. An old beat up photograph. Slightly torn. And he was standing next to a tree.

Rabiya said: 'This isn't the son we're talking about. We're actually interested in the one with the master's, your eldest.'

'Oh, the eldest one. Well, we weren't really looking for him to get married, but yeah, all right, okay, here's a picture of him.'

See, they figured if they married the second son off (playing politics), and he goes to England, they'll be bringing in money from both ends, from Bangladesh (through the firstborn) and England (through the second).

So she gives my mum his pic and my mum falls in love with it immediately. A black and white pic. Slightly faded. Somewhat worn. Curly hair. Sharp almond-shaped eyes. Full lips. Heard all good things about him too. 'Yeah, yeah, that's him!' my mum said. 'That's the one I wanna make my son-in-law.' So she comes back to Akrum's and shows me the pic and I thought, 'Well, he's the best so far, anyway. Thik acche. Do whatever you want.' Because at that point, I felt like I had it and wanted to go home.

**This is at the end of November.

His mum was only concerned about getting him a visa.

You see, if you're a Londoni, you're like a freakin piece of fucking gold and you get lines of guys dying to marry you so they can come to England.

I had twenty-three candidates that wanted to marry me. Do you believe it?

'He's a really good guy, that one,' Khala told me one day. 'He's got a really good character about him, but I'm not too sure about his mother.'

—But why did Aziboon insist on showing your family a picture of the second brother in the first place? I still don't get it.

—Because the second brother was the lazy one, that's why. At least the older brother's a professor and the earner for the family, so she felt like, 'Hey, let's marry this one off that's not doing anything, just walking around being a bum.'

—I see.

—But my aunty realized what she was doing. 'Hey, that's not the right brother. We don't want him. We want the other one, Hash'nuq.'

—Wow, they should have called it off after that. It was shady.

—Yeah, it was bad, but we didn't know the character of the family, and also, as soon as my mum saw the picture, she said for some reason that she really, really liked him, and that he looked like a good guy, so that's when she asked to see him in person.

—The plot thickens.

—Like a roux in broth.

—But hold on, do you really think all this was preplanned by your family? I mean ahead of time, from England? In other words, do you think your mum and dad phoned ahead to your aunty and uncle in Sunamganj, giving them the heads-up?

—Well, duh. I could hear Akrum saying, 'Just bring her here and I'll have tons of guys lined up for you, just waiting to get married.' You see, my mum and dad didn't realize His *whole situation, but it should have been a sign when they tried to show us the other brother's pic. My Khala always said, 'That lady's very slick,' but my mum must have told her, 'Well, she's not gonna live here forever, she's gonna get married and go back to England within a year.' Yeah, right. That didn't fucking happen. (laughs, looks to the floor and sighs).*

—If only they had insisted on you going back to England right after you got married.

—But they wanted us to come back together. They were afraid if I came back alone I might end up running away or something, and they didn't want that shit on their hands.

—Yeah, but everything they were most afraid of happened anyway, so what difference did it make? What goddamned difference did it make? By trying to prevent the future, by trying to suppress their most dreaded dream, their actions precipitated the events they were trying to prohibit.

7

How could my mum do this to me? No one asked me what I wanted. How could my uncle do this to me? I saw my cousins who were older than me and they weren't married yet, so what did I do that was so wrong? What did I do that was so bad? They figured I was gonna run off with a Pakistani. 'Well, yeah, I guess this is my punishment for what I did, then. This is my punishment from my mum,' but nobody respected my wishes. Nobody wanted to know how I felt about it.

Everybody knew I had done something. My mum told them, 'She's seeing some Pakistani guy and I have to get her married off.' She told my cousins who were already married, and my cousins who were already married told me, 'Oh, we didn't wanna get married either when we were your age, but we all have to get married one day, it's written on our foreheads,' and I just didn't wanna hear it anymore. I hated 'em.

'You told them?' I said to my mum.

'What was I gonna do?' she said to me. 'I had to.'

The only person I liked was Ruthna cuz she'd tell me things (she got married about a year after I did), and one day her older sister, who I couldn't stand for nothing, who was such a bitter bitch, said to me, 'Come here. A woman's fate is under a man's feet. She gets married, and that's it.'

She was just a big fat bully.

—Okay, let's back up a bit. When your mum and aunty came back with the picture you?

—Just sat there. 'We brought you something,' they said, and my mum pulled out this black and white pic from her sari and told me to take a peek. At that point, I wasn't even bothered anymore. I knew I was gonna go back soon anyway. 'It's okay,' I said. 'Better than the others.' Of course he was no Tom Cruise or anything, but compared to the other filthy bastards, eeewww! yuck! he was like Prince Fucking Charming, and my mum had this little tiny smile of hope attached to her face that bothered the fuck out of me, but you wanna know the worst part of it? She never even confirmed the whole thing with me or anything, never asked, 'Is it okay if we tell him that you want to marry him? Is that a yes?' 'No, it's not a goddamn yes,' I wish I would've said. I just said he was better than the others, and she took that for a yes!

—So tell me more about this Hash'nuq.

—Like what?

—His looks.

—I already told you. Dark curly hair, not very good looking, but better than the alternatives. Light skin, though I blame the photographer for that one. Almond-shaped eyes, *sharp features, thick mustache like Charlie Chaplin. I thought, 'Well, if he shaves that mustache off, he'll look a little bit better, and then you'd be able to see his lips and jaw line.'*

—And then?

—My mum told Khala and the other women who were there, 'Yeah, yeah, it's fine,' and the next few days were really busy in the house. There were people coming and going, his side of the people were coming to take a look at me, and my mum kept telling me you gotta always wear a nice sari and have your hair combed and have your hijab on your head, and I was like, 'Fine,' then his sisters and mum came.

—Ah, yes, Aziboon. Would you describe her?

—I'm reminded of the two women.

—Which two women?

—The ones my friend told me about.

—Who are they?

—One of them went to the king with a complaint.

—Which king?

—Don't know which king. Some king. An ancient king from long ago maybe, not sure, but the woman told the king what happened.

—What did happen?

—There was an agreement.

—An agreement?

—Yeah, you see, everybody in this woman's town was dying of starvation, and so she and another lady, her neighbor, came up with a pact to survive.

—Which was?

—To serve up each other's babies for dinner in hopes of forestalling death.

—You're kidding?

—*And the first woman followed through with her side of the bargain, but the second woman reneged.*

—*Which is why she went to the king?*

—*Exactly.*

—*And the king's solution?*

—*He never gave her one; after hearing the tale he flipped.*

—*I don't get it? How in the world is this story analogous to Aziboon? Connecting the two makes absolutely no sense.*

—*That's because you're missing the point.*

—*Which is?*

—*That the second lady not only ate the first woman's son but her own as well, in secret, after stashing it somewhere. My friend told me the whole story is written in your book of Du'tronomy. Why don't you look it up?*

—*Again, how does this relate to Aziboon?*

—*She's the second woman incarnate, stupid. Forget about the babies; she'd eat every goddamn thing worth ingesting. And do you think she would ever share? Ha! If she ever did that the world would stop spinning and implode from confusion and the residents of that other place would receive air-conditioning and ice water. I tell ya, if there was ever a log full of termites and a race between her and an anteater to get to that log full of termites, she'd eat the anteater, the log and the termites in one giant inhalation! And those are her best qualities! God. She's like a nightmare when you're already in hell.*

—*How so?*

—*Picture four-foot-seven-inches of ugliness at its acme, all round and plump with bulges popping out from everywhich-where. Now visualize a large black chasm—that's her mouthhole. Scary. And sometimes you don't know if she's the devil laughing at you or a hyena getting whacked to death, and sometimes she starts off and goes into this little hissing tangent, and her skin's so black that when she enters a room you'd swear midnight just stopped by for a visit, and when she sits on her ass, she has to pack in her stomach the same way you would a loose t-shirt—ew, throw up and vomit—she's such a fucking fat pig! Oh my God, how I prayed that she'd just burst open like the Hindenburg, kaboom! or that she'd blamm-pop! that one day I'd wake up, hear a loud noise, and kapow-dow! I don't know what my father-in-law ever saw in that fat bitch cuz my father-in-law was such a nice tall man with silver gray hair and a good heart. He had such a rich look about him and perfect smooth skin and eyes. I don't know, he must have loved fat pudgy women with warts.*

    —So Aziboon came over?

    —Yep.

—*And then?*

Aziboon looks at Luky's face from every conceivable angle and facet. She looks at her nose, under her nose. She squinches either cheek in succession. She audits, with pristine precision, the intricacies of her earlobes. She pulls up her sari to better examine her feet. She loiters over both hands, taking them into the meatiness of her own, turning them, first one way and then another, so as to determine whether any deformities are present, and when she finds something acceptable, she giggles, which, if you haven't heard her giggle lately, sounds like fingernails on a chalkboard.

The inspection is complete, and Aziboon has this big smile stapled from ear to ear and her daughters are wearing it as well. They say to Sunia, "Masha'Allah, masha'Allah, she's so pretty." Then Aziboon adds, "Yeah, I wanna make her my son's wife, definitely."

So the question arises: "How soon can we do this?" So Akrum and everybody from Luky's side, Leelu Miah, Amma and Rabiya, meet with *His* representatives to hammer out the arrangements, and after a few rounds of negotiations they agree on a date for the engagement: the twenty-second of December, nineteen hundred and eighty-six. *And from there on everything was a commotion, buying extra saris, jewelry, putting together a list, everything that we needed. Akrum took care of the catering, the engagement accessories; the sari and makeup were taken care of by the groom. About one hundred and fifty people had been earmarked for attendance. Then several days passed; then two weeks. And there I was, totally detached from the arrangements, isolated away from the details and the daily to-dos.*

As usual, the bride's last moments are spent in containment, complicated further by inner dread and bouts of quiet depression. *I thought of Idris a lot during this time and felt sad I wasn't doing this with him.*

A few days before the end of herself, Luky gets fitted for a blouse.

"What size, what size?" someone asks. "What size shoes? What size petticoat?"

"The sari is one size fits all," another person says.

"What's this?" someone asks.

"What do you mean 'what's this?'" someone replies.

"It's exactly what I mean," someone shouts.

Oh God, just kill me Luky thinks. *I only want to hide and* cry.

Mum—

"You're all grown up now and you're gonna have responsibilities, and you're gonna have to respect your in-laws. I won't be here for long after the engagement, so if your in-laws come and visit you in Rangarchur, because that's where you'll be staying till the actual wedding day, you're gonna have to respect them as you would me and Abba. They're your parents now; *we* are no longer your parents. Of course we'll be there if you need us. How could you even wonder such a thing? But *they* are your real parents now, so you have to be devoted to them in everything and be respectful in every way."

Luky—

"You mean you're not *staying*? You're leaving me after the twenty-second? But why do you have to go so soon for?" (panicking, breathing heavy.)

Mum—

"Because your Abba is all by his lonesome, and the rest of your sisters are—"

Luky—

Spinning, burning; my forehead feels hot and her words are jumble-jargoned in a heaping mass of quickshit down the toilet. Whaat? Her incomprehensible phrases are incoherent and this can't be happening to me. No, no, not in reality. This scene should be cut-snipped. Fuck! Never been left alone before and I can't understand the words or their meaning or hers or my understanding of the syllables. Spinning-falling shooting stars. Enclosing in on my mind. Am I fainting? or just aching?

Mum—

"—and I've never been away this long before, since September..."

Luky—

"But I'll be going back after the engagement, won't I?"

Mum—

"Yeah, yeah. You're gonna go back. Don't worry. You'll go back as soon as the wedding is over; after the engagement will be the wedding [when you're sixteen], and then you'll go back."

Luky—

"A whole year? But what am I gonna do [without you]? Why can't I just come back after the engagement [with you]?"

Mum—

"Because you don't belong to us anymore. You belong to your in-laws now; they're your real parents, not us, so I can't just take you with me. At least after the real wedding, when you're sixteen, you can apply for your husband and you and him can come back as a couple."

I never thought I'd have to stay in Bangladesh without my mum. It was bad enough living there with my mum, but she had said, 'Don't worry. Everything will be fine.'

Akrum negotiates with *His* representatives for the dowry. The gold. But how much will they hand over? How much of their purse will they yield? Back and forth they dicker. Back and forth they haggle.

Akrum shouts. People stare. He smashes his fist onto the table. The bargaining continues. More terms are presented. *His* side deliberates; minutes pass. *His* side confers; one hour has come and gone.

Tick-tock. Deadlock.

Tick-tock. Gridlock.

Akrum demands his demands and pounds his fist into his palm. His henchmen stand aflank as wings.

The other side redeliberates; they huddle together and agree to agree. Their aim? To regain once more Akrum's favor. And why wouldn't they wish that? After all, sane men do sane things, don't they? And does not prudence demand placation in instances such as these? If not, a man like Akrum whose notoriety as a shuudkur (a Bengali thug) precedes him in all the district, may resort to base level antics (as usual), or mafia style violence (as needed). Why, just last week he split a man's jaw in two for reneging on his loan!

But Amma doesn't like Akrum's mode of operandi or his forceful ways of one-upmanship, especially since she knows their side is dabbling in the red, and she doesn't want to take everything that they have.

—Amma said, "We don't need their gold or anything." (You see, she had gold stashed away in her armoire in Bradford, the same gold given to her as a wedding present for her own wedding many years before, and from that cache she swore the better part to Luky). But Akrum refused that statement with a sideways flicker of his hand. "No! We're not gonna give our Luky to those wolves just like that. *They better* give us some gold!"

—"But that would put a strain on them financially," Amma said. "So forget it. They don't have to give us any of their gold. We're not marrying her off for the money." *"They better* give us some gold!" So they agreed to part ways with two earrings and a ring, *and my mum gave me bangles for my wrists.*

Now time moves forward hazy, foggy, dimly, and the twenty-second day of December fast approaches. *And oh my God, am I gonna be engaged to this man? But I don't know a thing about him, and he hasn't even spoken to me. And what am I gonna do when my mum goes back to England? I'll be stuck here. 'But why can't I just go with you after the engagement?' I asked her. 'Because you can't,' she said. 'You belong to—'*

and tomorrow brings the engagement at noon

But for to-day, Amma and Rabiya bathe Luky in turmeric and oil.

"It'll give you a nice healthy glow," they say, smiling. While random women from the bari exclaim, "It'll give you a nice healthy shine!"

Other women come too, opining to Luky how a bride is supposed to sit on the dais, with her head tilted downwards and slanted slightly to the side, and how she never takes a peep at her surroundings. Never.

"At all times, beti," they say, "a bride's head is kept downcast in reservation, and never does she smile." Then some elderly lady, some distant granny from someplace, says: "No, no! She doesn't just look downwards, she has to keep her eyes closed the whole time too!"

Night falls and a weary worn girl of fifteen passes to the floor in a wilted mass of many petals. The wind blows and someone screams. Some women come runningtalking. "Get water, get cloth!" No one answers.

The girl not moving. But sleeping.

And dreaming.

In a dream.

"BORO AFFA, BORO AFFA! Come on, boro affa, wake up, wake up!"

"Salena? What are you doing here?"

"It's time."

"For what?"

"To go."

"To where?"

"Away."

"To where?"

"To there." Salena points to the window.

"To the window??"

"To beyond the window. Outside. On the road. To the block after the next block; to the beyonder-yond after the beyonder. Remember, boro affa, you're running."

"I am?" (Luky closes her eyes and tries to remember the plan of action, then opens them again with a blank expression; yet the cobwebs remain) *"I—???"*

"Boro affa, come on, quit playing around. It was *your* idea to—"

"Salena, how did you get here?"

"What?"

"How did you get here? I wanna know."

"What do you mean, how did I get here?"

"Well, mum never said you were visiting."

"What are you talking about, boro affa? We share the same room, we sleep just meters apart."

Luky blinks and peers to her surroundings, blinks again, then notices her room. "But I thought—wait, this can't be happening. I thought—how the heck—?"

"Boro affa, are you feeling all right?"

"I guess so." (as thoughts of Idris flash like lightning) "But I thought I was in Bangladesh." She sits up, alert. Places a hand on her chest, breathes and rescans the room.

"Well, good. Because—"

"Salena, where's mum and dad? Are they sleeping?"

Bam! (a dream in a dream)

A door slams in the distance and a deluge of moonlight falls aslant through the shades, alighting a portion of the floor in the room.

Belam!

"Salena? Is that you?"

No answer.

"Salena???"

Echoes bound from invisible canyons and ebb away into the stratosphere unseen, leaving only still sounds.

Luky removes herself from the bedside and moseys to the closet, her barefeet skimming across the floor with a hush. Realizing that she is already dressed and wearing a bright green sari, she strolls to the door atiptoe and reaches for the doorknob in a whisper, but stops when her hand touches the coldness of it; she seems to be listening for someone's wakefulness, for someone's feet to come running and end her excursion, for someone's fist to ground her body to smithereens, and she really hopes that her sisters, especially the nosy one, Taz, are sleeping and counting sheep and unaware of her spur-of-the-moment doings. Otherwise...

Still dreaming.

She's running away. Down little Horton Lane. Streetlights, carlights. The wind blows at her back. It aids her along. Can't you see? How it pushes her, urges her onward, so closer, closer to—. Old ladies sitting on the curbside, staring, wagging their fingers, hissing. She hears their vain callings, but bismillah (in the name of God) she's running away. Down Little Horton Lane. Wearing only her barefeet. Though what are people gonna say? About her head-coat that's missing, about her long black tresses that resemble the mane of Hidalgo? A kitten meows there. "Goddamn them!" she hears herself say. "Goddamn those—." Suddenly, she sees stars, shooting, falling like meteors, spinning backwards, exploding. Her eyes can't focus and her lower half feels completely empty. As she lay writhing in the middle of the lane. Blood oozing from somewhere. But where? That's when it hits her: this whole time she'd been running without any shoes on. Wearing only her barefeet. *How can this be happening?* she wonders. No one answers. Though the autumn breeze, out of niceness, blows westerly across her face and tells her all is forgiven, that everything is okay. But no! Everything is not okay; it just isn't. So she crawls back to house number eighty-eight, closer, so closer to—. Prison. Her home. Her room. God, she was so close to freedom. So near to liberation. Yet back to her old life she travels. *But how could I be so stupid?* she wonders in anger amid tears, *to run away from my— and my— without any footwear? I was barefeet******* End dream.

8

The day of the engagement at Akrum's.

They decorate everything with shiny balls and tinsels and the village betis sing their wedding songs. A tent is set up underneath those trees there, each tree adorned with ornaments, the trees tall and skinny and the red and white table cloths nice over the tables.

The scene looks like a happy one.

A few girls Luky's age rush to her side. All the time smiling, jumping up and down and giggling. "Oh my God, you look so pretty!" they say.

I wish Idris could see me so pretty.

"You look so gorgeous as a bride! Your skin is glowing! Your face is glowing! You've got the look of a bride!"

Bullshit.

"Aww, you're gonna get married and have a baby."

"Aww, you're gonna get married and have a family."

They were so excited. You could tell it in their voices. How they were wishing they were me.

"And your virginity's gonna fall on your first night!"

"I heard it hurts!"

Then they'd giggle their heads off, but I was fighting back tears.

The girls and Rabiya and Amma dress Luky in a sari. They apply makeup and gloss. A bit of powder to either cheek. "And here's some for your brow." Next, they hand her a mirror into which she peers and thinks of the raja and wonders who the girl in the mirror is now.

She shakes her head.

She does not know.

So she places the mirror back into Amma's hands and sighs. Or was that a tremble?

"There. All finished," Rabiya says.

Downtrodden and broken, Luky is aided to her feet and led to a certain room in the house, where, it is said, the groom's party will first aspire to. There they make her sit atop a bed decorated with freshly cut flowers whose wonderful aromas offer no consolation to her sadness; and in her painfully difficult situation she wonders why she was ever born, why she did not remain in bud and never bloom.

Above her head and behind her back is a canopy of sewn together saris trimmed with brightlights and garlands. She doesn't mind the brightlights but hates the garlands.

"Nonsense!" they say after offering her a bite of food and being put off by her refusal. "We insist." So she relents upon the insistence and opens her mouth wide enough for a set of fingers to insert some food in, and when the food enters her mouth, so too does the feeling of nausea.

More guests arrive. "Look," they say. "There she is! Wow! So beautiful!"

—*How long did that scene linger?*

—*About an hour. My mum asked whether I had to go to the bathroom. 'Because they're gonna be here soon,' she said. 'No, no, I don't have to go,' I said, because I was too nervous to do anything. So my mum said, 'Well, just keep your head down and don't move.' Then I heard someone say, 'They're here! They're here! They're coming! They're here!'*

—*And then?*

—*Everybody started clapping and singing wedding songs and hollering, and I could hear all kinds of voices. 'He's here! The bridegroom! Everybody! Get out of the way! He's here!'*

—*But how were you—?*

—*Faring? Feeling? Not too fucking good. How do you think I was—?*

—*My opinion is irrelevant.*

—*Yeah, well—*

—*So then He came?*

—*Yeah.*

—*And then?*

—*Some kids started yelling, 'There she is! There she is! The bride's over there!' and after that I felt somebody sit next to me on my right (Hash'nuq?) and then two or three other somebodies squinching in behind me (His sisters?), and people touching my face and moving it. Saying, 'She's so pretty, so gorgeous. Just look at her!' 'But what about my eyes?' I wondered. 'Should I open them now? Or keep 'em closed?' Because I couldn't remember what that old lady told me. Flash. Flash. 'Pick her face up.' Flash. Flash. 'We want a picture of them both together.' Flash. Flash. 'It's okay to open your eyes now,' someone said. 'No way!' I thought, then someone grabbed my head and turned it (for him to take a good look at, obviously). 'But hello! Is someone gonna put my face back, or is it gonna stay like this forever?' 'So what do you think of your new bride?' someone asked him. 'Do you think she's pretty?' And I guess he nodded because she said, 'You have to say one or the other, you can't nod.' 'Yes.' And then the mullah came in, and that's when I opened my eyes a bit and saw his knee there and his left hand on top of his knee and the henna on top of his left hand and the ring my mum gave him on his ring finger, and then the mullah asked me if I agreed, and if I agreed, to say alhamdulillah, so I said, 'Alhamdulillah.' Well, actually, he said alhamdulillah first; I just sat there in tears. And then my cousin grabbed me and said, 'Luky, you can say alhamdulillah, you know. It's okay. You can say it.' Then my mum said, 'Oh, Luky, my heart, please say alhamdulillah. Please say it. Please.' So it took a while, but I said it. 'Alhamdulillah.' And then they said we could feed each other the mishti and exchange garlands, and that was it; it was over. Everyone went to eat except for me. Because that's when his sisters crowded me like vultures and said, 'Bhabhi, bhabhi, you're ours now. You're ours now. You don't have to keep your eyes closed anymore (being sarky). We don't bite. Our brother's gone to eat, so you can open them with us. It's okay.' But I was scared to death of that fucking old lady, so I kept my eyes closed, and then my mum came over and said, 'Luky, Luky, it's me. Open your eyes now. It's okay.' So that's when I opened them, and that's when I could see.*

Later that night, the stiffness in her neck is aching and Amma chides her for her folly.

"You didn't have to keep your eyes closed the whole time, you know, or your head bent like that."

"Yeah, but that old lady told me *I had to*. She said it was disrespectful for me to look up or open them."

Amma shakes her head. "No, you could have left them *slightly* open." Amma uses her thumb and forefinger as a measuring device to indicate the ideal amount of openness.

"But that's what she told me," Luky says, reaching for her neck in agony. "Can I just go and get changed now? I'm tired."

"Yeah, you can go in the other room and get changed into something lighter now that everyone's gone."

Relief.

"And when you come back, I'll give you a massage."

In bed, Luky thinks about the engagement. Oh, how jovial her frontal lobe had been when it ended, after the last remaining houseguest had exited through the doorway, leaving her in a state of utter peace and, quite honestly, indebted to a higher power. Why, just before that moment of complete luxury, the mere idea of relaxing in private, of escaping from the throes of her itchy sari, of sleeping in and waking the following day, preferably around noontime, had been a much coveted vision within her troubled mind. Now she… Suddenly, her oasis of reverie goes up in flames. "Oh, bhabhi," his sisters buzz after coming back again, "you're ours now," and his mum right behind them, "All mine!"

Eventually, they leave and Amma comes over to Luky and says, "Masha'Allah, the whole engagement went really well, don't you think?"

For whom? (I didn't want any part of this).
Years later: 'You did, though. I showed you his pic.'
'I just said he was better than the others.'

The next day, they leave Akrum's and set out for Nanu's bari, Luky's home till September, but Amma's for only another week.

"Luky, are you listening to me?" Amma continues. "In seven days, I'll be leaving."

"Why though?" Luky asks, sobbing. "Can't you take me with you?"

"Na," Amma replies. "You're engaged now, and being engaged is the same as being married." She sighs. Repositions her daughter's hijab, reconcealing a few visible locks. "Please don't worry, accha? You're going to be sixteen in August and the wedding day is in September." Amma pauses, clears her throat. "So as soon as the ceremony is finished and He gets his visa, which shouldn't take too long, you can go back [to England]."

"But I don't wanna live here for a year [by myself], why can't I just go back with you and then come back for the wedding in September?"

"Na! We've already talked about this. Na, it's not good. Once you're engaged, you have to stay close to your husband and his family."

In Rangarchur, the days pass by like fleeting memories of Nanu's smile. *When it got close to the time of my mum's departure, I saw her packing her belongings and started to feel really sad about it, and I think she understood the way I felt inside and how hard I would have it by myself. 'Now you're gonna have to do some things for yourself,' she said. 'But remember, your cousins and aunties and uncles are here if you need them, and if you ever need anything specific, you can contact Akrum. And don't worry, Hash'nuq is a very good man and his family will come and visit you once in a while to see how you're doing. Are you listening to me, Luky? You'll have more than enough support here, so don't worry.' But I did worry because, after seven days, my mum's bags were ready and we were taken to Akrum's.*

"Get dressed! Get dressed!" Amma says the following morning. "Pick out something nice. Ooh, wait! What about this sari? Do you like it? I think he will."

"Who?" Luky squinches her eyes and tilts her head to the side. "What are you talking about?"

"Him."

"Who?"

"Him."

"*Who?*"

"Your husband."

"*Him???*" Luky looks to her surroundings and gasps for air like one who is drowning. "He's coming here?"

"Yes..."

Whaat?

"...coming with us to the airport..."

the heck?

"...to say his goodbyes and..."

Shit.

"...farewells."

Oh no. (*sick*) Oh no.

Hash'nuq arrives to Akrum's and steps off the ricksha, his face beaming with pride. He turns and helps his parents down while his two brothers and five sisters help themselves. Together, they walk to Akrum's door and enter.

Inside, Hash'nuq sits on the bed.

Amma says, "I'll get Luky," and disappears to another room. "Are you ready?" she asks her. "They're here."

Luky—

"I'm dressed, but—"

Amma—

"Hurry! They're waiting. And don't worry about the cha or the snacks. They're set out already. You can thank your Khala and Ruthna."

Luky—

"You mean I have to sit with him and talk?" (eyes widening.)

Amma—

"Well, yes. He is your husband after all. You're allowed."

Luky—

(at a loss for words) "…"

Amma—

"Come on, you look pretty and everything will be fine. Your makeup looks fine. I know you're nervous, but that's your husband out there, so breathe. Relax. He's a good man."

Luky—

(walks forward through the doorway to see her future husband, the man who, technically, already is, yet won't be officially labeled so till September) *the sixteenth? or when I'm sixteen?*

Amma—

"Here, let me help you to the bed." (takes Luky by the hand.)

It felt like a blind date. He smiled. I was shaking. But why did he seem so old? He asked me how I was doing and how the trips from Rangarchur to Sunamganj had been and how I was liking it here, and that was about it. Because mum said,

Amma—

"Please, son-in-law, please, you're gonna have to take care of my daughter since I won't be here for her anymore, and she's never lived alone, so if there is anything that she needs, please, son-in-law, please..."

Hash'nuq—

"Well, there's no need to worry. I'll write to your daughter every single day. I'll write to her with every chance that permits."

So he assured my mum everything would be perfectly fine, that he'd take good care of me. 'Don't worry,' he said. 'If there's anything she needs, all she has to do is contact me or my family and we'll help.'

Hash'nuq—

(turns to address Luky) "You know there are many girls who come from London and end up staying. (pauses momentarily to scratch upper lip) It's really not a bad place."

Then my mum grabbed each of our hands and put them together and said,

Amma—

"From now on, my daughter is all yours. I have no authority over her whatsoever, so if anything happens to her..."

And there were tears in my mum's eyes.

Hash'nuq—

"Oh, don't worry. I will definitely take good care of your daughter."

Amma—

"I know you will, I know. That's why we picked you. (inches closer) And if you ever need anything, please call or write us. I see you as another son now; I no longer have two boys but three."

Then his sisters and mum came.

Sisters—

"Aw, bhabhi, it's okay. Don't worry about it. We'll take good care of you. What are you crying for?"

Then my mother-in-law started kissing and hugging me, and I thought, 'Oh my God, I've got a family or something here. Maybe they are nice people, maybe I am gonna be okay after all.' Then, before I knew it, we were leaving.

They gather Amma's things and carry them to the rickshas and hoist them into an open seat. "We're ready," they say after boarding.

Now they're off, speeding away at human power. Akrum next to Hash'nuq, Rabiya squished in alongside Sunia, tickling her little niece's face and chin, and Luky, that poor little thing, wedged in the middle of Aziboon and His second sister, the bitch. (Aziboon's other daughters are in the seats of two others).

At the bus stop, they pay the ricksha-wallahs their fare and buy bus tickets. On the bus, Amma says to Hash'nuq, "Here, sit next to Luky," and when Luky sits by the window, he takes the aisle seat and Amma sits next to him but in the seat adjacent.

Next stop: the airport.

Luky peers through the window and sees the same horrible scape, but doesn't know what to do about it. Certainly, she can't look to her left—oh no—because that would mean. Oh yes. That would mean she would have to look at him, and no, no, no, that's not an option right now.

"Luky!"

Instinctively, she turns to the direction in which her name is being called from and sees him staring at her face. Oh God. She feels like dying.

"Whaat?" she cries real snotty. And why wouldn't she? Wasn't it Amma's fault that made her look that way in the first place?

"Your sister," Amma comments. "She's crazy for him!"

They arrive to the airport and Luky's nostrils are greeted with malodor.

Though by now I was used to it. I knew what to expect.

They leave many words left unspoken as they inch along to the gate. Many strangers and passersby rove up and down the terminal. Some look one way and then another. Some stand staring, with arms outstretched and palms facing upwards, staring, still staring, but no one makes a sound. Yet wherefore all this noise? This commotion? And who holds the answer if no one replies? And like a forsaken soul after death, lacking hope and God's good ear, Luky walks to the gate, her tongue aphonic, her eyes slightly downcast, seeing only the tops of her sandal straps and feet veins, feeling her beating heart inching upwards, forcing its way against her sternum, pushing it, shoving it, hammering it, as it wishes to break through, to escape, to spill out in a gush and speak in words of red on the floor, on the ground, at Amma's feet. For who knows, maybe Amma will rescind her flight plans and forgo her plane ticket? But now the loudspeaker brims with static and a little man pulls a cart of belongings there, but no one sees him except for Luky, and the tug of fate pulls the group closer to Amma's destiny, the goodbye. So they walk, oblivious to Luky and her unspoken plight of agony. They walk.

Now they stop.

And that's when Luky has this sinking heart feeling in her throat that her mum is really gonna go, and when her mum says goodbye to Rabiya and Leelu, then to Hash'nuq, his sisters and Akrum, followed by Aziboon, it gets even worse.

"Please take good care of my daughter," Amma says. "It's my only request, so please." After that, Amma starts to cry because, last of all, she comes to Luky. "Don't worry," she begins. "His family's a very good family and they'll take good care of you. Remember, if you ever need anything, don't hesitate to ask, and if you ever need to talk with us, you can call when you visit Akrum's."

And then my mum grabbed me, and all I heard was this loud weeping sound, and that's when I broke down too.

"Oh, Luky, my heart, don't cry. Everything will be all right. I promise."

Then He stepped forward, telling me not to cry, that everything would be fine.

"I have to go," Amma says, wiping her eyes. "They're boarding."

Then I hugged my little sister and my mum gave me a tabiz, an amulet containing verses from the Quran for good luck. 'To keep you safe,' she said before leaving. 'Goodbye,' I tried to say, but my voice wouldn't let me. 'Goodbye,' but her ears were too far distal. 'Goodbye,' but again no sound. 'Goodby—' and she kept turning around too, waving, wiping her eyes, then turning around again. And my sister was crying; she was stretching out, screaming, 'Brafa! Brafa!' I tried to run after them, but my feet wouldn't let me. I tried to say something like, 'Wait! Don't go, don't leave me!' but my mouth wouldn't open. And when I turned around to face the others, I couldn't see. I was crying. 'Where is everybody?' So I ran to a place where I could see the plane. I ran. I watched it. My mum going up the stairs, Shanu crying. I waved but they couldn't see. The door was sealed after that. The plane taxied. The wheels rolled. And then it just...just took off into the air and the clouds ate it. Out of sight. It was gone. And I couldn't see her any longer, only blue sky and clouds and nothing. Then He said we gotta go. So we left to go back and everybody was like a coffin on the bus ride home to Akrum's.

9

"Don't worry," Akrum says as the bus pulls to a stop, "everything's gonna be just fine. You're a big girl now." He pats her on the shoulder.

"Yeah, bhabhi, what are you crying for? You'll enjoy it when you come to our place. We can't wait to take you there. You're gonna be the prettiest bhabhi in the whole neighborhood, the whole district even! And did we tell you how pretty your sari is?"

They seemed all right.

"—and we can't wait to show you off to everybody."

Was I stupid or what?

They remove themselves from the bus and go to their separate ways, Hash'nuq and his family to their hole and everyone else to Akrum's. A day or two later, Hash'nuq says goodbye to his kinsmen and returns to his teaching post at the college, and four days after that Luky returns to Rangarchur.

Now I realize I have to do everything for myself—my bath; my mum would usually warm hot water for me in the yard, but now Ruthna would do my water for me. She was very helpful like that. She'd even wash my clothes for me. 'Luky affa, you can go and have your bath now. Your water's in the yard, and give me your clothes. I'll wash 'em for ya in the river and—' she'd bring my food for me too. 'Luky affa, your food's ready.' So we became really close friends, and most of our days were the same: we'd get up, have something to eat, and then I'd bathe while she washed my clothes for me. At twelve, I'd eat again, and then we'd hang out on the porch together until dinnertime, though sometimes we'd pick fruits in the woods or sneak to the river and watch the boat races, while at other times we'd beg Heron bi-shab to buy us things from the bazaar. Ruthna would ask him, 'Please bhaiya, when you go to the bazaar, would you buy us some craft materials?' Because she was always making these little birds or flowers, or something or other out of sequins, or cutting material to make salwar kameezes for her younger sisters and cousins; and they were always sewn by hand. Or she would say to me, 'Do you want anything to eat from the bazaar, cuz Heron bi-shab's gonna go there and he can get you mishti?'—she knew I liked gulab jamin a lot, and if I smiled, she'd say, 'Oh, bi-shab, can you bring some gulab jamin back for Luky affa? She likes it a lot, you know,' and he'd bring it for me, but the thing she loved the most was my makeup from England. 'Oh, you have such nice makeup, affa. Can you do my face for me?' So I'd give her a makeover, and then she'd look in the mirror and say, 'Wow,' cuz she'd never worn makeup before. But we had to take it off before namaz. Otherwise, Leelu'd murder us. 'Hey!' he'd shout. 'You're not married. You can't wear lipstick like that!' Well, I could wear lipstick like that, because I was married, but I didn't want her to get in any trouble, so I washed it.

And sometimes Ruthna would serve me the best pieces of meat or fish at dinner, but her mum was such a bitch, and if she ever caught Ruthna giving me any extra she'd say, 'What are you doing? Sit down! I'll get Luky's plate today,' and the days she got my plate for me were the days one tiny weenie speck of meat or fish sat staring, with lots of vegetables on either side of it. I tell ya, she was trying to be tight like a scrooge, but I know my dad sent them money.

And sometimes, maybe twice per month, He (Hash'nuq) would send me letters, and Ruthna would say, 'Luky affa, what did he write to you? What did he write?'

'He says if I need anything to let him know, and he thinks I'm so pretty and can't wait till we're married.'

'Really? He can't wait till you're married?'

'Yeah.'

'What else?' (she was so excited to know).

'I don't know. He says that he misses me and thinks of me all the time,' and then she'd cover her face with her dupatta and laugh as if we were talking about sex or something.

'What else?'

'He can't wait to take me home.' Gosh, it was the most exciting time for her; every time Heron bi-shab would go to the bazaar to pick up the letters: 'Oh, Ruthna look!' he'd say after getting back again. 'I've got a letter for Luky affa,' and she'd run and snatch it from his hand and bring it to me.

'*Luky affa! I've a letter from dula-bai.*' A letter from brother-in-law. '*Look, Luky affa, a letter, a letter!*'

So both of us would sit somewhere, and sometimes Shutna, one of Ruthna's younger sisters, would join us.

'*What did he write? What did he write?*' she'd beg.

'*Hold on. Let me finish.*'

'*Come on, we're dying here.*'

'*I'm so sorry I can't come and see you right now, but they don't really want us to meet up or anything until the actual wedding day, but deep down in my heart I miss you,*' and they'd be giggling their heads off. Then, yeah, Heron bi-shab was always so helpful to me too. '*Luky affa, do you need anything before I go to the bazaar? I'm going to buy the fishes for the day and a few other items, but if you want something from there, I can get it for you. How about some mishti? Or maybe you'd like some mangoes or fruit?*'

And once a week, he'd travel to Sunamganj for me and purchase oranges, biscuits or whatever else it was I needed from Akrum's store, things like jelly, candies or other types of supplies; and sometimes, every now and then, we'd all go back together, me, him and Ruthna, for a few days to visit, but the whole time there I'd just be waiting for the phone to ring. I had so much to say but... Oh God, did they forget about me? When are they gonna call?

Ring *Ring*

'*Amma?*'

'*What are you crying for? There's no point in crying now. You're married, you're engaged, and you'll be coming back after the ceremony's finished, you both will. So don't worry. Once he gets his visa, you'll come back.*'

'But can't you just come and get me? I don't wanna stay here anymore. Please.' And when my dad got on the phone, he was very basic and straight forward. I knew deep down inside he wanted to talk to me like he used to, when I was little, but he never showed any emotion, nothing.

I lost the connection with my father after I ran away, and I could never get it back again. I envied my sisters, how they could just sit and talk with him like normal.

I could never do that.

It just felt like no matter how much I apologized, I just couldn't... I knew deep down inside my dad's heart he loved me to death, but there was this boundary there.

—So tell me, what was the very first phone call from your parents like?

—The first one?

—Yes, after your mum left, you went back to Rangarchur to your uncle Leelu's place, but on several occasions, all prior to the wedding, you went back to Akrum's, where you waited for their ring; so please describe the anticipation you felt, the questions you wanted to ask.

—Well, every time Heron bi-shab came back from Sunamganj, I'd ask him, 'Did mum or dad call for me? Did they talk to Khalu? Did Khalu say anything to you about them?' Most times he'd say no, and I'd wonder why they weren't calling and feel let down, but there were times, maybe three or four, when he'd nod and say, 'Yeah, they talked to Khalu. They asked about you and said they wanted to speak with you next weekend,' and I would get so excited.

—And that was?

—At the end of January, I think.

—*Of '87?*

—*Yep.*

—*And how long was the trek from Leelu's place to the launch?*

—*About forty-five minutes on foot.*

—*And how long was the boat ride from Leelu's to Akrum's?*

—*Another three or four hours.*

—*So after three or four hours you arrived in Sunamganj?*

—*Yep.*

—*And then you went to Akrum's on a ricksha?*

—*Yeah.*

—*And how long did the ricksha ride take?*

—*About twenty or thirty minutes.*

—*And then the phone call?*

—*No; the phone call came a day or two later.*

—*So it rings, you pick up, it's for you.*

—*And a million and one thoughts zip through my mind like a hurricane. 'How soon after the wedding can I come back? Who's coming in September? Are you gonna come, Amma?' Then each of my sisters had a go at the line. 'Hi, boro affa, how are you? We miss you.' But I thought I was gonna have this big long conversation with each of them. 'Did you hear anything from my friends or from Idris?' But no, none of that, just 'Boro affa, I only have one minute. How is everything? We miss you and saw the pictures of the engagement. They look really nice.'*

—*So the first call was the hardest?*

—*Excuse me?*

—*The first call. It the hardest, correct?*

—*Yeah, and as soon as I heard my mum's voice I lost it, and she said, 'Farayni!' That's forbidden. 'Married women don't cry like that on the phone. What are you crying for? You'll be back soon.' Which made me feel even worse. I mean, my own mother just abandoned me to rot. I know she had to leave the country in a hurry for Abba's sake, but why did she have to lie for? 'Are you listening to me, Luky? How is everything? Does Heron bi-shab go over from Rangarchur to Sunamganj, to Khalu's store, and get your stuff for you on a regular base, your food and everything?' 'Yeah, he does.' 'Well, if there's anything you need, just ask your uncle and he'll get it for you.' And the whole time, I could hear my sisters giggling in the background, and they sounded happy. If only they knew I had to sleep on the ground every night.*

—*Well, it seems like your sisters were rather naïve throughout this whole affair. Did they really think you were happy? that you found yourself a handsome prince? that you were gonna live happily—?*

—*Ever fucking after? Yeah right, but that's the impression my mum gave them, that's how she interpreted it to them; she wanted them to see how boro affa went back to Bangladesh, got married, and now she's so happy; she wanted to create that image in their minds, but it's bullshit.*

—*You should have told them straight out that you hated Bangladesh and wanted to come home.*

—*Yeah, right. How was I going to do that? My dad would have said, 'We spent all this money on your daughter, and now she wants to come back? She's ruining everything!' and my mum would have said, 'Don't be a disappointment, Luky, you've already embarrassed your Abba enough,' which was just killing me inside. And I hated the fact they were*

*punishing me for running away with Idris, but I didn't want
my dad shouting at my mum either, so I just kept my mouth
shut. When September came, all I heard was, '10,000 pounds,
10,000 pounds. He spent 10,000 pounds on your wedding.
10,000 pounds.' He wanted it to look big, but I didn't want it
at all.*

—What was Ruthna's whole take on your situation?

—What do you mean?

—I mean, what did she think about him and his family?

—'Oh, I don't know about his sisters, affa,' she'd say.
'They're a bit slick.' 'No, they're not,' I'd say. 'They're nice.'
'But you haven't lived here your whole life, affa. There's
certain aspects of the language you don't understand.' Cuz
they'd say certain things.

—Such as?

—'Bhabhi, we want some good food at our place when you
come over, so you gotta learn how to cook,' and Ruthna would
say, 'No, she doesn't need to learn how to cook. She's from
London, remember? So you lot can cook for her.' 'Oh, we're
just joking,' they'd say. 'Don't take it so seriously.' Then later,
'They're not really joking you know.' 'Yeah, they are. Why
wouldn't they be?' 'Cuz they're being sarky, that's why. But he
seems like a really good guy. It's just that I'm not too sure
about them.' After that, time went by and all the arrangements started for the wedding.

10

In the evening, Ruthna goes to the tube well.

"Come on, affa. Let's go."

"Okay," Luky says. She thinks again of the day Ruthna had told her the tube well was situated near the home of some cute college guy named Sai'een Miah who came back to the bari every once in a while on break.

"Hurry, affa, you coming?"

"Hold on, my sandal."

And how, after a short walk in the well's direction, Ruthna had cried, "There he is! That's him. Isn't he so shada?"

"Yeah, he's so nice looking...and young. How old is he?"

"Eighteen or nineteen, I think."

"And he stays full-time in the city?"

"Yeah, but that's where he grew up." Ruthna had pointed to the location. "See the home over there with the clothes hanging on the line, the one that's just a stone's throw?"

"Yeah."

"But he's normally never there, except for holidays and the occasional break."

"Oh." *I thought damn, he's nice looking. Why couldn't they have married me to him? Someone young and...well, young. He was even better looking than the guys from England were, with light colored eyes and wavy brown hair. I said to Ruthna, 'You have guys that look like that in Bangladesh? He looks like a foreigner, like one of the guys from England.'*

'I know he does, affa, he just has a different look to him.'

I thought, 'Man, if I was married to him, I'd never wanna go back to England.'

Luky also remembers the first time Sai'een Miah waltzed up behind them at the tube well on a slightly overcast day.

"Hey Ruthna. Hey Ruthna's friend," he had said, causing a minor panic attack within their abdomens. "What are you guys doing?" While Ruthna, whose face had reddened to the shade of Rudolph's nose, had replied, "Umm, we, er, umm... We were just getting water, and oh, this here is my Luky affa, Luky."

"Salaam alaykum, Luky. It's good to meet you."

"Wa alaykum asalaam. It's good to meet you too."

"Do you need any help with that? Here, allow me."

Without hesitation, Ruthna had allowed him to fill the kolshis; first the one with the slight chip missing from its lip and then the one with the faded design.

"So how are you liking it here?"

"Me?"

"Has it been hard for you to adjust?"

'Not after meeting you it hasn't.' But after a few days, he went back to his school, and every time we carried our kolshis to the tube well a piece of life was absent from each of our hearts.

Now it's July. Now it's August.

Suddenly, it's September, and the preparations have been going on since July. *And all I kept hearing was, 'Hey, you goddamn monkey! Are you listening to me? We need this many pounds of rice; and you, you son of a goat fucker, make sure you get this kind of flour; and you, did you process the food yet?'*

'I thought you wanted me to slice the fruit?'

'No, you stupid jackass. I told you to slaughter the cows.'

And there was so much confusion.

'Here, Luky. Try on your new blouse, your petticoat, your sari.'

'But how many saris do we need for the wedding?' someone asked.

'What?'

'I said how many saris do we need for the wedding?'

'Who knows how many saris?'

'This many?'

'That's not many.'

'This many?'

'That's a better many. After all, he did say he wanted the best wedding ever.'

And the cooks even got into it.

'What will they eat?'

'What will who eat?'

'The guests, you idiot, the invitees.'

'Well, I suppose they'll eat anything and everything.'

'We need something more specific.'

'What suits your fancy?'

'Rice suits my fancy just fine, thank you, but it has to be basmati rice, and chicken roast, but it mustn't be overdone chicken roast, and korma.'

'What kind of korma?'

'Excuse me?'

'You said korma, but what kind of korma?'

'Chicken korma. How dare you suggest an alternative.'

'Anything else? Or are you finished?'

'Some polau would be nice, but if we have polau, we're going to need bhuna.'

'What kind of bhuna?'

'Excuse me?'

'You said bhuna, but what kind of bhuna?'

'The beefy kind, as if there's another.'

'Will that be all?'

'No, that will not be all unless you've already jotted down mishti.'

'Shandesh or doi?'

'Neither.'

'Neither?'

'That's what I said, neither. Are you deaf?'

'Then what, goddammit?'

'Gulab jamin, you crazy old fucker, and lots of jalebis.'

'But for how many people?'

'200.'

And then Abba came.

"He's here," someone screams.

Luky runs.

"He's coming across the field!"

People assemble en masse at the edge of Leelu's boundary, eager to see the Londoni in his white polyester suit. They watch Luky and Abba meet in a touching embrace.

But Luky wishes to pull back, to turn away, which she does, quite unexpectedly, only to burst like a grenade, though instead of flying shrapnel there are tears.

"What's wrong, beti?" Abba asks. "What's the matter?"

"Just leave me alone! I don't wanna talk to you."

Abba reaches for her arm. "Please tell me, what is it?"

You disowned me, you left me to die.

Leelu steps forward. "Yeah, why are you crying for? We didn't abuse you or anything. Your dad's gonna think we beat you up."

Luky pitches herself an angry eye and bats it to him.

"Luky affa, don't cry," Ruthna says. "What are you crying for?" She pats her cousin on the shoulder.

"Well, I guess you'll have trouble listening to this then if you're angry," Abba tells her. He kneels down, opens his briefcase and pulls out a small rectangular object, black in color, attached to which is a pair of earphones.

Luky's eyes gravitate to the Walkman.

"Here, I thought this would make you happy," Abba says, dropping the brand new apparatus into her palm. "Oh, and you can thank your sister, Lahbi, for these."

"My tapes!" She pops one into the player and two seconds after that Madonna's voice fills her ear holes. *Thank you, Salena.*

Inside the house, Abba sits on Leelu's bed and begins conversing with the adults in the room. Leelu's wife serves tea.

"How's mum?" Luky butts in, feeling much better after getting the Walkman.

"Oh, she's fine, everybody's doing well." He pauses for a sip of tea. "You know," he starts up again after putting the cup down, "you'll be able to go back soon. Are you excited?"

"I really miss it," she says.

"What?" Abba asks.

"Home."

Now it's three days before the wedding and the workers are busy in the yard putting up decorations, tables and folding chairs. Also a red and white tent. A dais is constructed there for the groom and bride to sit on and be stared at; a canopy is placed over the top of it and a mishmash of floral saris, some silk, chiffon, and georgette, all of them pleated, make up the backdrop. Freshly cut flowers litter the structure, and even more will be hewn on the morrow. Tinsels and glittery balls and Christmas decorations from England and more saris of all colors cover the house, the trees and any other thing lacking brightness. Extra sacks of rice and flour are stacked on top of one another on the floor next to Leelu's bed. *I looked out and saw men putting poles in the ground, hanging canopies, fiddling with tents. I was shaking. 'What the hell is going on?' I wondered. 'Is this a daydream? Or is this really taking place? Cuz in three days' time, I'll be gone from this place, led away by strangers.' It was scary. Then I remembered something my mum had told me once, something about a woman when she goes to her husband's place, that her freedom gets taken, and she has to do exactly what He tells her, exactly as her mother-in-law tells her. And I thought, 'Oh my God, why can't I just stay with Leelu?' Not because I wanted to; he was Pilton's doppelganger for God's sake. But I figured living with him couldn't be worse than living with them. And I never got to spend any time with my dad; he was always so busy with the outside workers in the yard.*

Now it's two days before the wedding and inside the house and without commotion abounds, and pockmarking the dais are more flowers.

(enter Ruthna and Shutna) "Look, Luky affa." They point to the dais and eye the pretty flora enveloping the platform.

Luky blinks.

"That's where you and dula-bai are gonna sit, that's where you're gonna get married. And look, Luky affa—" Ruthna points to the bamboo archway latticed on both sides with jute strips— "that's where brother-in-law's gonna come in through."

Luky examines the structure. Its middle is distinguished by a wooden gate draped with a bright orange sari, and its latticework is decorated with strings of lights and flowers in lieu of vines. The entire setup, which is situated not too far from the house, serves as the main entryway into Leelu's front yard, and everyone who comes to the extravaganza will enter via this arbor, as will the party of the groom.

Now it's one day before the wedding and Leelu's wife says, "You see how nice it's set up? Nobody's ever had a wedding like this before."

Yeah, but I don't want it.

"Your dad spent so much money, you know. That's all he talks about. Are you okay, Luky? What's the matter? There's really nothing to be afraid of. Dula-bai's a really nice looking guy and you'll be really happy with him. I'm sure of it. And look how gorgeous everything's gonna be. You wouldn't have any of this stuff if your father wasn't Londoni."

But I don't want it.

"…it gives you extra privileges."

Later that night, the bari women come and sing the wedding songs. They sing the mehndi night songs as they paint intricate henna designs on Luky's hands and feet. They think she looks so pretty in green.

Depressed.

Upset.

I didn't have my mum.

Just then, the bari women get interrupted by the arrival of the mahr, the traditional wedding present from the groom.

"It's here!"

Some men from the groom's side bring the chest of goodies in and set it on the floor and Leelu's wife digs into it.

Luky tries to breathe but her breath flitters away from her lungs and her heart crashes into her sternum.

"Look at the gold!" someone exclaims. "Look at the saris!"

More women come running.

An elderly lady reaches for something shiny. "Here's her tikli," the piece that hangs from ear to nose. "Isn't it wonderful?"

Ruthna and Shutna join the rumpus.

By now, women of all ages from everywhere are drooling over the mahr, howling and digging through it with abandon and glee.

All except Luky.

It was such a big deal to them, but I didn't want any part of that shit.

The women take turns holding each item with relish, but Luky slinks to the shadows, away from the moment.

I have to wear that stuff tomorrow?

She feels dizzy, like she wants to faint.

"Oh my God," someone says, "you're right. That sari's so gorgeous, and the tikli too. They're gonna look so pretty on her. Masha'Allah, look at the dupatta," the scarf.

Everybody was going nuts.

Next, they pull from the chest a big box of makeup. After tearing it open, the contents scatter to the floor.

Ruthna helps pick it up.

"Come on, Luky. See if you like these."

"Yeah, they're so nice, affa. What do you think?"

"They're all right."

"But you haven't even looked yet."

Some lady holds up a sari. "What about this one?"

"It's okay."

She pulls out another. "This here is your number two sari...your number three sari...your number four sari...your number eight sari."

But I don't want any saris.

At 2am, Luky fights with her eyes and the mehndi still covers her hands like a tattoo. The ladies of the bari have long since departed, but their echoes remain:

"To-day is the last day at your parents' place.

For to-morrow you'll be taken away from your home.

Why, here comes the groom now, entering through the gate.

He comes with his party to gather his bride."

She tries to console herself with sleep but cannot; the voices of Ruthna and her mother keep intruding. "Gosh, I love that sari, the number two one."

"Yeah, me too. It's so pretty."

When they finally cease, Luky closes her eyes knowing the following day will be her last, and the thought makes her so terrified that she feels like one waiting on death row, getting ready to take that long and quiet walk toward oblivion before the warden flips the switch; at that point there is no more delay or hope or further ado, and you realize no one is coming to save you and superman isn't real and the cavalry's been extinct for ages and eons and the governors are just figments of everybody's mind and imagination, with the biggest fallacy resting in the belief that they can issue stays.

At 3am, Luky wakes Ruthna: "I'm so scared," she says. "I can't believe this is happening."

"Go to sleep, affa. Tomorrow's your big day."

11

Around 5:38 in the morning, the booming voice of the muezzin belts out the azaan, the call to prayer, and Luky, in darkness, rises and does her namaz. A little while later, sometime after first light, dark-skinned workers with knives begin slaughtering bovines.

At 9:23am, Luky is taken to the pond by Ruthna and other bari women.

"It's time for your wedding ghusl, Luky affa. You need a full bath."

"Why can't we just do it in the yard?"

"Because all new brides do their ghusls in the pond," some lady says. "That's how it is."

After the ghusl, they dry Luky's wetness with cloth towels and apply turmeric to her body, to make her skin appear more shiny, to give it that yellow golden glow so prevalent among Bengali brides.

They call it the brides glow.

But Luky can't stop crying. She misses Amma and her sisters, wishes there was someone she could talk to—really talk to—someone like Nanu or...

Her insides feel lonely, even as women hover.

She thinks about the shada weddings back home in England, how the mothers there spend the day with their daughters and the fathers pop in every once in a while to say *hello, how are you feeling?* She thinks about the afterparts of the shada weddings too, how the bride and groom, after kissing each other in full view of their elders and acquaintances, walk hand in hand to the exit, smiling each step of the way for pictures, the excitement of the moment pulsating through their veins. She pictures the crowd cheering, tossing rice-grains, and little flower girls tossing flowers. Such a celebration, a day to remember for all time. She can almost see the bride and groom hurry to the limo or to some other fancy vehicle in waiting and speed away toward their honeymoon, which is almost always some exotic locale or tropical paradise, chosen solely for its sandy white beaches and cool posh drinks (you know the ones with those little umbrella thingies poking out of the glass), not to mention no worries. Together, they'll sit and sip at the oceanside and chat and stare into each other's eyes, each thinking I love you about the other.

A sigh. Luky fills her lungs with a breath of warm Bangladeshi air and wipes her eyes. This is no celebration. She feels like an empty box of cereal, one that's been tossed aside in favor of the free toy.

She wonders why Abba just once doesn't take the time to ponder how she's feeling, guesses he doesn't understand that part of it. But surely someone must have told him, "Your daughter is unhappy." Well, maybe they tried to. It's just that his main concern lies elsewhere. Besides, aren't brides in Bangladesh supposed to cry all the time? It's natural.

They clothe Luky in clean clothes, then bring her back in.

At 2:44pm, the ladies redo her makeup and hair, for each time she cries her appearance becomes a bit more disheveled than—

Suddenly, they hear voices. "They're here, they're here! The groom's party is here! They're coming from the jetty. They're almost to the gate!"

Ruthna and Leelu's wife lead Luky from the house to the dais. Within minutes, the well-wishers press forward, wishing Luky a happy wedding.

What's this? Someone sits behind Luky on the dais; it's Ruthna. "He's gonna come up now, affa," she whispers. "Are you excited?"

No, she wishes she could say, but the words never materialize. Instead, she feels movement, which sets into motion an acceleration of her heartbeat. Faster and faster it pounds the organs around it with agitation. Can you hear it?

Is that Him?

More movement.

A shiver parades up her backbone and her body warms to an unknown degree. Out of one eye, she espies a folded leg. Quickly, she jilts the image from her retina with a slight twist of her noggin.

The crowd undulates. *Flash. Flash.* Like giant pissed of fireflies. *Flash. Flash.*

Men's voices fill the air. "Congratulations," they say.

Are any of those his friends?

Women zero in. They touch the bride's face with their fingers and sample sections of her sari. They touch each individual bangle and every piece of jewelry. They grope it; they eat it with their eyes. They move the bride's chin one way and then another. Upwards, then downwards. "Oh, she's so pretty," they say before dispersing.

Luky's relatives step forward. They introduce themselves to the groom. "I'm aunty so and so."

"And I'm..."

Another voice.

Abba's voice? giving Him a hearty salaam; and when Abba speaks the words *I hope you look after my daughter for the rest of her life* tears fall from the pretty bride's face.

Guests scatter to the tents in search of comestibles and a few bari ladies redo Luky's makeup and eyes while Ruthna brings over a small plate of bhat and bhuna. All at once, everybody starts saying, *"It's getting dark. It's time to leave,"* so the crowd thins while the groom's party gathers the presents.

The bride opens her eyes.

The groom rises and thanks everybody for the wedding. "I promise to take good care of her," he says. But Luky doesn't want to go; fear and angst surround her like two opposing armies and she feels cornered.

"I'll carry her," Leelu says.

"Noooooo!" the bride starts screaming. "Don't touch me. I don't wanna go!"

Guests stare.

"What are you doing?" Abba shouts. "Stop it! Why are you crying?"

"Please don't make me." She clenches her hands around one of the dais' posts and digs in.

Whack. Leelu hits her fingers.

She swears she'll never to let go. Whack. Harder and harder she sobs. Yet her grip is slipping.

Whack. Blood oozes from her nail bed. "Farayni!" Leelu screams. "You don't do stuff like that. You're being disobedient!" And that's when Abba realizes his daughter's apprehension runs contrariwise to the normal unfolding of marital emotions, which is why he latches his arms around her body to console it, to ease the panic.

"Please, please," he says, "my fhoot, my fhoot." My child. "Calm down. You can't be doing this. Not here. Not now. Or it's gonna be a shame on me."

But all she can do is...

"Everything's gonna be at the tips of your fingers, sootoh Amma," Abba continues, "so why are you even crying?"

And before she knows it, Abba is leading her to the river, his hand encasing the smallness of hers.

Abba didn't plan on going to Sunamganj this night, but given the dreary circumstances, what were his options? He was supposed to say farewell at the river-boarding place, along with the others, but how could he have done so, when she wouldn't let him go?

"We've never seen anyone cry like that," some lady says to another as the launch departs and drifts away on the water.

Onboard, His sisters approach from the rear. "Oh, bhabhi, you don't wanna come to our place? We're not that bad."

311

"Yeah, we'll all get along. *We promise.*"

By the time the boat reaches the river-landing place and the people travel ashore with their belongings and head toward the spot where the rickshas are waiting to pick them up, the onset of nighttime is upon them. Abba helps Luky board one of the carriages and two of His sisters pile on for company, and away they go.

Luky closes her eyes and wishes she were in another venue, not this open-aired hearse. Oh, why does it continually play her requiem, this unsung death ode, in commemoration of the fairy tale life she always wished for, in notes played from the ricksha-wallah's dinging bell?

They eventually get to this alleyway, and on the opposite side of this alleyway there's this strange looking house, this dark house, and standing in the doorway is a woman, and in her hand is a candle. A few dwellings are nearby, but not many, and none lit.

The ricksha-wallahs come to a complete halt and Abba, after helping himself down, helps down his daughter.

His family, now semi-visible in the dim candlelight, tosses handfuls of shada bhat over each of their heads as they enter. Inside, His dad bids them over and has them drink some concoction, some sweet delectable substance because, as he puts it, it's some tradition or something and has to be done by the bride and groom on their wedding night, so of course they drink, after which Abba says, "I'm going to go to Akrum's now, but I'll be back in the morning. Try and get some rest."

"Accha, Abba."

Outside, night swallows him.

"Are you hungry?" someone asks.

"Just tired," Luky replies.

"But you can't go to bed without eating anything. Here." The woman hands Luky a bowl of rice curry. "It'll make you full."

"Thanks," she says.

After eating, she glances around the room. In one corner, sitting cross-legged on a mattress is His father, his white hair and punjabi matching in color. In the other three corners is nothing. Against one wall is a display case minus any glass. On the earthen floor, also sitting cross-legged like their father, are His sisters, while standing next to them with both hands pressed as if praying is Aziboon, her rugged smile akin to a dark cavern lined with coal.

Off to the side, there seems to be a small room whose inside is concealed by dowdy curtains made from discarded saris and cloth. An hour or so later, Luky is led to this room, which is only large enough for a bed and a dresser. There she eyes the adobe-like floor soiling the bottoms of her barefeet, the clay walls intermingled with bamboo and tin staring her dead in the eyes. She walks to the small solitary window, which is stationed in the northwest corner of the room, and peers through its tiny opening. The view is unexciting and bleak, not to mention black, and the window has no shutters, not even a small screen, to bar mosquitoes from entry.

"Bhabhi, this is your and bhaiya's room. Do you like it? I'm sure you'll get used to it. At least you don't have to sleep on the floor like *we* do." She hands Luky a candle, its flame already burning. "And remember to change your sari before bedtime." She smiles a sort of half-assed smile that speaks of mischief, then leaves, while Luky, all alone, sits at the edge of her bed too tired to move, even to speak. Her quietude lasts only a minute, however, as His youngest sister, Cookie, arrives unannounced and uninvited. "Bhabhi, do you need anything?"

"I have to go to the bathroom."

"Follow me."

She leads Luky to the rear of the house along a well-trampled footpath, the only light coming from their candle and the dim glow of the moon.

Where the fuck is she taking me?

They walk through a small patch of what appears to be forest before they finally get to the toilet, the restroom, which has no walls, which is only a hole.

"There." Cookie points to the place. "See it?"

With utmost care, Luky walks. Just a few more meters to go. She positions her feet on either side of the hole while holding onto her breath. She squats. Terrified and afraid that something is going to jump up her fanny, she pees and barely does she use any water to wash. With frantic desperation, she races toward home, Cookie right behind her.

When they enter, the first thing they see is His father motioning to Luky from his mattress perch. "Ma," he calls her, "don't worry. Everything will be okay. We'll try our best to keep you in the best and take good care of you."

"Salaam him," whispers one of His sisters. "It should be done upon entering and exiting, and every night before you go to sleep."

So she gives him obeisance by touching his feet, followed by her chin three times in rapid succession, each time saying the words asalaam alaykum when she does the touching.

"Now hurry, Ma. My son is waiting."

Cookie takes Luky by the hand and pushes aside the curtains. "Come on," she says, leading her across the threshold.

The curtains close.

They see Hash'nuq pen the last word of an unimportant sentence in his journal and close it. They watch him rise from the bed and readjust his trousers.

Cookie giggles like a school girl who has just been reminded of something filthy and again brings up the bit about the sari. Hash'nuq waves her away, and after another sarky smile she leaves. But Luky is still by the curtains.

12

—*How come you didn't run away?*

—*I didn't have my passport. What could I do? I just couldn't leave, and how could I get to Dhaka in a country full of men? I wished it, but obviously I didn't have the courage to do it. And what if I got caught running? How would I ever get home?*

The fajr azaan goes off and in comes Cookie, the smirk on her face telling of her maturity. She sees the bloody sari, its fabric all ruined. "Aw, didn't I tell you to take it off, bhabhi? How could you?" She pulls it from Luky's hands and holds it to the light. "Now it's worthless…great."

"Just go and wash it in the river," Hash'nuq tells her, "and let me know if it comes clean."

It doesn't.

Later, they doll Luky in extravagance and sit her in an armless chair like an exhibit and tell her to keep quiet, with her head slightly aslant.

The people of the village come.

The next morning, after fajr, He says to her, "In four days' time, I'll be gone. But I'll try and come back next weekend." He pauses, spits on an empty patch of grass and watches it bubble. "You know, maybe you can come with me someday and I'll show you around."

Four days later.

"What am I supposed to do when you're gone?" Luky asks.

"Make tea. Hang out with my sisters."

"I don't mind making tea."

"Good." Hash'nuq steps closer. "You know my family's a really good family and they'll take good care of you. It may not be the same as you're used to in England, but they'll try."

Hash'nuq boards the ricksha and waves.

"Allah hafiz," he calls.

"Allah hafiz."

"This is *your* house now," Aziboon tells Luky when she enters. "And since *He's* gone—" she gestures to the doorway— "well, that makes you the head."

What the fuck she is talking about?

"...and *you're* gonna have to take care of *us* now." Aziboon gestures to the others in the room, the lips of her face in a grin. "So get started."

That night, Luky creeps into bed exhausted. She stretches one way, lengthwise, then another way, crosswise, ever thankful for Abba's wonderful purchase (for in addition to buying them furniture and kitchenware, Abba presented them with flashlights and a bedroom-set). But wait. What's this? Why are his old ass sisters (the youngest of whom is three years older than Luky) coming into the room without even asking and saying something about taking bhaiya's place in bed?

Fucking bitches.

When morning comes, Aziboon comes with it. "Why are you sleeping in so late for, bo?" My bride. "You know the bride of the house doesn't sleep in so late. It's haram," forbidden. "She's always up before the crack of dawn making breakfast."

Fucking bitch.

Sometime later, neighbors and strangers visit the bride. They do so daily. Like clockwork. Luky hates their alien-looking bodies, their dumb stupid faces. "I'm so and so from someplace," they say. "And I'm that-this from somewhere." God. It's always the same old baloney. The worst though is when she has to sit there like a marble fucking sculpture, silent and immobile, compelled really (by Aziboon of course), to stay in the same unnatural position and listen to their bullshit.

Finally, the weekend arrives, Hash'nuq and his bags with it.

"How did it go?" he asks.

"All right," she lies. "Your mum was just teaching me a few things."

"She was?"

"Yeah."

"So it was okay, then?"

"I guess."

"But not perfect?"

"Well, it's just that…" But she doesn't finish the sentence. How can she when *they're* standing right behind her, breathing down her backside? So she keeps silent and doesn't say a word. Though she tries to find a quiet time to tell him, what an oddity it is to find such a thing. And two days later, he is gone, and never did she get a chance to tell him. Though before his departure, while he was yet waiting for the ricksha, she had had a small window of opportunity, a slight glimmer of hope, but didn't pounce on it; it was right after he told her not to worry, that he'd see her again the following weekend. But how in the world could she have spoken when a million-and-one worrisome thoughts were making her worry and choking her tongue in a stranglehold? Because it wasn't the following weekend as he had promised her; it was sometime the following month. Then it became every other month, and she began dreading and dreading the time without him even more. Not because she was in love with him or anything; she wasn't. Rather, it was her hate for the alternative, her loathing for the only other option—that of spending more time with Aziboon than without.

A different day.

"No, no, no," Aziboon tells her, "the bride of the house doesn't eat first. That's haram. She waits for those under her wing. No! You don't cut the fishes like that. Like this! What are you doing? Didn't your mum ever teach you anything?" Aziboon throws her hands to the ceiling. "What kind of girl are you?" And to make matters more exclamatory, she thrusts her finger as when a swordsman thrusts his saber, slightly nicking Luky's cheek. "And that mask you're wearing," meaning your pretty face, "isn't helping to make our bellies any fatter."

Luky blinks. She feels something on her face and touches it. Blood. Even more of it on Aziboon's finger. "I'll get better," she says, meekly. "It's just that my mum always took care of everything."

"*So what?* I take care of everything, and all my girls know how to cook."

Another blink. This time Luky casts her mind back to an earlier time when Amma was bent on teaching her cookery 101 and all its related entailments. The memory triggers a pain from the left side of her bosom, causing sorrow and remorse.

"Tsk tsk," Aziboon mutters as she lumbers through the doorway, carrying nothing save her own weight. *She must be going to the toilet* Luky thinks. *Oh God, please let her trip and die. At the very least, break a hip or something. Anything. But please God…something.*

Minutes pass and Aziboon, now a few liters lighter, trudges back to the house in one piece. *Goddammit* Luky mumbles.

She advances through the doorway and holds the door open as her two youngest daughters, including their three friends, file through.

How come they get to go out and have friends over?

Aziboon rotates a full one-eighty and faces the girls. "Maybe you can help my bo," she says, "slice the fishes?"

"Aw, what for?" asks the youngest. "Bhabhi'll do it for us. She doesn't mind."

Aziboon looks to her bo, then back again to the girls. "Thik acche," she says. "Fine with me," but to Luky she says, "Start cutting, my dear. My tummy's getting hungry."

The next morning, Luky rises with the azaan and begins making breakfast, so fearful is she of not pleasing her new mother.

"Luky!" Aziboon calls out, a mere hour removed from the morning. "What the heck are you doing in your room?" she asks as she pushes through the curtains and forces her way inside. "How's the kitchen work gonna get done if you're in here relaxing? *Whaat?*" she asks rather shocked. *"You're writing in a journal?* Girls don't keep journals, they—"

Look to the doorway. Where the voices seem to be coming from. They hear someone say, "How are you?" and someone else say, "I'm fine, alhamdulillah. Long time no see."

They hear laughter. Then someone say, "Hash'nuq!" And that's when Aziboon claps her hands like two brass cymbals and runs...wobbles rather, in an off balance manner, which, by the way, is quite appropriate given her mechanics and build.

"Ooh, ooh, it's my Hash'nuq," she chirps. "He's home. Hurry!" she says to Luky. "Go and change into your gold leaf embroidered sari and matching shawl and see if he wants anything to eat."

Relief. She changes. She's free.

"Do you want anything to eat?" she asks Hash'nuq a few minutes later.

"No," he says. "Forget it. Let's talk."

"I can't," she says. "Your mum wants me—"

"Never mind about my mum," he says sharply. He walks to where his mum is and says, "I'm talking to her now, so she can't help you with the cooking."

"Yeah, that's fine," Aziboon tells him. "Don't worry about it. It's okay, you know. It's fine. Go and talk with her. She's *your* wife." And as she says it, she gives Luky this little pissy glare, indicating "If looks could kill, you'd be dead."

Hash'nuq, quite oblivious to non-verbal cues, sits on a stool and asks Luky a question. "So what did you do when I was gone?"

"Helped your mum mainly, with the cooking and all that."

Hash'nuq laughs. "You, cook?"

"She was just teaching me."

He readjusts his spectacles. "And how did that go?"

Luky shrugs.

"Well?"

"I don't know. It's just the way she treats me."

"The way *who* treats you?"

"Your Amma," she whispers. "She thinks I'm stupid. But it's hard for me to cut those little fishes on the da'h, and your sisters won't help me—"

Hash'nuq rises from his stool.

Oh no. Luky remains motionless as he proceeds to confront his mother.

"What are you doing?" he asks in an upraised voice. "She doesn't know how to do any of this stuff. What about my sisters? What are they doing that's so important, that they can't contribute? They're the ones who've lived here their whole lives. Let them do it!"

Luky reaches for her mouth to cover it, to prevent a rather large gasp from escaping. *How could he have said that?* she wonders. *Is he so dumb not to realize I'll be the one left to suffer when he's gone? Unbelievable. She's gonna torture me. Can't he see the look in her eyes?*

Aziboon looks from her son to her bo, the intensity of her ire and the *I know you said something to him in private about me* look readily apparent on her lips. "Where are they, then?" Aziboon screams at the top of voice. "Call them!"

Again, Luky receives the stare of damnation. And from that moment on, whenever Hash'nuq came by for a visit, asking how everything was, she'd lie: "Yeah, everything's fine," she'd say, because she didn't want him confronting his mother again, which would only serve to make matters worse in the event of his departure. Why, the last thing she needed was additional duties charged to her person, or the sarky remarks his sisters would make on an almost daily base.

"Yeah," they'd say, "bhabhi can't talk to us about things, but she can tell everything to brother in secret when he gets back. And who does she think she is anyway, locking up her stuff like that, as if we're some kind of thieves? We don't steal anything."

But they *did* steal things, many things, which is why she started stowing her valuables in drawers and hiding the key in a handkerchief, which she always kept on her person. Guess they figured she'd be leaving soon and wouldn't need the stuff anyway. But the worst was when they took her cassette player. Shit, that was just downright nasty, even for a bunch of bandits like they were. After all, Abba had given her that before the wedding. It was one of those special kind of gifts too, one that a girl remembers forever, like a pair of brand new roller-skates. But what bothered her most was that no one ever admitted to the taking part. Yet who in

God's name besides them could have stolen it? Nobody. And though you wouldn't believe it, that conviction was upheld years later in a dream she had while in Tampa, Florida, and in that dream, after being transported back to Sunamganj and going through their belongings, she actually found all the things that they stole.

13

Aziboon—

"Oh, my Hash'nuq is so handsome…"

Huh? Which guy is she talking about? Cuz if that's her idea of being handsome, then maybe she should marry him.

Aziboon—

"…and he's so tall and light-skinned…"

Is she fucking blind? Please tell her her kid's not the hottest guy in the world.

Aziboon—

"…and he's got such a nice nose."

Yeah, he needs to get some of that shit cut off.

The Guests—

"Of course his physical qualities are superior to other men of similar age and pedigree. That's why he's with such a good looking girl. It's only reasonable he'd be married to a movie star."

What are they looking through, their asses? I appreciate the movie star comment but—

The next day, Rabiya comes for a visit.

"Oh, look at my bride! Isn't she wonderful?" Aziboon says. "Just look at her...so fair. Isn't she gorgeous?"

Oh God. Luky feels ill and the phony façade worn by her mother-in-law is close to making her ralph. "Oh, Khala," she says, "would you like something to eat or drink? Maybe some cha?" (meaning, *please say yes so I can escape this woman's crapola.* Unfortunately, Aziboon's interjection is quicker than her getaway).

"Oh, no, no, my dear," Aziboon says. "Spend some time with your Khala, talk to her a bit. Take it easy. Relax. It's not that often you get to see your relatives. So enjoy yourself. I'll get the tea."

Luky's jaw nearly crashes to the ground in confusion, so unsettling it is being the recipient of Aziboon's royal treatment. *I wish things were always this way.*

Rabiya leans in closer. Takes Luky by the hand.

"So tell me...how have you been doing? Is everything okay?"

"Yeah, everything's fine," she says. She has to. Especially when His sisters, that is, five female versions of Saqir, are sitting on either side of her, listening.

Later that evening, Hash'nuq says to his mother, "I'm going to a friend's and taking Luky with me."

"Why do you have to take her for?" Aziboon bellows while chomping on a drumstick. "I was hoping she could help me with all this work." She points to the work.

"Ask them," Hash'nuq says, gesturing to his sisters. "What are they doing?"

On the ricksha, Luky breathes in the outdoor air and listens to the ricksha-wallah's tiny bell. She smells the smell of incense when they ride past a certain home and sees a young man on his bicycle. She thinks she hears somebody call her name, but when she looks to the direction in which she thinks the name is being called from, all she can see is a woman in a burqa. Which makes her chalk the whole incident up to the wind. *God, it's great being out here. I hope this ride takes forever.* Why, the last time she'd been out in the open like this was the day of her wedding, when she made the long trek to Hash'nuq's via the launch, and that was nearly three months ago, give or take.

The following day, Hash'nuq waves goodbye.

"How long will you be gone this time?" Luky asks.

"Who knows?"

Three days later.

Aziboon falls ill and Luky is called upon to rub the scary woman's feet. And boy, does she hate it. Those crippled up toenails. Gross. Like an old man's wrinkly forehead. Nasty. With fungus and moss.

A week passes.

But the situation remains dire (in other words, Aziboon's milking the shit out of it).

"Ooh, ooh," she whines. "I'm not feeling so good. Could you feed me a little fruit, bo? Maybe some mangoes?"

A whole bag of fruit wouldn't fill you up.

"Ooh, ooh, my head's pounding. Could you rub it for me, and maybe dab some water on my face?"

Two weeks later, a terrible day.

Luky lies sick. Coughing. Shivering. Her nostrils partly crusty, partly runny. Her temperature's through the roof and climbing. But who comes to her rescue?

No one.

So she suffers alone while Aziboon, in the other room, chomps away like a swine. Yet if there is one glimmer of hope in all this it is that her father-in-law snaps into action and comes up with a plan, and now that his wife is preoccupied with the toilet, he puts his plan into motion and sneaks into Luky's room.

"Don't tell anyone," he whispers to her sleeping body as he lays two biscuits and a cup of cha on the dresser. "You can have these later when you wake."

But Aziboon, after her bowel movement, feels famished and sniffs out the goods like a hound would a rabbit.

"Your father-in-law brought you a cookie you know," she says to Luky the moment she wakes, "and this piece is for you." Snap. She breaks the thing in half without reservation and pops the bigger piece into her mouth and hands the smaller to Luky.

Why that fucking bitch. He brings me a cookie and all I get's a half?

"When are you gonna take my son to England?" Aziboon demands some days later. "It's been four months since the wedding, yet nothing."

"Well, your son hasn't gotten the papers."

Before going to bed, Luky writes a letter:

"Don't you think we need to apply soon, so I can go home?"

Eleven days later, a letter arrives in the post:

"Yeah, I think your dad did mention something about us applying before he left for England. I'll take a bus to Dhaka—that's where the consulate is at, near Elephant Street, I think—and find out the details."

But for Hash'nuq, the prospect of leaving behind his homeland wasn't met with much enthusiasm, but with sorrow and, as time went forward, with dread (which is why he deliberately chose to avoid the subject altogether, up until now). Nonetheless, his true feelings were closely guarded on the matter, so much so that he never gave Luky any indication otherwise, not even the tiniest little clue. However, even if an inkling had presented itself, nothing would've changed her point of view, as her sole focus was on getting home. Truth be told, the sole knower of his secrets was his mum. After all, wasn't it she who begged and pleaded for him to marry this Londoni girl in the first place?

It was their *last chance* she had said, their *only way out.*

"No, I…I can't get married now," he had replied. "I'm not even…and what about my teaching responsibilities at the college? How can I possibly—? And what about my sisters? Don't you think—?"

"Stop it," his mum had told him after grabbing him by the collar, "just stop it. I have never," she began before pausing and taking a measured breath. "I gave birth to you and want you to marry this girl."

"But…"

"Listen, you will never get another girl like this one. Trust me. She's our only way out, our only way to make the money. Just think, the amount you make here in a month, you'll be able to make there in a day. Can't you see? The suitors will come in droves just begging to marry your sisters then. Imagine how long the lines will be."

"Fine. I'll do it."

"Promise me."

"I promise."

14

A month after applying, a letter arrives from the consulate.

Luky tears it open.

It seems they have an appointment for an interview on the sixteenth day of the following month, which is a Wednesday in March at 10am at the consulate in Dhaka.

Their attendance is mandatory.

Luky rescans the letter. A date at the top reads: 25th February 1988. But when March comes, she falls ill with fever and vomiting becomes a daily occurrence, and most mornings she can hardly rise out of bed. His father summons a doctor from the city and the doctor administers a test.

"Did you know she was pregnant?" the doctor asks.

"Masha'Allah!" Aziboon screeches at the top of her lungs while wiping biscuit crumbs from her mouthparts. "I'm gonna have a grandchild!"

Oh God. I don't wanna be stuck here.

A new date is set for the interview.

Time remaining?

Four weeks, 6 days, nine hours...

April 20, 1988.

They arrive to the consulate in prompt fashion and are greeted coldly and escorted to separate rooms without delay.

"Please have a seat," some shada beta wearing a suit and tie says as he gestures from the doorway to an empty chair inside the room. "Someone will be with you shortly."

Fifteen minutes later, *that* someone arrives. Two someones, actually. Both white and both wearing suits and ties and carrying clipboards and mounds of files in white cardboard boxes and pads of paper for taking notes and pens.

They dump their items on the table and the shorter of the duo has a seat opposite Luky and starts up a conversation by saying, "Well, we went over your paperwork the other day, as well as all the other documents you sent us, and we'd like to ask you a few questions if you don't mind."

"I don't mind."

"Good. Then we're off to a good start."

The other man in the room crosses his arms and smiles.

"Are you ready for the first question?"

"I'm ready."

She rests both hands on her lap and briefly eyes the concrete floor, the chalky-colored walls surrounding them on every side, before glancing back to the man's face.

"Then let's begin."

The man opens a notebook filled with lined paper and folds the front cover to the back. He opens a manila folder that was previously in the white box and (randomly?) pulls out a packet of papers, which he scans, swiftly, one by one, before putting them on the table with the folder.

"So tell me," he begins after picking up his pen and leaning backwards in his chair, "how come a beautiful girl like you, a sixteen year old British citizen no less, who, I might add," he says, turning to his partner, "was only fifteen at the time of her arrival," then back to Luky, "has come all the way to Bangladesh to marry a man twice her senior?" He holds up two fingers just to be sure she understands what the word twice means.

"Well, my parents—"

"Forced you into it?"

"No, they—"

"What? Coerced you? Threatened you? Let me ask you this, did you have *any* say in the matter whatsoever? And let me remind you, young lady—" the man leans forward and rests his elbows on the table— "that your mum and dad could be detained and charged with a crime for endangering the welfare of a minor, as the legal age for marriage under *our* law, British law, is sixteen, not fifteen."

"But I wasn't fifteen," Luky says to the questioner. "You're thinking of the engagement."

The man gets up from his seat and circumambulates the table, pausing briefly at intermittent intervals. He puts both hands in his pockets, sits again and folds both arms across his chest and leans back.

"You don't happen to have any photos of this engagement, do you?"

"Umm…no. But I think my mother-in-law does."

"Ah, your mother-in-law. Well, does she have any pictures of the wedding?"

"I think so." Luky swallows.

The man pulls out another file from the box and hands it to his partner. "Now what I want to know is...why the sudden rush to marriage? You still had a whole year of school left. Why didn't your parents let you finish?"

"Umm, well, they..."

He bends forward to scribble something in his notebook and ignores Luky's response altogether. "Never mind. Just tell me why the two of you aren't living together? You've been married now, what? Seven months? Yet he's over there at Maulvi Bazar, living with some poor family in Barlekha. What the heck is all that about?"

"Well, Barlekha is where he teaches, at the college. And the family that he stays with gives him free housing in exchange for tutoring."

"That still doesn't explain why you're not together. Doesn't the wife usually go with the husband?"

"Yeah, but—" Luky shrugs her shoulders. "I don't know why he didn't take me, okay. It probably has to do with money. But he visits every weekend."

The man turns to his partner.

"Or maybe it's because you're not really married."

"That's not true."

The man's partner grins.

"Then why does he want a free trip to London so bad?"

"He doesn't want it so bad."

The man looks back. "But he wants it?"

"Yeah, but—"

"Not so bad?"

"Look, listen, he didn't marry me for the visa if that's what you're thinking."

"Who says that's what we're thinking?" He looks to his partner. "Maybe we're thinking about the big age difference here, or the fact that neither of you have anything in common." He looks back to Luky. "Why, any fool could see that this marriage is a farcical sham. And you know as well as I do that fifteen year old British girls don't normally travel halfway around the globe in search of husbands as old as their fathers."

The two men leave and Luky rubs her eyes.

One hour later, they return. This time the taller of the two sits opposite Luky while the shorter one stays standing, his back against the wall.

"Let me begin by telling you what is already apparent here," the taller man says, "and not in the least bit shocking. We believe this man you supposedly married, this Hash'nuq or whatever the heck his name is, did so with the sole intention of going to England and would have, in our opinion, if given the opportunity, divorced you as soon as he became a citizen. Do you understand what I am trying to tell you?"

"..."

"Young lady? Are you all right? I still have one more question to ask you. Was there any financial gain for you in all this?"

Meanwhile, in another room, Hash'nuq faces a barrage.

"Is it your desire to go to England?"

"I'm fine either way."

"What's your wife's favorite thing to do?" (and he couldn't answer because he didn't know).

"How long have you been married?"

"About seven months. But longer if you count the engagement."

"Should we count the engagement?"

"It's the same as being married."

"Yet you didn't live together?"

"Her family didn't want us to see each other until the actual wedding day, so she stayed with her uncle."

"And why was that?"

"Because of her age."

"Ah, I didn't know Bangladeshis followed British law when it came to the legalities of marriage. Are you sure it wasn't because you really wanted to go to England, and this was your only shot at doing so, and you didn't want to fuck it up by raping a minor?"

"How dare you."

"No? Then why in the world did you get married in the first place? And tell me the truth, you lying sack fodder."

"It was just one of those things. An opportunity arose and I accepted. It was time."

"Ah, an opportunity arose and you accepted? It was time? Well, isn't that the most laughable piece of bullshit I ever heard in my entire life. Voilà! A magic shake of the fucking wand and you're married to a movie star. Why, it's so very touching, truly. But if you will, you can cut the bullshit now and honestly answer me a question: is there a shortage of women in your country or something? I didn't think so. Yet you, a grown man, would have me, a humble servant of the crown, believe that a more suitable match, one closer to your own age and wisdom, is non-existent, which is so goddamn unbelievable as to boggle the mind. Do you really think I am so stupid as to believe any more of your lies? Because I am not, Mr. Hash'nuq, I am not. Roger Tate is no goddamn gullible dipshit. Never was, never will be. And you'll *never* convince me, Mr. Hash'nuq, not even the Queen of England herself could convince me at tea time from the stone steps of the palace, with God himself standing at her side as a witness, that a beautiful young woman like that—" he points to the doorway as if Luky is standing on the other side of it— "would willingly drop out of school and fly to a goddamn wasteland of a country like this one and marry the likes of you for no other reason than an acceptable opportunity presented itself and everyone accepted."

Hash'nuq stares Mr. Roger Tate in the eyes with ire. "It's not like that at all! I already told you, it's not like that at all."

"Then what's it like Mr. Hash'nuq? Please fill us in on the diluted thought processes driving your mad mind. We're all dying to know."

"It's not—"

"What, Mr. Hash'nuq, like that at all?" Mr. Tate rises from his seat and walks around the table.

Hash'nuq stays silent.

"Did you or did you not, Mr. Hash'nuq, marry this girl to go to England?"

"I did not."

"Was it your intention to go to England?"

"No."

"Did you ever wish to go to England?"

"No."

"Speak up, goddammit! You're beginning to sound like a fucking mouse."

"I said no!"

"Then why are you even applying when you don't even care about going?"

"Please promise me," Aziboon *had said. "I promise,"* Hash'nuq *had replied.*

The words feel like a hot burner underneath his palm.

"You're hiding something, aren't you, you bastard?" Roger Tate screams as he slams his fist onto the table.

Sometime later, the two men leave only to return shortly.

"We don't believe you're actually husband and wife, and I think you know that. However, you will still receive an official copy of our report in the post, detailing, to a tee, our decision. Are you clairvoyant, Mr. Hash'nuq? No? Well, don't worry about it. I think it's transparently clear here just what our decision will be."

15

Every day the same. Luky rises, hoping for a letter, her ticket home.

"If anything comes from the consulate," Hash'nuq says to her one day, "have one of my bhaiyas phone me from the bazaar."

The next day, a letter:

"Dear Mrs. so and so," Luky reads more quickly than her mind can process. "We are sorry to inform you that your visa application has been denied for your spouse, as there seems to be a strong wall (disconnect) between you and him, a barrier that, we believe, is directly related to a certain host of factors, with age being only one. We are of the opinion that this marriage was a set-up from the get-go, and that funds may have exchanged hands for the promise of a visa. Therefore, the application has been denied, as the groom's untruthfulness and lack of good candor in answering our questions marks him the sort of riffraff more suitable to England's jails than its streets."

Luky folds the letter and her body shivers. A flash of devastation pierces through her mind, and in the middle of her throat is a lump.

"What is it? What does it say, daughter-in-law? What does it say?"

"That we have to keep on trying."

"Whaat? He can't get his visa?"

"We have to reapply."

"I wonder how long it takes?"

Hash'nuq arrives home three days later.

"I told your parents it says we have to keep on trying."

"That's fine. Don't worry. We'll appeal. Just because they denied it doesn't mean we have to stop trying. I'll let your father know. He'll help us."

When Abba hears the news, he asks Hash'nuq to send him the letter. "I'll take it to a solicitor and get the ball moving. When it arrives, I'll let you know."

At the solicitor's office in London, a prominent man in a shiny black suit hands Abba a mountain of paperwork, the most important piece being the affidavit, Abba's written declaration under oath. In it, Abba states that the marriage was indeed an arranged marriage, that he was a witness at the wedding, and that he and Amma were the ones who arranged it. Furthermore, he declares that his son-in-law has already obtained pre-authorization for a job, and where matters of accommodations are concerned, he's already secured housing too.

The paperwork is sent to the consulate. Weeks dribble away without news. Finally, a breakthrough. An interview is granted, conducted. Fast forward the calendar one month. A letter arrives saying something about a strong barrier and something else in giant red letters stamped across the top of the page: APPLICATION DENIED.

"What does it say, daughter-in-law? What does it say?"

"That we have to keep on trying."

So they appeal and the days, like fleeting memories of a stranger's smile, pass from their eyes and the bitterness in their hearts toward Luky ever grows.

"I can't understand it," Cookie says to her sisters. "Didn't so and so's daughter take *her* husband to England in a matter of months?"

"I think so."

"Then how come bhabhi's situation is so screwed-up? Our brother's been in limbo for *ages.*"

"Yeah, it just goes to show a pretty face doesn't always get a visa."

The next time Luky sees Hash'nuq, she is furious. "I'm sick of it!" she says, "of every living person talking about that damn visa all the time and London. Just once maybe they could ask me about my belly or how I'm feeling."

Meanwhile, Abba calls the solicitor in London and asks him to write a letter to the British consulate concerning Luky's pregnancy.

"Of course the baby can come to England," the man in the shiny black suit says to the receiver. "All that's needed is a letter from her doctor attesting to the fact that she's pregnant and a list of possible due dates."

When the British consulate receives the letter from the solicitor and the doctor, they send out one of their own.

"Dear Mrs. so and so," Luky reads with hesitation, the skin on her back atremble. "Upon completion of your delivery, please feel free to visit the office with your baby. At that time, you may elect to have all the necessary blood work completed, including fingerprinting and DNA analysis."

Thank God.

That night, she dreams of voices:

How long is it gonna take for Him to get a visa? Ugly dogs got visas for their husbands and took them to London, but your pretty face is good for nothing. Are you even doing the paperwork right? And your parents, what the heck are they doing? They're not doing shit. You're supposed to take my son to England.

We're trying. My dad's got a solicitor.

Obviously, it's not working. You've been married now how long, and still no visa?

Fuck you. It's gonna happen.

Awake.

"What are you crying for? It's not like we don't feed you."

Yeah, right. I barely get water. But you, on the other hand, sit there stuffing your face.

More nighttime dreams.

No point in having a pretty face or a beautiful young wife if neither can get you a visa.

Oh dear God, please bury me alive if my only option is to be stuck here forever. Let Him get one [a visa] to any country. I'll go to Mars, Venus, wherever. I don't care. I just want out of this hellhole. Pleeease.

It's hard to believe that somebody, without hitting you, can be so brutal. Like how somebody, verbally, can be so...how it can be so painful. You think that when somebody hits you...

Sometimes I wish she'd just slap me, then it would be over and done with and I could move on.

October. 1988.

Luky topples over in agony and her father-in-law stumbles over from his bedside.

"What is it daughter-in-law? Is it the baby?"

"I don't know, but it hurts."

"I'll go and call the doctor."

The doctor arrives shortly before nightfall. Good news: it was only a false alarm.

"You're costing us money, beybootah," Aziboon shouts in between mouthfuls of rice and lentils when she finds out the news. "You don't call doctors for false alarms."

Several days later. Her father-in-law approaches from the rear.

"Has your mother-in-law got you cooking all this stuff again? Just leave it and come into the living area and rest."

"No, I can't. I gotta get it done."

The next day, while cleaning, Luky feels something leaking from her...so she reaches for a slab of sari and presses it there in order to hold the concoction at bay. With a free hand, she hides the puddle beneath a jute mat and sits on it and doesn't move.

One hour later, the men clear away from the area and one of His brothers sputter to the market for the phone.

The day ends and nighttime approaches. The dead hours ensue.

At 5:22 in the morning, the sun starts to rise, and not long after that the bari begins to stir with movement, and not long after that everything becomes...

A mess.

And fourteen hours later the story is no different except for the rain, which is coming down like bullets, bashing the house-sides, not to mention the rooftop.

Still pushing. With sweat rolling down either cheek. Feels like dying.

—"The baby's not coming," someone says.

—"Stuck," says another.

—"Not much time," says a third.

—"So we better hurry."

—"Yes, better hurry."

—"Or else."

—"Yes, or else."

—"It'll be too late."

For what? she wonders. *FOR WHAT?*

She tries to speak but cannot. A low groan is heard but disregarded as buzz. A fly lands on the tip of her nose.

"Read your surahs," someone says.

"Recite Allah's name."

Thirty more minutes tick from the clock. A man's voice inquires about a blade (is that the doctor?). "Yes," someone says. "Here." And the last thing she remembers is the maghrib call to prayer and a stubby little man (is that the doctor?), stepping forward with a…

God is great the muezzin calls. *He is great.*

And there is no God but he.

And Muhammad, peace be upon him, is his messenger.

So rush to your prayer mats.

Rush to your success.

For God is great. He is great.

And there is no God but he.

Soon real time events become hazy blue and gray.

"Do we have any more blankets?" someone screams. "We have to stop this bleeding and wipe away all this red."

"Over there," an old lady points to their location. While Luky dreams *how's the baby?* but never dreams of the answer.

Oh God she prays, *please give me a boy. Otherwise, I pray you just crack the floor open and push me...*

A week or so later, she sees the birth certificate, a flimsy piece of paper with hand written details, and wonders where her name is at.

UPDATE: ANOTHER DENIAL FROM THE CONSULATE. ALL SIGNS OF PROGRESS DIM

STOP

—*You went to the worst prison.*

—*I used to tell myself, 'This is it, this is the end of your life. You're supposed to live at your husband's feet forever, and this is my punishment for embarrassing my parents and ruining my father's name.'*

—*They say your mum took a step up, so to speak, when she married your father. And you—*

—*Took a downgrade?*

—*Precisely, and ever since that time you've been dubbed the semi-Cinderella.*

—*The what?*

—*The semi-Cinderella. You remember the girl with the wicked stepmother and stepsisters who went from workhorse to rider, from simple drudge to future queen?*

—*I remember.*

—*Well, compare your two stories: both you and she put up with hellish female antagonists who hated all things beautiful and got married to complete strangers. Which shows that you're kind of the same, yet different in that she went from rags to riches and married a future king, while you went from London to poverty and married Methuselah; hence the name 'semi-Cinderella.'*

—*Well, I did get my prince, eventually. It just took a little while to reunite my foot with the correct glass slipper, over twenty years in fact and a Ruby Tuesday restaurant in Tampa, Florida.*

—*Moving on, you once said you never wanted to grow up and be like your mum. Do you remember that?*

—*I remember.*

—*Yet you ended up becoming just like her. Was there ever a certain moment in time when you thought, 'Oh my God, I'm just like her?'*

—*Well, everything my mum did was for her family, which was okay. It was something she wanted to do, something she felt good doing, whereas I didn't have a choice.*

—*You must have felt stuck?*

—*At least my mum had a modern kitchen, not some third world...what is it? where you had to... It wasn't a stove, it was a hole in the ground where you had to keep on blowing through this little bamboo stick-thing in order to get the fire up, which took ages to light, and forget about a rice cooker.*

Over the phone, Abba tells Hash'nuq, "There's still hope you know, however small or dim. Though I think if she came to England with the baby, our chances of success would be much greater, what, with the media and all that nowadays. We can protest in Westminster, we'll go straight to Whitehall Road, us and others in the same situation. Who knows, maybe they'll grant us the visa. It's worth a try, anyway. After all, they have hearts, don't they? And if they see a little baby without its daddy, maybe they'll feel sorry and show some pity, maybe empathize a bit and come to their senses, that the baby needs its father. Understand, dahman, the goal is to put a public face on the issue, because the more personable we make it to them, the harder it'll be for them to ignore, and the harder it is for them to ignore, the harder it will be for them to avoid. In other words, they'll be forced to deal with it head on and react."

16

Bradford, England. 1989.

June.

The protests failed. Even the TV show about young brides trying to bring over their foreign husbands on visas, which Luky went on as a guest, drummed up no interest in her case. Not even months of phone calls and meetings with various government officials and letters addressed to the consulate on her behalf aided one iota of muscle, but instead fell on deaf ears and blind eyes.

The solicitor was at a loss.

Dead ends and walls surrounded them at every corner.

I can't believe this is happening.

Hash'nuq calls Abba on the phone:

"It's been four months now, yet nothing. So no more trying…please."

"But—" Abba begins.

"Listen," Hash'nuq says sternly, "I'm taking leave in few weeks and I expect to see their faces."

I can't believe this is happening.

"We can't keep you here any longer, beti," Abba says to Luky. "But don't worry, we'll keep on trying. That's a promise. And we'll hire new lawyers so that your case goes through."

Luky—

"I have to go back? You told me I could stay. You're both liars! You both played a big trick on me. How could you do that to your own daughter?"

Amma—

"We never thought…"

Abba—

"It's all those bastors' faults back in Bangladesh, the shada people at the consulate."

I can't believe this is happening.

Luky—

"You said we'd be gone for two weeks. Two weeks! We'll, it's been nearly three fucking years. You're not human, and you lot say that you're Muslims? You're not Muslims, you're liars. Do you know what I went through there, what that rakosh fett li," that monstrous fatty, "did to me? She tortured me, goddammit, treated me worse than a fucking slave, and I had no one to talk to, no friends, no nothing, and I couldn't even use the cutlery Abba bought me, not even the potato peeler. 'Oh, this is Londoni stuff,' they'd say. 'We have to put this on display,' as if their freaking home was a museum."

Amma and Abba—

"We know their place wasn't brilliant, which is why we gave you the furniture and the cutlery in the first place. We thought, 'What's the big deal? Dahman's a professor. He's got his masters. And one day he'll come to England and she'll never have to go back.'"

Luky—

"Well, now you know otherwise."

Amma and Abba step forward, tears drowning their pupils.

"Don't worry, sootoh Amma," Abba says, "I'll do everything in my power, I promise. I *swear* I won't give up."

At the airport, everybody walks.

At the gate, everybody stops.

"We'll miss you," Abba and Amma say to Luky and their grandson.

Abba leans in to hug his daughter, but she turns away so he pats her on the back as an afterthought. He does the same to the baby's head.

"Oh, don't worry, little grampa," he coos. "You and your mummy'll be back soon. I promise. I'm gonna make some…"

They say this happens at the end of your lifetime, how everything flashes like a fast-forwarding movie reel, how it keeps on spinning turning and the details of your life play on your eyelids like shadows on a wall from a candle flame, and what you see are the good times and the bad times, but the only emotion you feel is regret.

—So you never saw Idris?

Luky boards the pyre and Amma and Abba wave. The baby's head bobbles against its mummy's shoulder.

On the aircraft, Luky sits and stares, blankly, as though transfixed, through a tiny little window.

A stewardess locks the cabin door and the captain's voice streams from a loudspeaker, and into that place where only birds and angels thrive, they disappear.

Goodbye, England. Goodbye.

While on the ground Amma waves and Abba wipes the corner of his eye and Amma waves.

17

17 years later…

Tampa, Florida. Fall. 2006.

All this and for what? For nothing. I gave him my best years, my youth, when I should have been…

You know, I never really got to enjoy…

It's best for a woman not to be born. No mother-in-law equals no abuse.

'Can my niece come over and stay for a few days?' my *aunty'd ask. 'Yeah, yeah, she can go over,' Aziboon would say. 'But only for the day. Otherwise, I might miss her too much.'*

Bullshit. She just didn't want me to talk.

…and, yeah, for the entire time we were married He always made me feel like that, that it was always my fault. Like if anything ever happened to our…and he got sick, which he barely ever did, but if anything ever *did* happen to him, he'd say, "Well, you know what, God takes things out on the kids to get back at their parents for their wrongdoings, and I know I've never done anything wrong, at least not intentionally."

So who does that mean?

Hello?

So if any sickness would occur either to him or our son, he'd say, "I wonder why God's punishing me? What did I do that was so wrong? I know it's the result of one of *our* sins. But I've never betrayed God in any way, or my culture. I stuck to my roots and my religion."

Well, if his misfortune or our son's is the result of one of *our* sins, and I'm pretty sure he's saying he's not the sinner, then who do you think that leaves as the guilty culprit?

Hello?

"You know, maybe God's not punishing you. Maybe you're just getting old."

"No, it's the result of one of *our* sins. That's why this is happening."

"Well, if you did what you were supposed to do…"

"I did everything for the family."

"For that other family. What about this one?"

"I'm not doing anything for them now."

"Well, now it's too late." *When you're waiting for the judge it's too late.*

The gavel smacks the bench loudly and a little man in the rear of the courthouse, who'd been dozing in and out of dreamland, wakes.

"It is finished," they hear the judge say, his voice echoing through the chamber. "And such a remarkable little tale too. One for the ages, I suppose."

All these years, my teenage years, my 20s and 30s, you constantly made me work; you made me work so hard, full-time, and I had to put my kid to the baby sitter; and that's all I did was work, work, work. And you told me we'd have something of our own one day, a home, some savings...

And I believed you.

And I was waiting for that one day to happen, year after year after year, and it never...which only made me more...

And when I asked you, "When are we gonna do something for ourselves?" you said, "When my sisters have husbands, and when everything seems to be in order with my family."

Then what? We'll help them open business after business, build home after home, and snatch up land parcel after land parcel? I don't think so.

God. It was never enough.

"You know there's no difference between staying in Bangladesh and slaving away here in America for your family. It's just doing it in a high class sort of way. A posh sort of way. Either way, it's still slaving."

"That's not true."

"You know what, by the time we finish working our asses off, we're gonna be white-haired skeletons, living in some side-gutter with only jack shit to our name, and your brothers are gonna be sitting there like kings, owning everything, and it's *our* money and *our* earnings."

"No, they won't."

"You'll see. One day you'll realize it."

"Who cares?"

"Fucking hell, you know what? Here I am slaving, not so your fucking brothers can sit there like rajas."

"They're not."

"No? Then why are they living in *our* home, the one *we* paid for?"

"Listen—"

"No, I'm not gonna listen. You listen. Do you honestly think they're just looking after it?"

"Well, what do you want me to do, throw my mother out?"

—*You were their shovel.*

—*I was so reluctant to spend money too, because I wanted to save something, so that one day we could buy a home, which is why I never went on a shopping spree or spent any of his money, then fucking got nothing at the end. Though now I wish I would've spent every goddamn penny of it. At least then I would have known it all got put on me instead of those idiots getting it, and the worst part was that they always used to assume that 'Bhabhi is the one who doesn't let brother send a lot of money because she wants a car.' Well, you know what? A car is necessary in this country, you need it.*

—*When did they say that?*

—*I can't remember, but it got back to me.*

—*How much was he sending?*

—*At the time, I think, on a monthly base like four-hundred dollars, but it was never enough for them. 'You know, mum's really sick,' they'd say, 'and needs to see a specialist, and it's gonna cost...' or 'There's this really brilliant piece of property for sale in the next bari over. Can you wire...?' as if we got the money. 'But aren't the both of you earning?' 'Yeah, but we're barely making it.' 'Then borrow it from somewhere. It'll be really good for us.'*

—*They never got it, did they?*

—*They thought that money grew on trees, that you just plucked bills from plants like fruit.*

—*You should have told his brothers to get a job.*

—*They did have jobs, leisurely jobs. Are you kidding me? They barely lifted a finger.*

—*I'm surprised you never cursed them out over the phone.*

—*At the end, I was so pissed about everything, and whenever they'd call, I'd get so angry. 'You know what?' I'd think. 'Fucking bitches, all you do is sit on your fat asses while I grind away and toil. And for what? Just so you lot can get married?' They had no appreciation. It was like I owed them or something, like I was their slave.*

—*You were sending them tons of money and they were getting rich.*

—*See, what happened was, after we came to America, their status hit the roof. They came into this…this gold status. Now they're Americans, able to hang with the upperclasses, and the upperclasses didn't give a damn that His sisters were oldies, that they're in their 20s. Their goal was to position themselves so that one day, should the opportunity ever arise, they'd have a pathway. You see, there's always this hope of going to America. But they would have been nothing without me. I swear, their titties would have been touching, sweeping the floors.*

They say it's better for the ones who stayed behind. Even my mum said that, "That it's better…"

Just think about it. Who's getting the best benefit?

It's them.

And yes! I know about my tailbone sticking out, because when you're working your ass off all the time, you lose weight from sweating and not eating, and your tailbone sticks out, not that they would know anything about that because they were so used to sleeping on custom made beds in a castle and enjoying the shokari foiysha, the free government money, and getting something for nothing. Those lazy pieces of ass. Those good for nothing bums living like kings.

"I heard that they're building..." "Oh yeah, I heard that too." "...and that they've just opened up another business, and your mother-in-law's gained another 20lbs since July, and your eldest brother-in-law's belly is popping out even farther than it was before, and your other brother-in-law's khumbol is smacking the roof, and it's all because they're eating the shokari foiysha."

They thought it was our duty or something to support and feed them because we were a joint family.

"You know so and so sent back so many thousands last month to his family, and so and so sent back so many grand. How come you lot don't send us that much? And what about...who bought his family a large home and a business? How come you lot don't treat us?"

As if I care. Because nothing we ever did was good enough for them. You think they would have been thankful, but no.

"When did we wire this?" I'd say (because I'd find debits for so many grand on the statement). And he'd be like, "Oh..." (and make up some excuse).

"You know we barely have any money to survive on and you keep on sending... You're taking what is ours, what we're supposed to be getting, and shipping it to those vacuums."

God. They were barely making ends meet when I met them, going downhill fast, about to drown. Yet they got to live the life of fantasy, the life of kings and queens, while I never got to live at all.

When I'd go shopping, I'd pick something up like a nice blouse or a purse that I wanted to buy, only to put it down again and walk away. I had to calculate, "Well, I only make a hundred-something a week. I can't spend 10 dollars, 20 dollars, on a pair of pants or a blouse or a nice pair of shoes or a purse. That's 20 dollars I have to give to the baby sitter. That's 20 dollars I have to pay for food. That's money for the bus fare. I can't waste it."

I always felt like…and I used to hate myself for it.

—So he sends them all of this money, but he can't give any to you?

—That's what makes me so mad, you know, and when I think about it, I wasn't even able to buy… It was horrible.

And whenever we visited His family, they expected every piece of luggage to be filled with treasures from America.

Honest to God they did.

"What the hell is this shit?" they'd say. "We can get better stuff here in Bangladesh."

They didn't even appreciate it. And I used to think, "I don't even get to wear things like that. I don't even get to buy things like that for myself."

"Oh God. That's all I'm ever doing is working and looking after this kid," and I started to hate myself for it. "Is this all I'm ever gonna do with the rest of my life, forever?"

Then another 5 years goes by, then another: "So when do you think we can do something for ourselves?"

Then another: "Oh, we will, we will. Don't worry. We will. I want to but my family needs it so bad."

Initially, we were trying to…but why?

Then I became resentful. Then disgusted. Then I was like, "Fuck it, that's it for me."

All this money, all this spending and buying. Year after year after year. *Of using my innocence.*

—Tell me how you felt about coming to the U.S.?

—I kinda liked coming to the U.S. cuz it was a freedom for me coming from Bangladesh obviously and from England too cuz I always felt like my family would've restricted me so coming to America was the best thing that ever happened don't know what I would've done differently knowing what I know now probably would have gotten out of the marriage a little bit sooner like as early as possible yeah I definitely would have gotten out of it sooner had I the courage to do so without worrying about the whole damn ijudth thing now it's like I'm my own person and no one's gonna come and give me anything to help me with so back then if I knew what I know now I definitely would have gotten out of it a little bit sooner cuz at the end of the day even after 19 years I've caused enough heartache and embarrassment for my mum and dad so now I think I should have just done it sooner.

When his sisters got married, they were able to move into their own homes with no mothers-in-law, and when his two brothers got married, they were able to move into our castle home, the one built with my hard work and money.

"Why do they get to move in there," I said, "when I had to live with your mother?"

They never had to slave for Aziboon. They were set up from the get-go.

"I worked hard, gave my blood for this, not so *those two* could come and enjoy..."

When they got married into that palace, I was so...

"I know, I know," he said to me one day. "I understand you worked hard for it, but don't worry, you'll get swab for it (blessings), you'll get rewarded."

"Yeah, right, when am I gonna get rewarded? When I'm fucking dead? I didn't slave so they could come and..."

What was he gonna say to me?

(nothing).

It was the truth, and I fucking hated it.

—*His sisters lived the life of riley.*

—*Of course they had it easy. Why wouldn't they, when they had Cinderella? 'You know, not everybody can be your brother or sister,' I told him. 'Not everyone can be on easy street. They're the lucky ones, you know. They're the ones wearing the golden shoes.'*

—*God, they made all of their earnings off your sweat.*

—*But they'll never appreciate it. And one day they're gonna screw him out of everything. I always said that to him. 'One day your brother's gonna pull a slick one, and you'll be left holding your dick and two balls.' 'Not true,' he said, 'because everything's yours, the house, the land, the... It's all been registered in your name, so he won't be able to...' Yeah, right, because when it came down to it at the end nothing was mine, not a thing. That shithead. Everything was His brother's. And it really hurt my dad's feelings too, that he married his daughter off to that family, and all she ever did was work and slave and fight all those years, only to be cheated out of everything at the end.*

"I'm what made you in this country," I said to him one day. "And if it wasn't for me and my help, you'd be in the gutter," and somehow he had the gall to turn around and say to me that I didn't have any part of it. "After all these years of helping you, you're gonna stand there and say that shit to my face?"

You took advantage of my childhood.

"You know what?" I told him. "You can have all that shit back in your country, the home, the land, the... I don't care about it anymore. You can have it as a charity."

"Who are you to give me a charity?"

One day, one day. Well, how much longer was I supposed to wait for that one day? 5 years? 10 years? 19 years? Because that one day never came. And do you know what else he said to me? "When you die, you're gonna have to answer for your own sins. I won't be there to save you." "Oh yeah," I said. "What makes you so special? What makes you think you're going to heaven and I'm going to hell? Who knows, you might end up going to hell and I might end up going to heaven. Maybe God up there will end up liking me more."

After divorce. Luky on phone with mum. "You married me off to someone as old as my dad." *Two years later, after marrying a guy from America. Luky again on phone with mum.* "Now is everything okay?" *like being sarky, hinting that I've got a younger dick.* "Now is everything all right?" "Yeah, everything's fine." "Well, make sure you spend the rest of your life with him." "Okay, I will." "At least it's different with the English," *she went on.* "They may be a bit more selfish about things, but whatever they make in terms of earnings, it's for them and their wives and children. There's no other relatives to fuss over."

ABOUT THE AUTHOR

L.A. Sherman grew up in Bradford, England where she learned how to sneak out of the house without making the door creak. At the age of fifteen, she was tricked into going to Bangladesh by her parents and forced to marry a man as old as her father. After four years there with a wicked mother-in-law, she won the visa lottery for America and moved to the Big Apple. Now hard at work on her second book, she lives in Tampa, Florida with her family near a pond full of gators and spends her time doing all the things that Bengali girls don't.

PHOTOS FROM MY LIFE

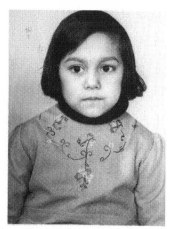

Me in 1977. I was six.

Me in 1979. I was eight, going on thirteen.

The only surviving picture of my Nanu, my grandmother;
probably taken in the 1970s. She is the lady in the first
row, front and center.

Me at thirteen in my oversized, father approved, ugly as hell "I-wouldn't-be-caught-dead-in-front-of-my-white-friends" dress. But don't worry; my real clothes — my mini-skirt and tank top — were underneath.

Me in August of 1986, getting ready to depart for
Bangladesh with my mum, to see my uncle Leelu Miah,
who, supposedly, was on his deathbed. We were only
supposed to be gone for two weeks.

My engagement in December of 1986. I was only four
months removed from my fifteenth birthday. My eyes
were closed because some old lady, some distant granny
from some place, told me I had to keep them that way.

Notice the henna on the back of my hands. It was done with nail polish.

Notice His auntie's fingers on my chin. She was turning
my head so he could take a good look at my face,
obviously.

This is when I started to get a neck ache.

My marriage in the fall of 1987. I just turned sixteen. His
side of the family, everyone from his freaking village,
swarmed me like mosquitoes. I couldn't stop crying. I
missed my friends. I felt sick to my stomach. I missed my
mum and wanted to go home.

"Oh my God," I thought. "What's happening to me? What am I gonna do?"

They changed my sari for this photo. The first sari I wore was actually the number two sari. This sari was the actual wedding sari. After that, they carried me to the river. Then to the boat, and then we sailed to His place, which was in the middle of freaking nowhere, in the late evening.

This was taken twelve days after the birth of my son. I was so skinny; I think around ninety pounds. I was so thankful I gave birth to a boy. Otherwise, I think my mother-in-law would have killed me.

After my parents saw a picture of how skinny I was (the previous one with the baby), they flipped, and so my mother-in-law started feeding me extra food to fatten me up. I felt like a balloon.

Me and my mum at Heathrow Airport in 1991. I just landed after winning the OP-1 visa lottery for America. I was so glad to see her and thankful I wouldn't have to go back to Bangladesh again. In a few months, I'd be in New York.

Me at my first job in the U.S. at Metropolitan Lumber & Hardware. Notice how skinny I was. I was so happy to be 8,000 miles away from my mother-in-law.

Me in our one bedroom, basement apartment. At heart, I
was still just a little girl with a teddy bear.

Me and my first friend in the U.S. in 1992 or 1993. We thought we were so cool, that we were rebels. Oh, the things you do when no one is looking!

Dressed in black, this is me wishing I had a car and getting ready to be mischievous.

Me visiting my parent's place in England after being in the U.S. for a few years. Notice the pink walls and carpet, the cheesy decorations: the tinsels and balloons. It was like a carnival. Can you believe it? The decorations stayed up year round.

A low point in my life. I wished that things were different, that my husband would understand how I felt inside, how sad I was, and that I just wanted out.

Me thinking I was the Bengali Joan Jett.

Me coming down the steps at my dad's place in England as though I were an actress in some Hindi film, trying to be the next Aishwarya Rai.

Goofing around at my sister's house warming party.
Notice the can of whipped cream in my right hand.

Posing on my dad's staircase that leads to the attic. In
three days, I'd be back in the U.S.

1998. Having my morning cupper at my dad's place, making the most of my time away from the U.S. and my arranged marriage.

1999. Yay! I finally got my U.S. citizenship.

My dream job as a glorified cocktail waitress...er, I mean, flight attendant for Tower Airlines. It was great. I got to see the world for free!!

The big 3-0. Me celebrating my 30th birthday with cake on my face. If you look closely, you'll see that the balloons say "Happy Anniversary" instead of "Happy Birthday." To be honest, they were the cheapest ones we could find.

Posing in my mum's new renovated kitchen. After all those years in England (over thirty), she finally got the kitchen she deserved.

2005. This was the last time I visited Bangladesh. I'm in the maroon and gold sari on the right standing outside the walls of my dad's masjid, or mosque, in his home village of Rajanpur.

Riding the escalators in New Jersey. Sometimes me and my best friend would do this at the casinos when we were bored. My God. We were living the dream in the good old US of A.

I'm finally my own woman now, finally free, finally out of the marriage.

My new love.

A picture from my second wedding. Now I could look up and not worry about getting a neck ache, or that some old Bengali lady was gonna tell me to keep my eyes closed.

In New York on 42nd Street in Manhattan on vacation.
We visited Canal Street (for the purses), the Empire State
Building (for the sights), and Chinatown (because we were
freaking starving).

My second baby. He was just a few weeks old. Most people can't believe I have kids, let alone two kids who are twenty years apart.

In Dedham, England, which is near Colchester in Essex
County, at the Sherman's house, where my hubby's
ancestors used to live prior to their coming to the new
world in the 1630's. By marriage, I'm related to General
William Tecumseh Sherman, Civil War hero; Roger
Sherman, signer of the Declaration of Independence and
Constitution; General Sydney Sherman, the first person
known to have said, "Remember the Alamo!" and Stuart
P. Sherman, the famous writer and critic of Henry Louis
Mencken.

I'm more confident now. I know what I want.

I'm no longer running.

I finally have the fairy tale life I always wished for, the happy ending that most people only see in the movies.

Finally at peace with my parents.

GLOSSARY

Abba — Dad or father

Abba kita korbo? — Dad will what?

Accha — All right

Alhamdulillah — Praise God

Allah — The Arabic word for God

Allah hafiz — May God be with you

Allahu Akbar — God is great

Am — Mango

Am achar — Pickled mangoes

Amar shahtay dui-jon mammon ai-say — I've two guests here with me

Amar sootoh Amma — My little mama

Ami — I or me

Ami bujhte na — I don't understand

Ami farr tam na — I can't do it

Ami goro ai see — I'm home

Amma — Mom or mother

Amra ai see — We're here

Arabic — The Semitic language of the Arabs and also the language of the Quran

Ar-ami dosh minute foray aye-moo — I'll be back in ten minutes

Asalaam alaykum — Peace be unto you

Asr — Late afternoon prayers

Ayats — Verses from the Quran

Azaan — The call to prayer

Bangladesh — A country located in South Asia. Formerly known as East Bengal, then later as East Pakistan, it became a sovereign state in 1971

Barlekha — A subdistrict of Maulvi Bazar district in the division of Sylhet, Bangladesh

Barmy — Crazy or foolish

Bastors — Bastards

Bata sandals — Bata is an Indian company that makes footwear

Batash — Air / wind / oxygen

Bazaar — Market

Bay-deen — Unbelievers or disbelievers

Bay-deen jadth — You rowdy cast of disbelievers

Bels — A type of fruit, native to South Asia

Beta — Guy / man

Beti — Lady / woman

Betel nut and paan — A type of leaf and nut, most commonly chewed in South Asia much like tobacco

Beybootah — Dummy

Bhaiya — Brother

Bhalo — Good

Bhalo kori-cha ar-nastha bah-now — So make us some good tea and some snack

Bhalo nam — Good name

Bhat — Rice

Bhat thear motton shada — White like the rice

Bhuna — A type of curry

Bideshi — Foreign

Bideshi shickarr — Foreign pig

Bi-shab — Another word for brother

Bismillah — In the name of God

Boonies — Titties

Boro affa — Big sister

Boro bi-shab — Big brother

Bradford — A city in West Yorkshire, England

Bundoh ho — Be quiet

Bura beti — Old lady

Bura manoush — Old people

Buraq — The name of the winged horse that carried the Prophet Muhammad from Mecca to Jerusalem and back again during the night journey

Burqa — An outer garment worn by some Muslim women to cover their bodies

Cha — Tea

Chapattis — Unleavened flatbread from the Indian subcontinent

Chull — Come with me

Da'h — A curved, raised blade attached to a piece of wood that is used for cutting fish, meat and vegetables

Dahman — Son-in-law

Dal — A thick stew of lentils

Danda — A Sylheti slang word for the male genitalia (i.e. dick)

Deshi neeyah beeyah deemo — If you don't settle down, we're gonna take you to Bangladesh and get you married

Dewsbury — A town in West Yorkshire, England

Deywah — An oversized wooden spoon

Dhaka — The capital of Bangladesh

Dhikr — Repeating Allahu Akbar, God is Great, while thumbing through prayer beads, a type of rosary

Dhonyobad — Thank you

Doi — Yogurt

Dula-bai — Brother-in-law

Dupatta — Scarf

Dur'ho — Get lost

Eid — A festival marking the end of Ramadan

Eid Mubarak — Happy Eid

Ek — The number one

Ek taka — One Bangladeshi dollar

English hoisos — You think you're an English person

Ere foray kita hoibo? — Then what happened?

Fahgol nees — Crazy girls

Fairista — Angels

Fajr — Morning prayers

Farayni — Not permitted

Ferrotte nee ekta — She's one filthy / dirty girl

Ferry-wallah — A Bangladeshi door-to-door salesman who sells things such as saris out of suitcases

Fhoot — Child

Jee — A paid escort who escorts Londoni children to school and back

Genji — An undershirt, more commonly known to Americans as a wife-beater

Ghazal — A type of poetry invoking melancholy, love and longing

Ghum — Nap or sleep

Ghusl — A bath

Goonda — Thug / villain / bad guy

Gorom batash — Hot air

Gulab jamin — A popular dessert throughout the Indian subcontinent

Gunah — Sin

Gurushpur — A village in Bangladesh

Ha du du du — A chant that players must repeat over and over again while holding onto their breaths when playing Kabadi, Bangladesh's national game

Haram — Forbidden

Hasan Nagore — A subdivision of Sunamganj

Henna — A type of dye used in marriage ceremonies to adorn a bride's hands and feet

Hijab — Head covering worn by Muslim women

Hookahs — Water pipes used for smoking

Ijudth — Prestige

Imam — The prayer leader in an Islamic community

Innit? — British slang for "Isn't it?"

Insha'Allah — God willing

Isha — Nightly prayer

Ittah farayni — It's not permitted

Ittah ki? — What's this?

Jackfruit — The national fruit of Bangladesh

Jah — Go

Jai namaz — Prayer carpet

Jalebis — A popular South Asian sweet that, to Americans, resembles orange pretzels

Jam-e-khans — Jamaicans

Jam-e-khans ai-say — The Jamaicans are here

Jam-e-khans bai ray roi say — The Jamaicans are still out there

Joy Bangla — Victory for Bangladesh

Jute mat — A mat made from long, shiny vegetable fibers that can be spun into coarse, strong threads

Kabadi — Bangladesh's national game

Kajol — Eye liner

Kafirs — Unbelievers or disbelievers

Ke bai ray? — Who's out there?

Khala — Aunty

Khali baby ho-wow — You keep making babies

Khallah bandors — Black Monkeys

Khallah nee — Black lady

Khalu — Uncle

Khaynay farr tay na? — Why can't you do it?

Khumbols — Asses / butts / rear-ends

Kita? — What?

Kita hoisay? — What's the matter? / What's wrong?

Kita koro shaub? — What are you all doing?

Kita kuboor? — What's the news?

Kitcha — A story

Kitchu hoi-boh ni? — Does it matter?

Kitchu na — It's nothing

Kit kita mangi — Dried pussy / coochie girl

Kolshi — A clay water pitcher

Korma — A type of curry

Kufi — Skullcap

Kushiara River — A river in Sylhet, Bangladesh

Lahbi — Lovely

Lamba suilie — Long headed (i.e. haired) dirt bag

Lilts — A type of soft drink by the Coca Cola Company that is sold in the United Kingdom

Londoni — Bangladeshi expats who live / spend most of their time in England

Londoni affa — The sister from London (i.e. England)

Londoni bi-shab — The brother from London (i.e. England)

Lungi — A traditional garment worn by men around the waist much like a skirt

Lychees — A type of fruit in Bangladesh that has a whitish pulp

Madrasah — An Islamic school

Maf korben — Forgive me

Maf nai — No forgiveness

Maghrib — Sunset prayer

Mahr — The amount of gift money to be paid by the groom to the bride at the time of marriage

Maithtoe na — Don't talk

Manchester — A city in North West England

Maulvi Bazar — A district of Sylhet Division in North-Eastern Bangladesh

Masha'Allah — God has willed it

Masjid — Mosque

Mehndi — The art of henna painting

Meju — Middle

Mishtis — Sweets

Morahs — Two round woven seats made from cane and bamboo

Muezzin — The person who does the call to prayer in an Islamic community or Mosque

Mullah — A Muslim man, educated in Islamic theology and law

Muslims — Those who follow the religion of Islam

Na — No

Naan — A type of bread

Nam — Name

Namaz — Prayers

Nana — Grandpa or grandfather

Nanu — Grandma or grandmother

Oofhtah — Upside down

Oy — Yes

Papadums — A type of flatbread that is more like a cracker than bread

Parathas — Pan-fried flatbread

Polau — Rice cooked in a seasoned broth. Also known as pilaf

Prophet Muhammad — The last prophet of Islam as taught by the Quran

Punjabis — A traditional item of clothing that falls either just above or somewhere below the knees of the wearer

Quid — British slang for one pound in monetary currency

Quran — Islam's holy book

Rabbisher jadth — You belong to a caste of rubbish

Raja — King

Rajanpur — A village in Bangladesh

Raj kumar — Prince

Raj kumari — Princess

Rakh — Hang up, as in hang up the phone

Rakosh fett li — Monstrous fatty

Ramadan — The ninth month of the Islamic calendar and also the Islamic month of fasting

Rangarchur — A village in Bangladesh

Razakar — Literally, a traitorous Bengali. The term was applied to any Bangladeshi during the 1971 liberation war who sided with and / or aided the Pakistanis

Ricksha — A two-wheeled cart powered by a human

Ricksha-wallahs — Rickshaw drivers

Sago pudding — A sweet pudding, similar to tapioca or rice pudding

Salaam — The word for peace in Arabic

Salwar Kameez — A pair of light loose trousers and a long shirt which traditionally comes down to the top of the knee

Sari — A strip of unstitched cloth, ranging from four to nine meters in length that is draped over the body in various styles

School-o jai ram gi — I'm going to school now

Shandesh — A type of dessert in Bangladesh, created with milk and sugar

Shaub namaz for so-ni? — Have you all done your prayers?

Shada — White

Shangram — Struggle, as in Bangladesh's struggle for independence during the 1971 liberation war

Shaplas — Water lilies

Shaytan dorsay shopti — The devil has all of you

Shokari foiysha — Free government money

Shonapur — A remote village in Bangladesh

Shuudkur — Thug

Slag — British slang for slut

Sonali — Gold / Golden

Sooboh — Shut up

Sootoh — Little

Sootoh bi-shab — Little brother, as in the younger of Luky's two brothers, Saqir

Sootoh raj kumari — Little princess

Suil — Hair

Sunamganj — A city in Bangladesh

Surah Al-Fatiha — The opening chapter of the Quran

Surahs — Chapters of the Quran

Surma River — A river in Sylhet, Bangladesh

Swab — Blessings

Sylhet — A major city in North-Eastern Bangladesh

Tabiz — An amulet containing verses from the Quran for good luck

Tagore —A Bengali poet who won the Nobel Prize

The night of power — Also known as Laylat al-Qadr. Said to be the holiest night of the year in the Islamic tradition and also the night in which the first revelations of Islam and the prophethood of Muhammad began

Thik acche — Okay

Thirash kutah — A thirsty dog

Tikli — The piece of jewelry that hangs from a woman's ear to her nose

Uni — Short for university

Urdu — One of the official languages of Pakistan

Wa alaykum asalaam — And unto you be peace

Wellies — Boots

Whoonga bastor — A damn bastard

Whoonga rabbish — A damn trashy bastard

Wudu — Ritual ablution (Before praying, Muslims wash certain parts of their body)

Zamzam water — Holy water from Mecca

Zebra crossing — A type of pedestrian crossing in the United Kingdom, marked by alternating dark and light stripes on the road surface

Zuhoor namaz — Noon prayers